THE
EVER-
BLOOMING
FLOWER
GARDEN

THE EVER-BLOOMING FLOWER GARDEN

A Blueprint for Continuous Color

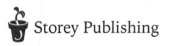
Storey Publishing

LEE SCHNELLER

To Richard,
and to
the memory of Lollipop

The mission of Storey Publishing is to serve our customers by publishing practical information that encourages personal independence in harmony with the environment.

Edited by Gwen Steege
Art direction and book design by Dan O. Williams

Cover photography by © Lee Schneller

Interior photography by © Lee Schneller, except for © GAP Photos Ltd.: 125 middle, 126 bottom, 131 bottom, 136 top, 155 top, 158 bottom, 164 bottom, 172 bottom, 174 middle, bottom, 175 bottom, 183 top; courtesy of Schreiners Gardens: 161 bottom; © James H. Schutte: 176 middle; Liz Stanley: 28, 29, 48, 53 top left, 63–66, 68, 69, 82 bottom four, 187 middle; Mars Vilaubi: 50

Color illustrations by Dan O. Williams, with additional illustrations on page 79 by Sarah Brill, top right; Beverly Duncan, top left, middle right; and Mallory Lake, bottom right

Diagrams by Alison Kolesar, pages 10, 11, 26, 52, 58–60, 87, 91, 95, 99, 103

Indexed by Christine R. Lindemer, Boston Road Communications

© 2009 by Lee Schneller

Printed in the United States by CJK
10 9 8 7 6 5 4 3 2 1

Library of Congress Cataloging-in-Publication Data

Schneller, Lee.
  The ever-blooming flower garden / by Lee Schneller.
      p. cm.
  Includes index.
  ISBN 978-1-60342-139-3 (pbk. : alk. paper)
  1. Flower gardening. 2. Gardens—Design. I. Title.
  II. Title: Ever blooming flower garden.
SB405.S36 2009
635.9—dc22
                                                    2009001392

CONTENTS

PART ONE

What **gardener** doesn't dream of blooms from frost to frost? For many, this is an impossible dream. Like other gardeners, I used to be humbled and dismayed as my best efforts produced gardens that burst forth with splendor in June but fizzled out into a dried-up mass of foliage as the summer wore on. In *The Ever-Blooming Flower Garden*, I share the techniques that I've developed to unlock the secret of continuous blooms and put it within reach, even if you've never gardened before.

My first continuously blooming garden marks the entrance of a beauty salon on a tawdry strip of U.S. Route 1 in Rockland, Maine. Surrounded by asphalt, fast-food joints, and a quick-oil-change shop, a more challenging location could hardly be found. Hired to rework a lackluster garden, I was able to create a traffic-stopping oasis bursting with perennial blooms from April to November in a very small space. Thanks to its fortuitous location, my first garden brought me a flood of business from the beauty salon clientele and many opportunities to refine my technique over the next decade.

When I started designing gardens, my first attempts felt like mortal combat with messy lists of plant information. Height! Color! Zone! Bloom time! Sun or shade? The bigger the garden, the more cumbersome and confusing the lists. It seemed impossible to remember and organize all the details, and making changes in midstream created even more chaos. I knew I wanted a broad selection of plants with different heights and bloom times, but getting a grip on the big picture seemed impossible. Then I came up with a simple system for taming the jungle of plant data by using a totally new sequence for garden design. My system delivers a detailed snapshot of a whole garden on a single page and even doubles as a shopping list, which cuts out another step. I've used it to design and rework over 100 gardens of all sizes and shapes. After finding it so useful, it occurred to me that I had something important to share with other gardeners, so I started giving four-hour workshops for gardeners of all skill levels, who told me they felt empowered by my technique and inspired to new levels of confidence and creativity.

AN INVITATION TO SUCCEED

Anyone can use my system. Here's the basic approach:

- ▶ **Create the "Blueprint"** by selecting short, medium, and tall plants whose various bloom times guarantee color through the season (chapter 3). Choose plants from the Plant Palette (part 3), a conveniently organized list of prescreened plants.

- ▶ **Buy all the plants** (chapter 4).

- ▶ **Lay out and plant** the new garden: place the plants in the prepared bed and move them around until you're satisfied (chapter 5).

My standard system involves planting everything very densely. This offers several advantages: The bed appears full and mature more quickly, weeds and unwanted seedlings are minimized (because they have little room to take root), and you get more blooms per square foot. You can still use my system of organization (the Blueprint) for beds that are not densely planted if you prefer that style.

Many books tantalize with promises of continuous blooms, but most merely catalog bloom times by season. Those books can be useful for choosing individual plants but fail to help gardeners organize the information flexibly to create the elusive season-spanning garden. This book has everything you need to plan and plant a successful, continuously blooming garden, whether you're a novice or an experienced gardener improving mature beds.

Gardening is a form of creative expression accessible to almost everyone. The materials to do it are relatively cheap and abundantly available — all you need is the smallest patch of ground. Unlike a painting displayed in a private interior space, gardens are generally enjoyed by many viewers. When someone creates a garden, it enriches many lives and inspires others to be creative, too. That's why I hate to see anyone fail, especially if they're new to the world of gardening. Admittedly, things can go wrong, and failure may sour people on gardening for good. They think they have no aptitude for it and give up after the first attempt. This book is my contribution to easy, successful gardening. Success encourages gardeners to experiment and create more, and I think that makes the world a better place for everyone. Good luck, and happy gardening!

Purple coneflower (*Echinacea purpurea* 'Magnus'), the buds of 'Muscadet' Oriental hybrid lily (*Lilium* 'Muscadet'), and catmint (*Nepeta sibirica* 'Souvenir d'Andre Chaudron') pick up the slack in late July when gardens tend to deteriorate in summer heat.

CHAPTER ONE

THE CONTINUOUS-BLOOM SYSTEM

In this chapter, we're going to jump right into my continuous-bloom system. If you need advice about where to put your garden, information about basic principles of garden design, or suggestions of favorite plant combinations, you might want to read through chapters 2 through 6 before actually filling out your own Blueprint. But if you already have some experience with plants, I invite you to plunge right in! I believe you will quickly discover why my system constitutes a giant step forward in perennial garden design.

Have you ever set out with enthusiasm and confidence to design a flower bed for that special spot, then ended up pulling your hair out a few hours later with pages of disconnected notes and dog-eared catalogs but no cohesive plan? My system puts you in the driver's seat by keeping track of all the cumbersome details so you can concentrate your energy on creativity. When I teach workshops, there are always long moments of silence as people digest the essentials of my technique, then pencils suddenly begin to fly, designs emerge, and enthusiasm is everywhere. I hope this chapter gives you that same sense of excitement and confidence about creating your own garden designs.

HOW MANY PLANTS?
5 EASY STEPS

To begin developing your garden Blueprint, you must first figure out how many short, medium, and tall plants you'll need to fill your new perennial bed. Most perennial design techniques instruct you to choose what *type* of plants to use first, so my technique departs significantly from the norm at this point. By doing it my way, you know exactly how many of which height plant you need to select, thus avoiding the situation where

Step 1

Draw your bed to scale on graph paper as shown in the example below. You can purchase a pad of graph paper or make copies of the samples provided on page 216. Make each square equal to 1 foot.

Step 2

Divide the bed into three parts (for short, medium, and tall plants). You can draw straight or wavy lines. *These divisions **do not** indicate plant placement in your final garden* — this step just establishes a rough proportion of short, medium, and tall plants. Setting aside about half the bed for medium-height plants is a safe bet, but you can try various ratios if you feel adventuresome. If your bed is less than 5 feet deep, you should consider just dividing it into two parts (for short and medium plants; see page 26).

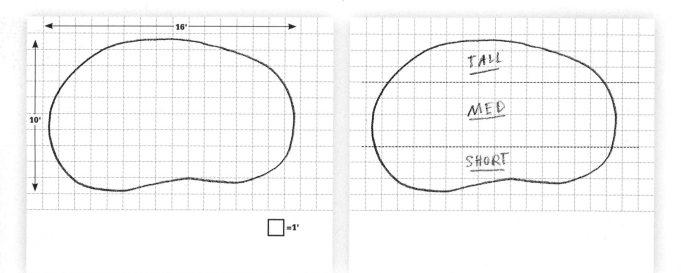

Draw a rough outline of your bed to scale.

Divide the shape into short, medium, and tall sections, based on proportion, **not design.**

you've fallen in love with and committed yourself to a bunch of plants that won't work in your flower bed. As you'll see in chapter 3, this method also allows you to change your mind infinitely during the selection process — something that with other methods is cumbersome and irritating at best.

The following simple drawings and calculations are designed to make it easy to generate a plant list that contains the right proportion of short, medium, and tall plants whose bloom times are balanced over the season.

Step 3

Use the formula to see how many plants of each height you need. Begin by counting up the number of squares each for short, medium, and tall plants on your graph paper drawing. (Count partial squares as a half square.) Enter your figures in the "Number of Squares" column. Divide by the figure in the "Plant Spacing Adjuster" column, which accounts for the spacing between plants. Enter the results in the "Target Quantities" column. Round up to the next whole number if necessary. This formula allows for about 15-inch spacing for short and medium plants and 17 inches for tall plants. This is tighter than is usually recommended, because I prefer to plant close together. When you get to the actual planting step, some plants should be placed closer or farther apart than this. (See pages 52–53.)

If you prefer not to use graph paper, you can skip steps 1 and 2 and use the alternate method described on page 198 in the appendix.

Steps 4 & 5
on the next page

	SHORT	MEDIUM	TALL
	24 ■ + 16 ▷	54 ■ + 10 ▷	18 ■ + 17 ▷
	32	**59**	**27**

	NUMBER OF SQUARES	PLANT SPACING ADJUSTER	TARGET QUANTITIES
SHORT ▷	32 ÷	1.5 =	21
MED ▷	59 ÷	1.5 =	39
TALL ▷	27 ÷	2 =	14

Count the squares in each section (partial squares are ½) and enter results into the chart. Calculate your final planting numbers by dividing by the spacing adjusters. Always round up.

Step 4:

Transfer the target quantities for short, medium, and tall plants to the boxes at the top of the Blueprint Form (example below).

ENTER # OF PLANTS	**21** ◄ SHORT	**39** ◄ MEDIUM	**14** ◄ TALL

Step 5:

Use the Plant Palette (beginning on page 106) as your reference to choose plants according to their bloom time. The Plant Palette is conveniently organized to present all the recommended plants that bloom in each season on a pair of facing pages. This lets you stay focused and shows you all the choices on one page so you don't have to flip around and try to remember what you're looking for. The shaded boxes indicating bloom data are particularly useful here, as you can see at a glance where you will have blooms and gaps even within the subseason itself.

As you're working with the Plant Palette, if you need more information about any given plant or if you want to look at a photo of it, just look it up in the alphabetical Flower Catalog (beginning on page 120). As you fill in the Blueprint, watch for gaps in the bloom schedule and keep checking across each row to be sure you haven't chosen clashing colors, because these are the plants that will be blooming at about the same time.

The rest of the book covers in more detail how to use the Plant Palette and Flower Catalog, as well as offers design principles and basic techniques for caring for your garden throughout the year.

ENTER # OF PLANTS	**21** ◄ SHORT	**39** ◄ MEDIUM	**14** ◄ TALL
FOLIAGE		2 SEDUM 'PURPLE EMPEROR	
SPRING	1 IBERIS 1 VERONICA 'GEORGIA BLUE' (25) IRIS RETICULATA 'HARMONY'	2 IRIS 'CRIMSON KING' (PURPLE), (25) TULIPA 'BEAU MONDE' (PINK/WHITE TRIUMPH)	
...ER	3 ALLIUM SCHUBERTII	1 IRIS SIBIRICA (BLUE)	1 PAEONIA (LIGHT PINK)

2

GETTING STARTED ON YOUR BLUEPRINT

If **you've ever fumbled back and forth** among piles of garden books and catalogs looking for photos, heights, and bloom times, you'll appreciate the concise and complete information in the Plant Palette and Flower Catalog. These tools are the precious result of many years' experience. They list about 200 low-maintenance plants that work best with my dense planting system. I've selected them over the course of my years of designing more than 100 gardens and planting more than 8,000 plants. In the Plant Palette, each season has its own section, which corresponds to a row on the Blueprint; the plants are further grouped into columns according to their height. The ideal candidate for the Plant Palette is a plant with these qualities:

▶ Attractive flower

▶ Hardy at least to Zone 5 or lower

▶ Long-lived plant

▶ Good foliage (or foliage that can easily be hidden if unattractive)

▶ Long bloom time

▶ Ability to survive close planting

▶ Readily available at retail

▶ Adapted to sun or part-sun conditions

▶ Grows well in ordinary garden soil and moisture conditions

▶ Not invasive

Obviously, only a few plants meet all of these criteria, so the list of 200 was created by weighing a lot of pros and cons.

The Flower Catalog contains detailed information and photos of each plant in the Plant Palette. I apologize for forcing scientific plant names on you, but common names are not accurate enough to identify specific plants. For example, there are dozens of plants called "sage" or "bellflower." When I started learning the scientific names, I did a whole lot of flipping back and forth between index entries, and so I created an Index of Common Plant Names (page 207) to make your job easier.

⊹ Keeping Track of Special Cases

Often, I need to keep track of some plants in a Blueprint for a special reason. I use parentheses, circles, squares, triangles, and dots to categorize special plants in my Blueprint.

For example, I want to include tulips in my Blueprint for design purposes, but I don't want to include them in the plant count because they go between perennials and don't really take up room. To remind myself to exclude them from the plant count, I put them on the list but enclose the quantity in parentheses. At the top of the Blueprint, I make a note that says "( ) = exclude from count."

Similarly, I might draw a circle around the quantity of any plants I'll be getting from my own divisions, and at the top of the Blueprint I write "○ = from divisions (do not buy)" to remind myself not to buy these plants.

✛ Just What Is Bloom Time?

Bloom time is affected by so many factors you might wonder why it's even worthwhile trying to pin it down. The answer is that a continuously blooming garden is a joy to behold throughout the growing year and it's worth the trouble to try to make it happen. Most plant tags, catalogs, and reference books offer pretty broad and vague information about bloom time. Weather — including temperature, moisture, and wind — is the biggest and most obvious variable. Bloom time is also affected by the amount of light a plant gets (that is, whether it's located in full sun, partial shade, or shade) and its proximity to the moderating influence of large bodies of water. Here in Maine, I've seen variations of weeks with identical plants located just 10 miles apart, one very near the ocean and the other just inland.

I'm not saying that by using this method you'll be able to crank out a garden that blooms unfailingly for your 4th of July barbecue, but you'll definitely get a whole lot closer to what you're aiming for. With this design technique, you use broad strokes to "rough in" a garden that blooms much more predictably than you might have thought possible. The goal in filling in the Blueprint (see page 217) is to create a balanced bloom schedule throughout the growing year. Foliage plants (the first row) are optional.

Occasionally, it makes sense to design a garden that blooms only in certain seasons. For example, if my clients spend the winter in Florida and use their house only in the summer, they don't care about spring bulbs or plants that bloom before July. I then use the Blueprint to plan a garden that blooms only at certain specified times.

A bold combination of purple smokebush (*Cotinus coggygria* 'Royal Purple'), 'Moerheim Beauty' sneezeweed (*Helenium* 'Moerheim Beauty'), drumstick allium (*Allium sphaerocephalon*), common monkshood (*Aconitum napellus*), and 'Coronation Gold' yarrow (*Achillea* 'Coronation Gold') perk up the garden in late July. ▼

◄ Using clusters of 'Purple Dome' New England asters (*Aster novae-angliae* 'Purple Dome') and azure monkshood (*Aconitum carmichaelii* 'Arendsii') is much more effective than using single plants in the fall when not much else is blooming. A single pink 'Alma Pötschke' New England aster (*Aster novae-angliae* 'Alma Pötschke') is tall and substantial enough to have an impact by itself, though.

QUANTITIES OF EACH PLANT

As you select plants, you also choose quantities. You might use just one or two of each variety of plant. All the books tell you *not* to do this, but it works with my system of densely planted beds (as long as they are not too big) and gives you maximum variety, especially if your space is limited.

If your bed is large (say, more than about 16 feet long), you might prefer to use masses of three to seven plants. A very large bed made of single specimen plants usually looks fractured and too busy. Massing allows the eye to rest on clumps of plants instead of individuals.

As you work on your design, periodically add up the number of plants you've tentatively chosen. Jot this provisional total in the blank space at the top of the column to the right of the column title and compare it to the number you wote in the box to the left of the column title (the "target number of plants"). I usually do preliminary totals like this several times during the course of designing a garden. You needn't match the target number exactly; just try to stay in the right ballpark.

APPROACHES TO DEVELOPING THE BLUEPRINT

With so many choices, it can be hard to know where to start. Just browsing through the Flower Catalog or the Plant Palette for inspiration is a great way to begin. The Flower Catalog has the advantage of offering photos of each flower and detailed horticultural information, while the Plant Palette gives you all the plants that bloom at once on a single page (but with abbreviated information and no photos), so each resource has its pluses and minuses. A number of different design approaches have worked for me. Choosing one of the following can help focus your efforts. Whichever approach you choose, the design process is one of trial and error, choosing and erasing. (You will find basic plant design choices in chapter 3.)

WORK WITH WHAT YOU KNOW AND LIKE

Start with a favorite combination of flowers that bloom together and build the rest of the garden around them. To carry out this approach, think of a favorite flower and look it up in the Plant Palette. This gets you on the page that lists all the other plants that bloom at the same time. For example, you might start by writing in 3 delphiniums and 5 Asiatic hybrid lilies on the Blueprint form in the row labeled "Midsummer." Next, choose a few complementary plants that also bloom in midsummer. Finally, choose the rest of the plants that bloom during the other months to create a continuously blooming garden.

CHOOSE TEAM PLAYERS

Base your design on plants that mix well with others and bloom for a long time. Even if you don't use this as your starting point, be sure to include some good team players, such as solitary clematis (*Clematis integrifolia*) and patrinia (*Patrinia gibbosa*), in your design. Plants like these help sustain the bed before and after the superstars like delphiniums and peonies have their burst of glory.

'Magnus' purple coneflower (*Echinacea purpurea* 'Magnus') and 'Souvenir d'André Chaudron' catmint (*Nepeta sibirica* 'Souvenir d'André Chaudron') make an exceptionally long-blooming combination.

DARTBOARD METHOD

This way of working might sound ridiculous, but it actually works. Since the goal is a continuously blooming garden, you can start by simply choosing one plant from each category of the Plant Palette for each empty box in the Blueprint. Continue choosing plants this way until you've reached the target quantity for each height. Check across the rows to be sure you haven't chosen clashing colors within each month, and be sure to include some plants that provide good structure and good foliage.

USE YOUR FAVORITE CATALOG

This approach substitutes your favorite catalog for the Plant Palette. Most plant catalogs contain all the information you need about height, bloom time, and color (although the bloom data is usually not as specific as that in the Plant Palette). When you're done filling in the Blueprint, you can simply order the plants from the catalog. This approach requires more experience as the plants are not prescreened for ease of growing and tolerance for close planting as are those in the Plant Palette.

Lancaster geranium (*Geranium sanguineum* var. *striatum*) and Serbian bellflower (*Campanula poscharskyana*) bloom together from early summer to midsummer.

You don't have to copy every bit of information onto the Blueprint — just write the minimum you need. For example, I might write "*Campanula* 'White Clips'" or "*Campanula* 'White Clips' – Midsummer +" to remind me that it blooms beyond its bloom category (midsummer). Sometimes I note the plant height if it is especially tall or short. If you have trouble remembering colors, you can write the plant names using erasable colored pencils.

You are well on your way to creating your own garden! You have determined the size of your garden (page 10), then used the formula on page 11 to calculate how many plants of each height you need, and finally, you have used the Plant Palette and Flower Catalog as references for your plant choices. Your Blueprint is now ready to take along to the nursery or garden center to help you purchase your plants.

Before you leap in and start designing, however, you'll want to decide on the best size and shape for your garden (chapter 2) and consider some suggestions on designing with flowers (chapter 3). In addition, study the detailed plans and photos of the five actual gardens in part 2, which can be used as a starting point for your own design. This book is filled with suggestions to help you design and plant a garden that can bring you joy throughout the seasons and for years to come.

Cushion spurge (*Euphorbia polychroma*) delivers an explosion of early color, good structure all season, and a fanfare of red fall foliage.

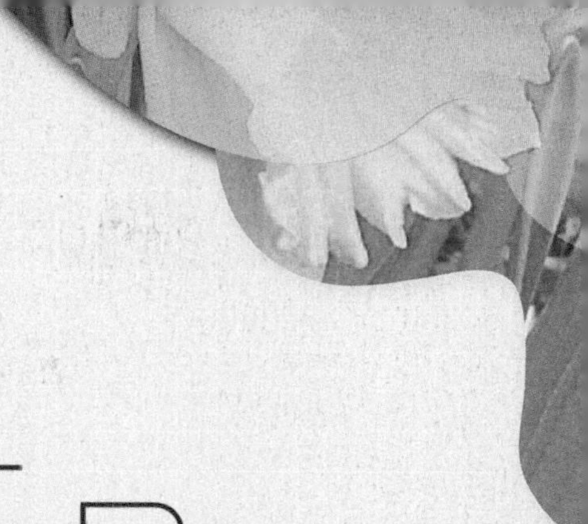

CHAPTER TWO

BEAUTIFUL PLANS LEAD TO BEAUTIFUL GARDENS

Since gardening is a creative endeavor, doesn't all this planning out ahead defeat the purpose? The temptation to rush in without a plan is often overwhelming. Like everybody else, I sometimes succumb to the lure of lovely plants at the nursery and drag home my prizes with no idea where to put them. New holes are hastily dug, and the beautiful new plants disappear in the mishmash.

Why do gardeners so resist the task of planning? In my case, I suffer from the delusion that I know and understand my yard. I think I don't need to plan because great gardening ideas will spontaneously arise in a beautiful creative process. Unfortunately, this is not the case. Instead, my mind zeroes in on details and I tend to miss the big picture. I think of adding or subtracting little things in corners and empty spots. Unless I make a special effort to be objective, my imagination is constrained by existing patterns born of habit, not inspiration. In this chapter, I'll help you see the big picture by taking an objective look at three important components of a successful garden: its site, its size and shape, and the condition of its soil.

THE IDEAL SITE

If you're about to create a brand new garden, your first consideration is where to place it. This is a time for a thoughtful, objective look at your surroundings and how you want them to work for you. Step back and try to see your property as a stranger would. Ask yourself some basic questions about the site and your design objectives.

WHO IS THE GARDEN FOR?

This might seem obvious, but confusion on this point leads to mediocre landscaping that pleases no one. Ask yourself, is the garden a treat for myself, or do I want to dress up my yard for neighbors or friends? Will my family enjoy looking at or working in the garden? Am I trying to impress someone else or to create something uniquely mine? For example, a screen of tall perennials can be enjoyed from both sides, giving privacy during prime outdoor activity months while also offering the neighbors something nice to look at.

The ideal spot is a place where your garden can easily be viewed and tended. You should avoid places where high winds or bad drainage could stress or even kill the plants. Choosing a site in full sun (one that receives six or more hours of direct sunlight per day) gives you the broadest choice of plants. This small raised bed complements the ocean view from several vantage points outdoors and from inside the house.

At my house, tall hollyhocks (*Alcea*), Culver's root (*Veronicastrum virginicum*), and yellow waxbells (*Kirengeshoma palmata*) screen a narrow front yard from the road.

HOW CAN I TAKE ADVANTAGE OF THE APPROACH?

What stands out when you drive up to your house? Most of us come and go by car, yet we often ignore this view when planning gardens. Putting a garden where you'll see it every time you pull in or out of the driveway can be very satisfying.

Traveling the route from automobile to front door can be a journey to enjoy each day rather than a boring chore.

ARE THERE UGLY FEATURES I SHOULD MINIMIZE?

Don't let existing structures hobble your imagination. The temptation to simply embellish a strong element like a telephone pole or the side of a driveway may be powerful. But doing so just emphasizes an ugly feature and accentuates a line that probably works against a good composition. Sometimes the best way to handle an unattractive feature is to create beauty nearby to light up your yard and steal attention away from less desirable features.

1. This freestanding raised bed hides a concrete foundation and elevates a collection of low-growing coral bells. Purple foliage in the perennials and annuals ties the scene together. 2. The naturalistic streambed lined with moisture-loving perennials began as an unsightly drainage swale. 3. This freestanding perennial bed replaced a scruffy, rock-strewn spot.

+ Pitfalls to Avoid

Here are some common design mistakes to avoid:

- ▶ A long, thin bed along the edge of a driveway
- ▶ A circular bed around a telephone pole
- ▶ A tiny round island bed swimming in a gigantic lawn
- ▶ A bed of short plants along an ugly concrete house foundation
- ▶ A bed under a big tree (insufficient light, root competition)
- ▶ Short, medium, and tall plants packed into a too-narrow bed

The little cluster of flowers draws your eye right to the telephone pole and away from the lovely trees and field.

WILL I BE ABLE TO ENJOY THE GARDEN FROM INSIDE?

My favorite perennial bed lies directly opposite the kitchen window where I see it constantly. I used to stare out at a boring picket fence and strip of grass; now I'm energized by a constantly changing flower scene. Avoid the common mistake of locating a beautiful perennial bed along the foundation where it's invisible from inside the house. Ask yourself, "How often will I see a garden if I put it here?" Walk around inside your house noticing which windows you use most often. But avoid "wishing" yourself into different habits by putting the new garden outside a room where you *think* you should spend more time, like a little-used formal dining room. If you have to make a special effort to sit down and look at your garden, it can become a joy-killer, like a closet full of new clothes that will only fit when you lose a few pounds.

A profusion of campanulas and the ocean beyond greet the eye from the home office adjacent to this garden.

WHAT PRACTICAL THINGS SHOULD I CONSIDER?

A few practical considerations weigh into site selection, too. You don't want to build a garden where it might cramp future expansion of your house. The site should drain well and be accessible with a wheelbarrow. (If the site drains poorly you can build raised beds of stone or wood.) A flat spot or ditch at the bottom of a slope is usually too wet for a garden, unless you're using plants specifically adapted to boggy conditions. Watch out for places where water stands after rain or where water pools and freezes in the winter — the roots of most perennials can't survive these conditions. A very dry, sandy site (especially at the top of a hill) might also cause trouble, as the garden will tend to dry out too fast.

The garden should get enough sun and not too much wind. "Full sun" usually means six hours of exposure per day, and plants that grow in full sun tend to provide the most blooms. "Partial shade" is a little more vague, but it usually means several hours of sun per day. As for wind, if you see nearby trees or grasses bending constantly, the site is probably not ideal for a perennial bed unless you restrict yourself to groundcovers or other short plants. Constant wind dries plants out quickly and stresses their stems. If you put tall plants in a windy spot, they will usually grow shorter than normal and you will probably lose some blossoms (especially large ones) because of broken stems. You can build continuously blooming gardens on less-than-ideal sites, but your choice of plants is more limited and the results may not be as good.

+ Location! Location! Location!

Ask yourself, "How often will I see a garden if I put it here? Will I have to make a special effort to see it?" These locations usually work:

▶ Visible from the kitchen window

▶ Visible from the living room or TV room

▶ A freestanding bed in the lawn, visible from several rooms at once

▶ Where you'll see it every time you pull in or out with the car

+ Consider This . . .

▶ Who is this garden for?

▶ When will people see it?

▶ Where do you most often sit or stand inside your house? What windows do you use most often?

▶ Will the garden be convenient to water supply and tool shed?
  O yes O no

▶ Can you reach it with a wheelbarrow?
  O yes O no

▶ Are sun and wind exposures favorable?
  O yes O no

▶ Is the drainage adequate?
  O yes O no

▶ Will it be in the way if you want to build an addition on the house later?
  O yes O no

A CASE FOR RAISED BEDS

If the drainage is poor, if the soil is very clayey, or if you want to elevate the bed to provide a better view from indoors, you can build raised beds of stone or wood. Although the initial effort and expense is higher, raised beds also keep the grass out and provide a place to sit while weeding. (For more information, see page 79.) Keep in mind that a raised bed can increase the need for watering if you fill it with sandy soil or live in a dry climate.

If the raised bed is to be at least 12 inches deep, pour the topsoil right on top of the sod and allow it to settle over a winter. The sod eventually disintegrates without affecting the perennials above. For shallower raised beds (less than 12 inches deep) the entire interior must be desodded by hand or you'll run the risk of running into the sod when you dig the holes to plant your perennials. In addition, the rotting sod can produce heat that can damage the roots of the new perennials.

Whether the bed is deep or shallow, the perimeter must be desodded. (This is the area where the bed sides — stone or timbers — contact the ground.) To help prevent the bed from heaving in the frost in cold climates, lay a few inches of coarse, crushed rock around the perimeter before putting the stone or timber in place.

Raised beds outlined by wood, stone, or brick provide good drainage and make gardens more visible.

3

DECIDING ON SHAPE AND SIZE

Once you've picked a spot, you can experiment with bed shape and size. Here it's helpful to use a garden hose or a package of bamboo stakes to outline possible shapes. Look at your outline from various vantage points, including from your favorite windows inside the house, and adjust the shape and size. Consider how the bed will fit into its surroundings: Will it look nestled in and inviting? Will it be in proportion to the house, fences, and outbuildings, or will it stick out awkwardly or cramp paths and open spaces? Will you have time to maintain a garden this size?

GET THE PROPORTIONS RIGHT

If you plan to use plants in a variety of heights — short, medium, and tall — your bed should be at least 5 or 6 feet deep. Breaking this rule of thumb results in an awkward garden that appears collapsed or too "steep." If you have room for only a narrower bed, try limiting yourself to short and medium plants. The bed's length should also be in proportion to its surroundings. A common mistake is to make gardens that are too small or too short.

CREATE THE APPROPRIATE SHAPE

Rounded shapes like ovals lend a casual air, while rectangles and other angular shapes look more formal. Lay out various shapes to evaluate the effect. Try to "color outside the lines" instead of being constrained by strong architectural lines. For example, you can create a feeling of spacious elegance by letting your foundation borders flow beyond the corners of the house. Ending a foundation bed precisely at a corner can make the garden look squeezed in by overaccentuating the sharp vertical line.

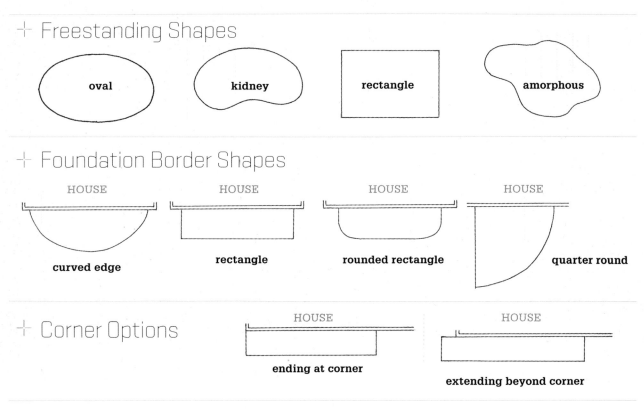

+ Freestanding Shapes

oval   kidney   rectangle   amorphous

+ Foundation Border Shapes

HOUSE — curved edge

HOUSE — rectangle

HOUSE — rounded rectangle

HOUSE — quarter round

+ Corner Options

HOUSE — ending at corner

HOUSE — extending beyond corner

+ Drama Through Focal Points

A well-placed focal point can make a garden come together. A single, dramatic focal point is much more effective than numerous small objects. In my own garden, I find it very difficult to follow this principle. It's much easier to pick up a lot of small, inexpensive objects than to take the time to research (and pay for) larger, more substantial pieces. But a good focal point rewards you every time you look at your garden.

The pair of freestanding trellises I designed for the Farnsworth Art Museum in Rockland, Maine, are loosely based on photos I saw of eighteenth-century spiral trellises in a historic Portsmouth, New Hampshire, garden. Besides displaying the rose to advantage from every viewing angle, these trellises provide good air circulation, which helps prevent the foliar diseases to which roses are so susceptible.

A strategically placed bridge or gate creates a sense of transition and entices the visitor to an unseen (and sometimes imaginary) destination. This device can be used to great effect in small gardens to create an illusion of greater space. In this steep oceanside garden I designed a bridge that goes nowhere to suggest a farther destination.

Trellises at the Farnsworth Art Museum (left); bridge at steep oceanside garden (right).

PREPARING THE SOIL

Don't try to work the soil too early in the spring when it's still wet and soggy; it should dry out enough so that you won't ruin the structure by working on it with tools. Good structure includes air spaces between the bits of soil, and this structure is improved in cold climates through the alternate freezing and thawing that occurs in spring. If you work the soil too early, you can collapse these important air spaces, and the soil cannot recover until it goes through another freeze/thaw cycle. If you're not sure whether it's safe yet to work the soil, ask your local Cooperative Extension Office or an experienced gardener in your area.

Once you've chosen a location and marked out the size and shape, any sod in the area should be removed to prepare the site for planting (see below). If your soil is pretty good (not extremely clayey or sandy), no more bed preparation is needed at this point. Later, when you plant each perennial, you will improve the soil just in each planting hole. By not fertilizing the entire planting bed, you not only reduce the cost of amendments, but you also discourage weeds because the soil between perennials is unimproved.

To see whether your soil is too clayey or too sandy, moisten a little patch of the soil, pick up a walnut-sized wad in your hand, make a tight fist, then open your hand. If the soil forms a tight ball that doesn't fall right apart when you poke it, it's too clayey. If it hardly holds

✢ In with the Good, Out with the Old

When you remove sod, you may be taking some precious topsoil with it. Here's how to reclaim the topsoil with a minimum of back strain:

1. Slice the bed outline with an edger, then cut the sod into a checkerboard of 8–16" squares.

2. Loosen and remove the squares with a spading fork and pile them on a tarp.

3. If the soil is very good, use the back edge of a Cape Cod weeder (**3a**) or other dull tool to knock off as much of the soil as possible (**3b**). Another good technique is to flip the sod so it's dirt-side-up on the tarp, chop at it with the blade of the edger to loosen the soil, then shake the loose soil off the scrap of sod. Either way, you should add the good topsoil back into the bed and toss the leftover sod scraps into a wheelbarrow for disposal or composting. (To compost, pile up the sod and cover it with heavy — 4 or 6 mil — black plastic or a heavy tarp; after about a year, you'll have topsoil for another use.)

its shape at all, it's too sandy. Compost is the answer to both of these problems.

If the soil is extremely clayey it must be lightened up by forking in 3 to 6 inches of compost to a depth of about 12 inches. Failing to do this can result in stunted plants whose roots cannot grow deep enough, the death of plants that need normal drainage to survive, and fissured soil that's really hard to rehydrate once it dries out. Some plants do tolerate heavy, clay soil better than others (see a list of them in the Appendix), but building a whole garden with only those plants doesn't give you many choices. It's worth the extra effort to dig the compost in deeply, as you'll never get the chance again to improve the deep soil once your garden is planted.

Very sandy soil should be enriched by mixing in a good 4 to 6 inches of compost before planting. Failure to enrich sandy soil results in excessive drainage and insufficient nutrients for healthy growth (except for plants specifically adapted to poor, sandy soil, such as bearded irises). If your soil is too clayey or too sandy and you have to enrich the whole bed, you need not amend the soil in each individual planting hole as described in the directions for a normal bed with acceptable soil.

If you suspect that pH (the acidity or alkalinity of the soil) might be a problem in your area, you should get a soil test kit from your Cooperative Extension Office to find out what amendments can help correct an imbalance. Again, ask an experienced gardener or the Cooperative Extension Office if extreme pH is a problem in your area. Most herbaceous perennials prefer soil with a slightly acidic pH.

+ What Lies Beneath

Don't underestimate the importance of good soil! Sometimes the reason your garden fails to thrive is a fundamental problem with the soil that you haven't identified. For instance, a group of office workers I knew tried unsuccessfully for ten years to grow annuals in a raised bed filled with sand by a dishonest landscaping contractor. The bed was too poor even to grow annuals, but they believed the contractor, who told them he had sold them topsoil, and blamed themselves for their gardening failure. I hope the basic gardening information in this book helps prevent this type of problem.

This bright and frisky 'Angelina' stonecrop (*Sedum reflexum* 'Angelina') is perfectly suited to the hot, dry rock garden.

CHAPTER THREE

DESIGNING WITH PLANTS

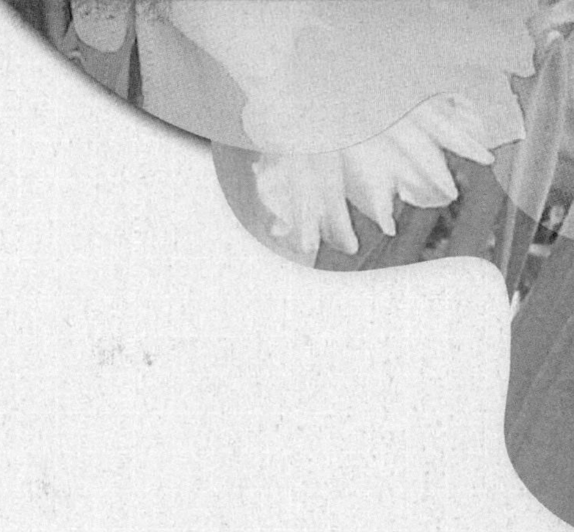

Choosing what plants to use in your garden can be a lot of fun! You'll quickly discover that there are many factors to consider, but don't let this discourage you because the Blueprint design method helps you keep track of all the details so you can enjoy playing around with different possibilities. It's okay to experiment, and everything you do in your garden is part of a learning experience. Besides the basic design approaches mentioned on pages 16 and 17, I outline a few of my favorite design tips in the following pages. You'll also find an abundance of great garden design information in other books, magazines, and even some of the better mail-order catalogs.

In this chapter you'll find my favorite perennial combinations for each season, as well as tips on site considerations and how to maximize the power of good foliage, flower shape, and bulbs. But first, let's start with everyone's favorite design feature: color!

COMBINATIONS THAT ROCK!

Garden books are full of photos and suggestions about good color combinations, and I encourage you to make use of these. When you're just beginning, the simplest way to unify your garden is to limit yourself to a few colors. Putting together exciting perennial combinations is a prized art. The more you garden, the more these good combinations of color and form suggest themselves, either by plan or by accident. Here are some basic dos and don'ts that I like to keep in mind:

▶ **DO:** The simplest way to unify your garden is to limit yourself to a few colors.

▶ **DO:** Soft yellow and greenish yellow blooms are easier to blend than gold or lemon yellow.

▶ **DON'T:** Orange and scarlet are generally hard to blend.

▶ **DO:** It sometimes pays to include some colors that might not be your absolute favorites in isolation if they blend well with the overall scheme.

▶ **DON'T:** Try not to introduce clashes with nearby flowering shrubs. I learned this the hard way after planting orange poppies next to an existing hot pink rhododendron, which was not in bloom when I designed or planted the garden.

+ Some of My Favorite Combinations:

Blue, soft yellow, and white

Purple, yellow, and deep red

Purple, lavender, magenta, dark red, and soft yellow

Pink, purple, blue, and white

+ Some Combinations to Avoid:

Pink or lavender with
gold, scarlet, or orange

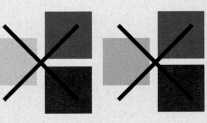

Powder blue or pink
with red and yellow

EVERY COLOR IN PROFUSION

I learned this approach from one of my favorite clients, a self-described "flower piggy." His mottos are "no colors don't go together" and "the more the merrier." Mixing all colors together indiscriminately produces an effect of joyful exuberance. It's one of the easiest types of gardens to design: don't limit your palette of colors, and don't resist any inclination towards subtlety or limits. One possible pitfall, though, is that not all the flowers bloom at once, and so you need to avoid particularly discordant combinations that aren't mitigated by the overall blend. For example, if all you have in early summer is an orange poppy and a pink geranium, it's going to look bad. If, however, you add some yellow-green lady's mantle and blue veronica, the overall effect works, because it includes a bigger mixture of colors.

⊹ Dying Well

If you want to minimize maintenance, try to choose plants that look good even when they've gone by. For example, red astilbes look good in bud and in bloom, and the seed heads gradually fade to an attractive reddish brown. In contrast, white astilbes go through an ugly brownish white phase before developing relatively attractive seed heads. In fact, white flowers generally die badly and go through an unfortunate phase.

The "every color in profusion" design scheme.

SPRING

'Sulphurea' basket of gold (*Aurinia saxatilis* 'Sulphurea') makes a good partner for 'Little Episode' dwarf bearded iris (*Iris* 'Little Episode').

EARLY SUMMER

'Mme. De Vernville' peony (*Paeonia* 'Mme. De Vernville') blooms with blue and white Siberian irises (*Iris sibirica*).

MIDSUMMER

'Purple Rain' sage (*Salvia verticillata* 'Purple Rain') and 'Rosea' solitary clematis (*Clematis integrifolia* 'Rosea') are both good at intertwining with other plants.

LATE SUMMER

'Rosy Glow' stonecrop (*Sedum 'Rosy Glow'*) (far left center), 'Purple Emperor' stonecrop (*Sedum 'Purple Emperor'*), 'Purple Rain' sage (*Salvia verticillata 'Purple Rain'*), and sea lavender (*Limonium latifolium*) bloom in mid-August, while the seedheads of 'Brilliant' stonecrop (*Sedum spectabile 'Brilliant'*) (top center) add to the effect even before bloom.

FALL

Azure monkshood (*Aconitum carmichaelii 'Arendsii'*) and 'Alma Pötschke' New England asters (*Aster novae-angliae 'Alma Pötschke'*) and white snakeroot (*Eupatorium rugosum 'Chocolate'*) (far lower left) put on a show in October.

NEVER UNDER-ESTIMATE THE POWER OF GOOD FOLIAGE

Successful perennial design isn't all about flowers. Starting with a framework of plants whose foliage looks great all season long is probably the single best way to create a good perennial bed. People find it hard to focus on this because good foliage sounds about as exciting as flossing your teeth, but (like tooth flossing) the payoff for attending to this detail is huge. Several of my favorite foliage superheroes are false indigo (*Baptisia australis*), peonies, and azure monkshood (*Aconitum carmichaelii* 'Arendsii'). You can also sneak in a small shrub such as purple smokebush (*Cotinus coggygria* 'Royal Purple'). (Where I live in Maine, smokebushes are marginally hardy and they usually die back to the trunk in winter. In late spring, I cut back the dead tips and then get long, purple new growth with lovely purple leaves. In southerly climates these plants can turn into big troublesome shrubs.)

USING FOLIAGE AS A COLOR MODERATOR

Repetition is a classic technique for unifying a design, and you can use it when you choose foliage plants:

▶ **Use a lot of plants** (25% or more of the total) with foliage in shades of purple, such as purple-leaved varieties of coral bells (*Heuchera*).

▶ **Tone down bright colors** with the liberal use of gray foliage plants, like 'Valerie Finnis' and silver mound artemisias (*Artemisia ludoviciana* 'Valerie Finnis' and *A. schmidtiana*), and 'Sulphurea' basket of gold (*Aurinia saxatilis* 'Sulphurea'). Avoid 'Silver King' artemisia (*Artemisia* 'Silver King', which should have been named *Artemisia* 'Invasion of the Huns'), as it is invasive and will wipe out everything in its path.

opposite:
A soothing and subtle mixture of golden creeping Jenny (*Lysimachia nummularia* 'Aurea'), variegated bugleweed (*Ajuga reptans*), and moss provides plenty of color without flowers.

+ Late Bloomers

Flowers that bloom later in the year tend to have superior foliage all season long. In contrast, the foliage of some spring-blooming plants often looks bad (oriental poppies) or even goes dormant (bleeding heart) after bloom. Some examples of late-bloomers with foliage that contributes all season are:

▶ *Aster* **'Schneegitter'.** Resembles a low-growing juniper.
▶ *Chrysanthemum weyrichii* **'White Bomb'.** Features low, dark, glossy foliage.
▶ *Nipponanthemum nipponicum.* Displays glossy, succulent-like foliage.
▶ *Aconitum carmichaelii* **'Arendsii'.** Has broad-leaved, deep green foliage that turns golden at the end of bloom time.
▶ *Sedum* **'Autumn Joy'.** Succulent foliage, attractive seed heads.

For additional plants with especially good foliage, see page 202.

+ Good Foliage Combinations

1. The foliage of this peony and 'Coronation Gold' yarrow (*Achillea* 'Coronation Gold') still looks good in late September. The yarrow was cut back to its basal foliage after bloom.

2. Lady's mantle (*Alchemilla mollis*) and gray-foliaged 'Valerie Finnis' wormwood (*Artemisia ludoviciana* 'Valerie Finnis') look good for most of the season but usually need to be cut back by early fall.

3. This purple smokebush (*Cotinus coggygria* 'Royal Purple') and azure monkshood (*Aconitum carmichaelii* 'Arendsii')* have dramatic foliage all season long.

4. Four good foliage plants: azure monkshood (*Aconitum carmichaelii* 'Arendsii'), Culver's root (*Veronicastrum virginicum*), 'Valerie Finnis' wormwood (*Artemisia ludoviciana* 'Valerie Finnis'), and 'Amethyst Myst' coral bells (*Heuchera* 'Amethyst Myst').

5. Two examples of exceptional foliage all season long for a garden in full sun: 'Purple Emperor' stonecrop (*Sedum* 'Purple Emperor') and 'Snowcap' wall rock cress (*Arabis caucasica* 'Snow Cap' (in lower middle).

6. The 'Blue Wave' hydrangea (*Hydrangea macrophylla* 'Blue Wave') hides brown foliage on lower stems of the 'Alma Pötschke' New England Aster (*Aster novae-angliae* 'Alma Pötschke') behind it.

GAIN VARIETY THROUGH PLANT HEIGHT AND FLOWER SHAPE

Tall plants can make dramatic statements in your garden, and they also can be helpful partners of other plants, as long as you place them in appropriate spots. Here are a few characteristics of tall plants to keep in mind as you develop your plan.

▶ **Shade creators.** Tall plants on the south side of a bed shade their northerly neighbors, creating conditions of partial shade.

▶ **Good edgers.** Some plants were just made for spilling over the edge of a bed, especially if you're planting in a raised bed. Some of my favorites are 'Snowcap' wall rock cress (*Arabis caucasica* 'Snowcap'), 'Schneegitter' aster (*Aster* 'Schneegitter'), basket of gold (*Aurinia saxatilis*), Carpathian harebell (*Campanula carpatica*), candytuft (*Iberis*), and soapwort (*Saponaria ocymoides*). You can plant them with their root ball directly touching the stones of a raised stone bed or rock garden planting.

▶ **Natural supports.** Shrubs (or shrublike perennials, such as false indigo (*Baptisia australis*) and garden phlox (*Phlox paniculata*) can be useful in a mixed border for supporting ungainly wobblers such as Russian sage (*Perovskia atriplicifolia*) or clematis vines.

▶ **Dense plantings.** Many plants, such as Maltese cross (*Lychnis chalcedonica*) and Asiatic hybrid lilies, "stretch" beyond their normal height to reach more light when planted densely.

Choosing plants whose flowers vary in shape adds interest to your garden: Choose spire-shaped flowers, such as delphinium, veronica, and salvia, or globe-shaped flowers, such as peony, trollius, allium, and hydrangea. Flat-topped yarrows add distinctive, triangular shapes (and make wonderful landing pads for butterflies), while sedums contribute masses of dense, succulent-like foliage with blooms at the tips.

+ Daylilies and Peonies: Garden Workhorses

For continuous bloom from just one plant genus, you can't go wrong with daylilies (*Hemerocallis*). You can start with the early-summer-blooming lemon lily (*Hemerocallis lilioasphodelus*) and end with the long-blooming 'Autumn Minaret', which blooms from late July through late September or even longer here in Maine.

Using multiple daylilies that bloom at the same time across a large bed can tie it together through repetition of the funnel-shaped blossoms. Specific bloom time is rarely indicated on plant labels (knowing that a daylily blooms "in summer" is not that helpful when you're trying to design a continuously blooming scheme), but you can research specific bloom times on some Internet sites, such as the site www.daylilydatabase.org (Web site of the American Hemerocallis Society).

Not only can daylilies offer continuous bloom, but they can provide other services in your garden as well. Place them in front of plants with foliage that goes dormant after bloom, such as poppies, true lilies (*Lilium*), and tulips, whose foliage must be allowed to ripen for six weeks after bloom to recharge the bulb for the following year, so you can't cut it back. Be sure the plant in front is not so tall it obscures the other plant when it's in bloom. Peonies are another good choice for this task, as they are still small when the tulips are in bloom.

In this garden, the reddish peony foliage at left will continue growing (and turn green) to help hide the foliage of the large Darwin hybrid tulips when they finish blooming.

4
DON'T FIGHT THE SITE

Choosing plants that suit the light, soil, and moisture conditions of your site will make maintenance much easier for you. Some plants grow almost anywhere, but most prefer either a moist site or a dry site and thrive only under those conditions. Trying to grow plants that like a light, sandy soil in heavy clay is very discouraging as the roots will fail to penetrate the soil and the plant can even die because of the poor drainage conditions caused by the clay. Matching the plants to the site makes for happy plants with lots of blossoms and good foliage. There are plenty of fantastic plants to choose from for almost any growing conditions, so why not use them and save your time for enjoying the garden?

This dry suntrap was originally planted with badly suffering roses. The sedums that replaced them produce abundant foliage in the spring and, with no extra care or watering, hit their stride in early fall and put on a great display to end the season.

Irises: One Name, Totally Different Requirements

Few genera have species with such varied growing requirements as irises. This summary will help you give them what they need.

Bearded irises. These include the bearded hybrids (*Iris germanica*) and dwarf bearded *Iris pumila*. They prefer alkaline soil and grow from fat tubers with a fringe of roots. Plant them with the tuber parallel to the ground and partly emerging from the soil like a duck swimming — half in, half out. Be sure not to bury the tuber completely, and press very firmly on the soil all around the tuber to eliminate air pockets, which will rot the tuber. Bearded irises love sunny, sandy, well-drained soil, require no fertilization, and don't like too much water. They multiply by fanning out in the direction of the sprouted end of the tuber, so point that end toward an empty spot in the planting bed. Avoid smothering them with groundcovers, as this can promote tuber rot and insect damage.

Bearded iris (*Iris* 'Crimson King')

Siberian irises (*I. sibirica*) and blue flags (*I. versicolor*). These like acidic soil and grow from matlike roots. Plant them as you would any perennial. They tolerate average dryness to boggy conditions.

Japanese irises (*I. ensata*). These irises require acidic soil and quickly perish with too much alkalinity. They prefer rich, moist soils, and can grow in standing water. Like Siberian irises, they have matlike roots.

Dwarf irises (*I. reticulata*). These irises grow from bulbs and reach 4 to 6 inches tall. Plant them in the fall in well-drained, average soil.

Siberian iris (*Iris sibirica* 'Caesar's Brother')

Dwarf iris (*Iris reticulata* 'Harmony')

Japanese iris (*Iris ensata*)

THE SECRET TO EARLIEST SPRING COLOR: BULBS

Few plants can beat bulbs for their combination of low price and flower power, assuming you buy bulbs that perennialize (that is, come back year after year). The autumn of your garden's first year is the time to add the spring-blooming bulbs, but you'll want to include them in your Blueprint right from the start. In the fall there will be convenient spaces between the perennials you planted in the spring, and this is where the bulbs will go. Sometimes I select specific cultivars during the design phase and sometimes I just put in a generic entry such as "(50) yellow and white Darwin hybrid tulips" and choose the specific cultivar later. The quantities of bulbs ("50" in this case) are listed in parantheses so I remember to exclude these from the plant count (see page 13).

Garden centers and colorful mail-order catalogs offer an irresistible array of glossy flower photos. Impulse buying can be part of the fun of bulb shopping, but taking a moment to digest a little extra information can help you choose the best bulbs for your purposes. Here are a few tips based on 20-odd years of bulb gardening in Maine.

By carefully selecting early-, mid-, and late-blooming bulbs of various sorts you can give yourself weeks of continuous bloom, even in the springtime garden. The bloom times given in the Plant Palette and Flower Catalog are averages for Maine and can be adjusted accordingly for other areas. Bloom time can vary tremendously from year to year, even in the same location, depending on the weather. Light conditions are also a very big factor. I planted some 'Hawera' daffodils (*Narcissus* 'Hawera') on either side of a fence one fall and the ones on the sunny side bloomed two weeks before the ones in partial shade! I recommend planting a large number of bulbs with overlapping bloom times to ensure a good display.

TEMPTING TULIPS

One of my pet peeves is how the tulip industry obscures from customers the crucial information about whether their tulips perennialize (that is, come back year after year). Most of the largest, fanciest tulips are meant to be grown as annuals, but on the packaging you won't read that; you'll just get tiny, droopy tulips the second year. Many people mistakenly conclude they have done something wrong. Tulips meant to be grown as annuals include the Darwin (also called single late), lily-flowering, and peony-flowering types. If you want maximum drama, these are for you. Generally speaking, the bigger and showier the flower, the less likely it is to perennialize and the later it will bloom.

Afloat in a sea of fresh spring foliage, the Darwin hybrid tulip 'Ollioules' (*Tulipa* 'Ollioules') and Triumph tulip 'Beau Monde' (*Tulipa* 'Beau Monde') complement common bleeding heart (*Dicentra spectabilis*).

If you prefer planting once and enjoying the blooms for many years (is there really anybody who doesn't want to do that?), Darwin hybrid tulips are excellent for perennializing and are nearly as large and elegant as the fanciest varieties mentioned previously. Emperor (also known as Fosteriana) is another good type of large perennial tulip, and Kaufmanniana hybrids and Greigii tulips are good perennializers in the small- to mid-size range. Some (but not all) Triumph tulips perennialize well.

Species tulips and their cultivars are deservedly gaining popularity. At 4 to 8 inches tall, these little gems perennialize the best and look fantastic in drifts or clusters. Species tulips have both a genus (*Tulipa*) and a species name, unlike most tulips that have only a cultivar name. Some of my favorites are *Tulipa humilis*, *T. batalinii*, and *T. vvedenski*. Like most small bulbs, species tulips are much more affordable than their larger, showier cousins.

DEPENDABLE DAFFODILS

Daffodils, as well as jonquils and paperwhites, belong in the genus *Narcissus*. All bulbs need good drainage, but narcissus are the fussiest. Many types naturalize well, some are fragrant, and all are shunned by deer and rodents. (When we say a bulb or a perennial "naturalizes," we mean that it multiplies on its own to produce more of its kind in the vicinity where it's planted. Bulbs do this by creating bulblets that become their own plants; perennials usually do it by self-seeding or by sending out runners.) Narcissus blossoms (like sunflowers) turn toward the sun, so don't expect to see their faces from a vantage point north of where you plant them (as I once did).

Narcissus come in fabulous forms from petite rock garden plants to stout trumpet or ruffled shapes in colors ranging from yellow, white, and orange to pinkish or even green. Two of my favorites are 'Ice Follies' (long-blooming, white/yellow bicolor) and 'Hawera' (a long-blooming yellow dwarf that puts out a big spray of blossoms).

These 'Kaufmanniana Type' hybrid tulips bloom early with the crocuses.

ELEGANT ALLIUMS

The flamboyant lollypop orbs of alliums, also known as flowering onions, have become a common sight in recent years. Dr. Seuss might have invented these plants. The Victorians, with their taste for big, weird flowers and foliage, used plants like *Allium giganteum* in beds edged with ornate wrought iron. Most alliums have attractive seed heads that persist after the flowers fade.

For a one-two punch of continuous summer bloom (mid-June to mid-August in Maine), try azure allium (*A. caeruleum*) and drumstick allium (*A. sphaerocephalon*). Both have blossoms under 2 inches in diameter on 24-inch stems, and you can sprinkle them in clusters throughout any perennial bed. Azure allium blooms first for several weeks, followed by drumstick allium. The larger allium bulbs can be expensive, but these two are a bargain.

For something completely different, try *Allium schubertii*. A full 10 inches of its total 16-inch height consists of a huge, fireworks-like flower, and the seed head remains splendid right into autumn. These and other large alliums are especially susceptible to rotting during wet springs, so don't be too discouraged if you have to replace them once in a while.

A mass of drumstick allium (*Allium sphaerocephalon*) produces three weeks of blossoms in July and August in Maine.

You can make your own July Fourth fireworks with the huge blossoms of this special allium (*Allium schubertii*).

LOVELY LILIES

Asiatic and Oriental hybrid lilies can be planted in spring or fall. They deliver two to three weeks of splashy, gorgeous flowers. The Asiatics (such as 'Lollypop') bloom first and usually have smaller blossoms and bolder colors. The Orientals (such as 'Muscadet' or 'Star Gazer') bloom a bit later and tend to be larger, fragrant, and multicolored or speckled. Besides the Asiatic and Oriental hybrids, many other lily varieties can work in a mixed perennial bed. For sheer quantity of vivid flowers in a small space, it's hard to beat a lily.

One caveat about lilies: the small, red lily-leaf beetle has become prevalent in some parts of the country in recent years, devouring lilies with heartbreaking results. Keep an eye out for them or your precious lilies might be ruined. Check with your local Cooperative Extension Office for the latest and best control methods.

One annoying habit of lilies is their proclivity to crank out tiny bulblets as the years go by. These bulblets send up feeble foliage and an occasional half-hearted flower, and they dilute the impact of the larger parent bulbs. Unless you're meticulously digging them up and growing the bulblets to mature size in a nursery bed, they're basically just in the way and should be weeded out.

'Muscadet' Oriental hybrid lily with purple-foliaged 'Chocolate' white boneset (*Eupatorium rugosum* 'Chocolate').

'Lollypop' Asiatic hybrid lily (*Lillium* 'Lollypop') offers several weeks of big, cheerful blossoms in midsummer.

SMALL BULBS

If I had to choose just one small bulb it would be the grape hyacinth (*Muscari armeniacum*). The various species and cultivars of grape hyacinth naturalize readily, tolerate conditions from sun to shade, and bloom for many weeks. Most have lovely bluish purple or white blossoms, which are not eaten by deer.

Crocus, glory of the snow (*Chionodoxa forbesii*), squill (*Scilla*), and dwarf iris (*Iris reticulata*) are all easy bulbs that perk up the drab spring landscape. All small bulbs should be planted in masses to maximize their impact. Although colors like deep purple look great in photos, small dark flowers are easily overlooked, while lighter colors pop out against the dark, moist spring soil.

▲ Masses of giant crocus light up the spring garden with vivid colors.

CHAPTER FOUR

SHOPPING FOR PLANTS

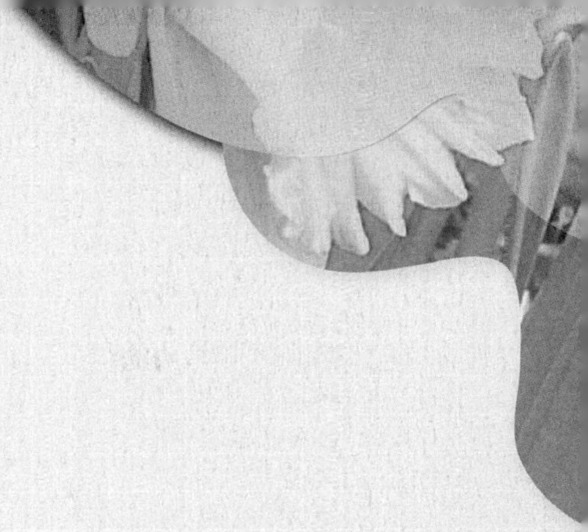

like to buy plants locally so I can evaluate their health. If there's not much selection near where you live, you might have to travel to find a good garden center or order the plants from catalogs or from online sources. If you do go the catalog route, avoid catalogs that offer lots of plants for bargain prices, as these are usually small, inferior-quality plants that will have trouble getting established. Mail-order plants are also usually more stressed because of traveling in a box through the mail under varying temperature conditions.

When you go to the nursery or garden center, take along your Blueprint and a copy of the Plant Palette. If a chosen plant is unavailable, you can easily pick a good substitute by referring to the Plant Palette. Your Blueprint helps you see what color, size, and bloom time will work.

Go ahead and indulge in some unplanned additions if you get inspired by especially beautiful or healthy plants at the nursery. Again, your Blueprint tells you at a glance whether the addition fits into your plan. If your heart is set on an unavailable plant and you want to try to find it later, plan on using a bamboo stake with a duct-tape label to stand in during the layout phase, once you're back in your garden.

TIPS FOR BUYING PLANTS

In the real world, there are few perfect plants, but a little extra care will help you get the most for your money. These guidelines will help you aim for the best.

PREBLOOM PLANTS

Look for healthy, sturdy plants that are preferably not in flower. A plant with a good crop of stems and leaves growing from its crown is better than a taller, stragglier plant that is already blooming.

GOOD ROOT STRUCTURE

If possible, slide the plant gently out of its pot to check the roots. The ideal plant has a spider web of roots showing on the root-ball. Blackened or mushy roots indicate disease, probably because the plant has been in the pot too long. Most nursery perennials are pot-bound to some degree, meaning that their roots have formed a mat lining the inside of the pot. These roots will be cut back when planting (see page 65), but it's best to choose the least pot-bound specimens.

On the opposite end of the scale, watch out for bare-root perennials that have been potted up but are not yet rooted in. Most nurseries buy at least some bare-root plants in bulk, then pot them up for resale. If not enough time has elapsed after potting up, their immature new root structure might not survive transplanting into your garden.

GOOD FOLIAGE, HEALTHY PLANT

Foliage should generally be tough and dark green, except for varieties bred deliberately with different colored foliage, of course, such as purple coral bells (*Heuchera*). Steer clear of any of these foliage problems:

▶ **Plants with overly abundant, light green, tender foliage** may have been overfertilized. These plants will struggle to get established, and the foliage may attract aphids.

▶ **Foliage that looks dusty and/or gray** may be suffering from powdery mildew. This disease can kill the plant and infect the rest of your garden.

▶ **Plants with wilting foliage** can indicate a fungal disease or pest problem, or neglect.

▶ **Plants with any sign of insect infestation** should be avoided. Look for insects and eggs on the foliage and soil. Snail eggs look like gelatinous masses and will quickly explode into a colony of hungry pests if they hatch.

The medium- and dark-brown roots are rotten. If you cut away as much of the rotten root mass as you can, the plant will probably recover if it still has enough good roots (like this one).

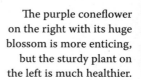

The purple coneflower on the right with its huge blossom is more enticing, but the sturdy plant on the left is much healthier.

WEED-FREE SPECIMENS

Avoid plants that have weeds growing in the pot. Weeds often indicate that the plant has been overwintered (sometimes repeatedly) at the nursery and is probably weakened and pot-bound. Some weeds are very difficult to disentangle without damaging the plant. Be especially careful never to buy a plant — or accept one from a neighbor or friend — that contains goutweed (a.k.a. bishop's weed or *Aegopodium podagraria*), as it is almost impossible to eradicate and quickly chokes out the other plants in your garden. Goutweed reproduces from small nodes on its roots, and the more you break it up, the more it multiplies. The variegated type is less odious than the solid green kind, but they should both be treated with fear and trepidation. I know gardeners who have moved because of goutweed.

2

WHEN YOU GET HOME

Keep your plants in a holding area until you're ready to plant, checking daily to be sure they have enough water. Ideally, your holding area should match the light and wind conditions of the finished bed to best prepare the plants for their final destination. If you live in a hot climate, though, you should keep black nursery pots in at least partial shade or the roots can be destroyed by the absorbed heat. Treat any slugs and snails that appear, and quarantine any unhealthy plants.

In spring, if you buy plants that have been raised in a greenhouse, you might have to move them in and out of a sheltered area (a greenhouse, garden shed, or garage) to gradually "harden off" their tender foliage before you transplant them into your garden. Hardening off is the process by which foliage that has grown in an artificially sheltered environment is prepared for life in the real world. Failure to properly harden plants off can result in frost kill, sunburned foliage, and dieback. Although this usually doesn't kill the plant, it sets it back and retards development.

If possible, store your purchases in a holding area where light and wind conditions match those of your new flower bed.

MULTIUSE 1" Round White Labels
Same size as template 5112™*

Item #

GERANIUM SANG.
'ALBUM'

MYOSOTIS

MYOSOTIS

MYOSOTIS

SAPONARIA

SAPONARIA

CAMPANULA
'DARK BLUE
CLIPS'

CAMPANULA
'DARK BLUE
CLIPS'

LIMONIUM

LIMONIUM

PRUNELLA

ASTER
'SCHNEEGITTER'

Laser/Ink Jet

Removable round labels and a large piece of
graph paper let you experiment with layout
schemes.

CHAPTER FIVE

GETTING YOUR PLANTS INTO THE GROUND

When I first designed gardens, I drew layouts on graph paper because I thought garden designers were supposed to do that. But I always felt defeated when I got ready to plant and had to change it all around because my paper layout didn't look right on site. I've realized that working in two dimensions on a flat piece of graph paper just doesn't help me visualize the garden environs and how the plants will look there. When I'm actually working on site on the other hand, key details leap out and solutions come intuitively. On site, I immediately see, for instance, how my original thought of placing a gigantic Joe-Pye weed on the left end of a bed would make an awkward, looming tower, while the same plant would nestle in nicely on the other end where a nearby tree could help temper the impact of its height.

My drawn design always ended up in the trash, and I decided that for me, at least, it was a waste of time. So I gave that up and developed my own layout system. It basically consists of doing the entire layout on site simply by placing the pots in the prepared bed. This requires quite a bit of concentration, because once you set a plant in the bed, it's easy to lose track of its attributes. If this seems too daunting, see page 58 for a paper-plan approach that may suit you better.

DECIDE ON PLANT PLACEMENT

Before you set out your plants, check your Blueprint to make sure you have all the plants for your design. I like to keep my Blueprint handy for easy reference by putting it on a clipboard inside a large zippered plastic bag to protect it from water and dirt. The following steps describe how to lay out your new bed according to my system.

A ziplock bag keeps the Blueprint and clipboard clean and dry.

1. Assemble all the plants in clusters in front of the prepared bed. The area will be organized something like this:

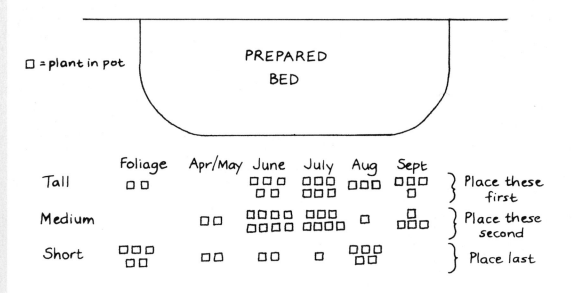

2. If any plants are missing, use a stand-in during the layout stage: Take a bamboo stake that's roughly the height of the missing plant, then top it with a duct tape "flag," writing the plant name in permanent marker to stand in during the layout step.

3. Starting with the tall plants, place the pots in the prepared bed, trying to keep bloom times evenly distributed. The tall plants usually form the framework. They generally go in the back third of the bed, but putting some in the front or middle can be exciting. For example, the 5-foot-tall daylily *Hemerocallis* 'Autumn Minaret' looks great at the front of a bed.

4. Leave a little extra room — maybe an extra 3 to 6 inches on each side — around tall plants as they tend to be broader. The detailed notes in the Flower Catalog section mention which plants in particular need extra room.

5. Once all the tall plants are distributed, move to the mediums, then to the shorts. The order of placement is not that important, as long as you use a system that helps you keep track of bloom time and size. Keeping complementary plants together is also a goal. For example, I always try to put basket of gold (*Aurinia saxatilis*) next to early-blooming purple bearded irises such as 'Crimson King' or 'Little Episode'. When I have an important combination like that, I sometimes place them at the very start to be sure they are well positioned. A cluster of several plants that look good blooming together (especially if the combination is repeated in the same bed) is usually more effective than scattering things that bloom at the same time evenly throughout the bed. Clusters provide a focal point where the eye can rest, while evenly scattered blossoms can make the garden feel unsettled.

UNDERSTANDING PLANT HABITS

When I was a newcomer to garden design, I usually chose my plants from those beautiful close-up photos you see in gardening encyclopedias and catalogs. What an unpleasant surprise I had when I discovered that the flower was not the only important part! I had inadvertently chosen a lot of plants with poor or unremarkable foliage, and the result was a flower bed without good structure. I also accidentally smothered some short plants by putting them too close to things that looked small in their pots but that developed wide, arching foliage as they grew in the bed.

The flowers and the foliage of each plant give it its "habit," or shape. I've identified twelve different plant habits and made a few notes about which types combine especially well or badly with each other. The following suggestions apply to placement of certain plant habit types.

1

Low or medium-height mound. Blossoms do not rise much or at all above foliage. Classic example: 'White Clips' Carpathian harebell (*Campanula carpatica* 'White Clips')

Campanula carpatica 'White Clips'

2

Low or medium-height mound with blossoms floating above on stems. Most or all foliage is at base. Classic example: 'Mount St. Helens' coral bells (*Heuchera* 'Mount St. Helens')

Heuchera 'Mount St. Helens'

3

Mound of basal foliage with blossoms on medium to tall stems rising above. Stems may have some leaves. When you cut off the spent flowers (or "deadhead") this type, you may cut it back to its basal foliage. Classic example: 'Türkenlouis' Oriental poppy (*Papaver orientale* 'Türkenlouis')

Papaver orientale 'Türkenlouis'

4

Fountain or fan-shaped foliage rising from base in a relatively solid mass. Blossoms rise not too far above foliage. Foliage may be cut back to within several inches of ground if it browns after plant blooms. Classic example: daylily (*Hemerocallis dumortieri*)

Hemerocallis dumortieri

5

Mound of basal foliage with leaved stems rising in a rather dense mass above. Usually needs extra space so basal foliage is not shaded too much. May be cut back to basal foliage. Classic example: purple coneflower (*Echinacea purpurea* 'Magnus')

Echinacea purpurea 'Magnus'

6

Vertical mass of intermingled foliage and blossoms. Medium-height true lilies are the best example of this form. Cut back foliage halfway at most after bloom. Classic example: 'Star Gazer' Oriental hybrid lily (*Lilium* 'Star Gazer')

Lilium 'Star Gazer'

7

Leaves primarily on stems, which form a rather solid upright vase- or oval-shaped mass. Might form a clump or multiply by creeping. Medium to tall height. Do not remove all the foliage if cutting back after bloom. Classic examples: azure monkshood (*Aconitum carmichaelii* 'Arendsii'), 'Venusta' queen of the prairie (*Filipendula rubra* 'Venusta'), garden phlox (*Phlox paniculata*)

Aconitum carmichaelii 'Arendsii'

8

Blossoms just at the top of a fan-shaped or vertical clump. Leaves primarily on stems. Short to medium height. Classic example: 'Autumn Joy' stonecrop (*Sedum* 'Autumn Joy'); cushion spurge (*Euphorbia polychroma*)

Euphorbia polychroma

9

Matlike creeping foliage with blossoms held above. Short to medium height. Classic example: 'Gaiety' bugleweed (*Ajuga reptans* 'Gaiety')

Ajuga reptans 'Gaiety'

10

Irregularly shaped stems that intertwine with neighboring plants. Usually has some basal foliage as well as leaves on stems. Usually does not need extra space to survive. Classic example: knautia (*Knautia macedonica*)

Knautia macedonica

11

Substantial vase-shaped basal foliage with stems. Blossoms may rise above or be nestled down in the foliage. Usually medium height; most bulbs fall in this category. Classic example: 'Apeldoorn' Darwin hybrid tulip (*Tulipa* 'Apeldoorn')

Tulipa 'Apeldoorn'

12

Substantial vase-shaped basal foliage with huge blossom head on short stem. The extremely large-flowered allium, *Allium schubertii*, is the only plant in the Plant Palette that has this form.

Allium schubertii

PUT PLANT HABITS TO WORK

Including plants with a mixture of the growing habits illustrated on pages 54–55 will ensure a dynamic design for your garden. Keep the following pointers in mind to ensure that your plants thrive. Remember that most perennials need sunlight to hit their foliage.

▶ **Mat-forming edgers.** A draping, mat-forming plant (type 9) can be planted with its root-ball right against the edge of a raised bed. The roots will get established inside the bed, while the foliage creeps and drapes over the edge of the raised bed.

▶ **Smaller sun lovers.** Be careful not to place a plant that develops a wide top (types 4, 5, 7, or 8) where it could smother and kill a short, mounding plant, especially one that requires full sun. For example, avoid planting a daylily right next to 'Snowcap' wall rock cress (*Arabis caucasica* 'Snowcap'). Similarly, don't put a plant that needs full sun in the shadow of a taller plant. An example is planting Joe-Pye weed (*Eupatorium maculatum)* on the south side of tall asters.

▶ **Good partners.** Plants with wide tops (types 4, 5, 7, and 8) can usually be planted right next to each other; their foliage will intermingle and sort itself out. Examples of this would be a daylily and a Siberian iris or two daylilies planted together.

▶ **Sunlight and foliage.** Plants with foliage that goes up the stem (like monkshood) can survive cramped conditions, while those that have only basal foliage (like anemone) die if planted too densely.

In late fall, 'Schneegitter' aster (*Aster* 'Schneegitter') sends a charming spray of tiny white flowers over the edge of the bed.

Grapeleaf anemone (*Anemone tomentosa* 'Robustissima') needs some elbow room but rewards you with six or more weeks of autumn blooms.

4

CRITIQUE THE LAYOUT

Once all the plants are in place, I carefully look over the whole scheme, checking for clashing colors, proper spacing, and balanced bloom times. Sometimes I decide to add or remove plants at this stage, making new bamboo/duct-tape stakes if necessary. Check to see that you haven't placed plants in straight lines; a zigzag pattern produces a more natural effect and maximizes flower visibility.

+ Nuts-and-Bolts Tips

As you do your on-site layout by placing the pots directly into the planting bed, it's easy to become confused and fail to remember the height and/or bloom time for each plant once it's placed in the bed. If you lose track of too much information about height and bloom time, it can be difficult to achieve a balanced layout. Here are some memory aids that I've found helpful.

To keep track of height: Cut bamboo stakes to match plant heights and stick them in or tape them to each pot. This allows you to keep tabs on heights even after placing the pots in the bed.

To keep track of bloom time: Flag the bamboo stakes (from the step above) with different colors of adhesive tape for different bloom times. If you're not using bamboo stakes, try tying different colors and patterns of surveyors'

tape (available at hardware stores and building centers) or fat yarn around each plant or pot. One of my workshop participants even suggested spraying or dabbing paint on pots to signify bloom time. If you can get colored plastic flags on short pieces of wire (like those used for invisible dog fences), they work perfectly. When I need to use color to establish a sequence, I usually use the order of colors in the rainbow because it's easy for me to remember. The sequence is "Roy G. Biv" (red, orange, yellow, green, blue, indigo, violet!).

To provide access for layout and for maintenance later on: Place stepping stones larger than your foot (10" or 12" diameter) throughout the bed during layout and planting. These allow access to the center for maintenance after the foliage has filled in.

An Alternate Method:
PAPER
LAYOUTS

If you prefer to work out your layout on paper ahead of time, I've found it helpful to draw the bed to scale on a large piece of paper or cardboard and use small sticky notes or removable color-coded dot stickers to play around with the layout. If you come up with a good layout but still want to try other versions, photocopy your work (with a large format copier at a copy center if necessary), then remove the stickers and try another arrangement.

The sequence and thought process I describe here is basically the same as what I do on site when I lay out the pots directly in the bed. This layout illustration is based on (but not exactly identical to) Garden One in part 2.

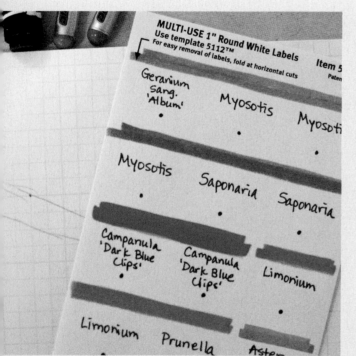

1. Using 1-inch removable labels, I color-coded each plant by month of bloom [you may prefer to use the seasonal terms: red (spring), orange (early summer), yellow (midsummer), green (late summer), blue (fall)]. I used plain white labels for foliage plants, and indicated height with small dots at the bottom of the label: one dot for short plants, two for medium, and three for tall.

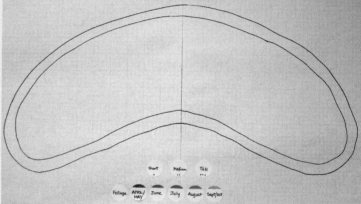

2. I draw the bed on graph paper at a scale of 1 inch to 1 foot of garden. (See the plan for Garden One, page 87.)

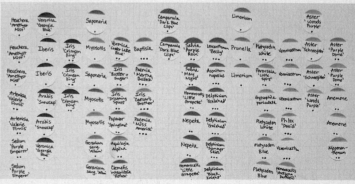

3. I arrange the plants by bloom time and height on another sheet of paper.

4. I like to place the tallest and/or most prominent plants first. In this example, the purple smokebush (*Cotinus coggygria*) is big and contributes all season, so I started with that. The azure monkshood (*Aconitum carmichaelii* 'Arendsii') and the clusters of Culver's root (*Veronicastrum virginicum*) came next because they all bloom relatively late, so their foliage is obvious all season long. Next, I placed the extremely tall delphiniums. My goal was to create little islands of tall plants in the back third of the bed. The delphiniums would be cut back after bloom, so their presence would be diminished after midsummer. I added the tall plants for early summer next, since no early summer plants were in the picture yet and I wanted to be sure to claim some prime space for them, and finally the rest of the tall midsummer plants to finish off that height category.

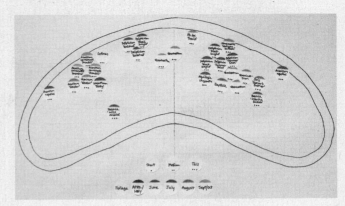

5. All of the spring plants in this garden were short or medium in height, and none of them were in the plan yet. I added most of them at this stage across the front and along the right edge, which is visible as you approach the house from the parking area.

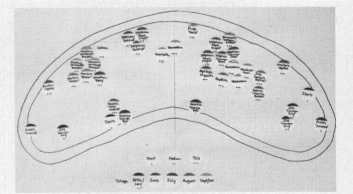

6. Since there were relatively few fall plants in the design, I wanted to add most of them at this point to ensure relatively even distribution. It's easy to make the bed really lopsided late in the season when not much is in bloom, so I prevented that by staking out prime locations for fall plants at this stage of the game.

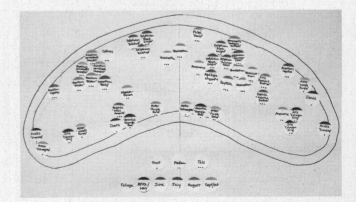

7. Next I started filling in large areas with bunches of early summer–blooming plants, then midsummer-blooming plants (taking care to ensure even distribution), followed by the late summer–blooming plants. You can lay out whichever month you want first, but just be sure you're working toward relatively even (or balanced) distribution of blooms for each month across the bed.

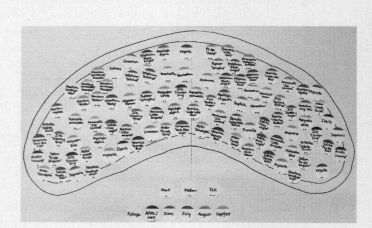

8. The foliage plants came next. At this stage there were still quite a few early summer–blooming plants left over, so I placed them next, followed by what was left of the late summer–blooming plants.

When all the stickers were in the bed, I did some final adjustments, mostly improving the spacing between plants. One location change I made was to move the catmint (*Nepeta*) and the wormwood (*Artemisia ludoviciana* 'Valerie Finnis') (in the lower right corner) farther apart since they both have grayish foliage that's wasted on each other. In the final arrangement, the *Sedum* 'Purple Emperor' is somewhat between them to improve contrast.

CHAPTER SIX

PLANTING YOUR CONTINUOUS-BLOOM GARDEN

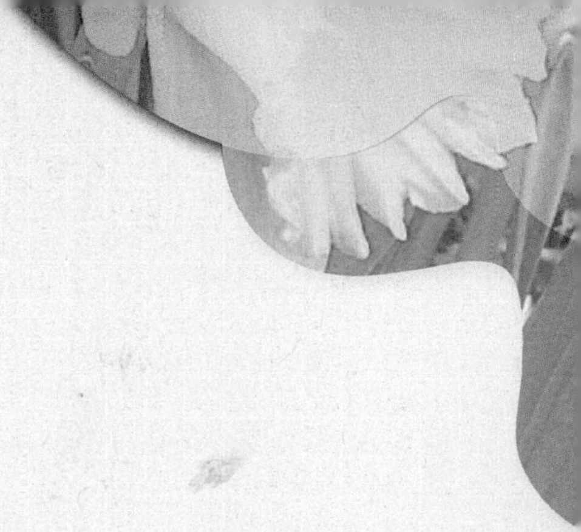

All the thinking and planning steps are now complete and it's time for some real gardening! Your new bed should be thick with pots ready for planting. I like to use small-headed shovels because they fit better in the tight planting space I favor. These shovels are sometimes called "florist shovels," though my friend Debby Smith affectionately dubbed them "girlie" shovels. I improve each planting hole with a compost/manure mixture instead of applying soil amendments over the entire planting bed. This not only saves on cost but also discourages weeds from springing up between plants. People are sometimes skeptical about this technique, but I've had excellent results with it over the 10 or more years I've used it.

1

IN DEFENSE OF DENSELY PLANTED BEDS

I **like to pack as many plants** as possible into the bed. Densely planting perennials provides several advantages:

▶ It maximizes blossoms.

▶ It discourage weeds, because there's no place to take root.

▶ Plants tend not to spread or need dividing as often as widely spaced plants. I've observed this clearly with Siberian iris, which I recently had to divide for the first time in a 10-year-old bed. Siberian irises usually develop a doughnut shape with a dead space in the center and require division every 3–5 years.

✛ When Mildew Is a Factor

Plants very susceptible to powdery mildew (including bee balm and many varieties of garden phlox) are not usually recommended for these dense plantings, although 'David' (*Phlox* 'David') is very mildew-resistant and works for me in these dense beds. If you simply must have a mildew-prone plant in your design, try to place it on an outside corner where it's exposed to maximum air circulation. It can also help to spray the foliage with an organic fungicide such as Serenade.

Phlox 'David'

2
AMENDING YOUR SOIL

If you're planting a whole garden at once, it's convenient to mix up a whole load of amendments in a wheelbarrow. I use roughly a 50-50 mixture of high-quality compost and composted cow or sheep manure. Good compost and composted manures contain no peat, which is a cheap filler. Poor-quality compost can actually kill plants, so I like to stick with reputable brands. Avoid free manure from the neighbor's horse or cow manure pile, because it usually contains nasty, uncomposted weed seeds that turn your beautiful new perennial bed into a maintenance nightmare. I allow 100 pounds of compost/manure mixture for 20 or 30 plants, and mix it as follows:

1. Pour equal portions high-quality composted manure and compost into a wheelbarrow and use a shovel to mix them together.

2. Save your back while mixing: Slide the shovel down the slanted surface opposite the handles, push the shovel forward, then, using the edge of the wheelbarrow as a fulcrum, push down on the handle to lift the loaded shovel head. Twist the handle to dump the shovelful back into the wheelbarrow. Repeat about 20 times to be sure all the material is thoroughly mixed.

╪ When Plants Need Help

Most herbaceous perennials prefer slightly acidic soil, but a few do best with more alkalinity. If your soil is naturally acidic, you can add a scoop of lime to the planting hole of alkaline-loving plants like baby's breath (*Gypsophila*), pinks (*Dianthus*), and bearded irises (*Iris germanica*). If the soil needs to be acidified you can add pelletized sulfur.

During the past few years I've been using a root enhancer on all my transplants. It seems to help in getting the plant established during the first year. My favorite is called Dyna-Gro K-L-N, and I use it at the rate of one teaspoon per gallon of water. I then do all my watering from a watering can.

DIG IN!

Once you've got the amendments mixed and ready, here's how to proceed with planting.

1. Place your pot in the desired location in the bed, then use the shovel tip to mark the exact spot and set the plant aside.

2. Dig a hole approximately as deep as needed: just eyeball the depth at this point.

3. Dump in about two heaping shovelfuls of 50-50 mix of compost and manure, and thoroughly combine it with the soil: Three to five churns of the shovel should be enough.

4. Scoop out enough amended soil to make room for the plant, and set it in a pile separate from the unamended soil.

5. Use two bamboo stakes to gauge the correct depth. First, mark the depth of the soil in the pot with your thumb on one bamboo stake.

6. Use the horizontal stake to mark ground level. It allows you to gauge the depth at the center of the hole. It's important not to bury the crown of the plant too deeply. Adjust the hole depth as necessary, by adding or taking away more soil.

7. Slide the plant from its pot. If it's very pot-bound, you might have to push, shake, or pry it loose.

8. For very pot-bound specimens, the roots need to be loosened up or the plant will be stunted. Use your fingers to loosen the roots. If the roots form a solid mat that you can't penetrate with your fingers, use a knife or hori hori to slice off the outermost layer, or make 1-inch-deep top-to-bottom cuts all around the sides.

9. If the roots have formed a mat on the bottom, be sure to slice or tear off the mat. Whatever method you use, you can be pretty brutal — the danger of the roots strangling the plant is much greater than the danger of ruining the roots. New roots can't pierce a root mat, and failure to break it up usually results in permanently stunted growth. A few roots might break off, but don't worry. Most people do this too gently, so don't be afraid.

continued on next page

10. Suspend the plant gently by the foliage and place it in the hole, positioning it so that its crown is level with or slightly above ground level. Add handfuls of the amended soil back into the hole, alternating the amended soil with unamended soil, until all the soil is used up.

11. Use a sweeping motion to draw in soil from the surrounding area and create a little saucer-shaped earth berm around the plant to help channel water to its crown while it's getting established. The inside of the saucer should be at or slightly above ground level. If it is below ground level, dig up the plant and elevate it so the crown is slightly above ground level. Don't make the saucer too sturdy, or you can cause crown rot from too much moisture concentrated on the crown. Over the course of a year, the berm should gradually disintegrate, leaving a level garden.

12. Water in the transplant immediately after planting by gently filling the saucer with water, especially if the weather is sunny or dry. Take care not to use too much water pressure or you'll destroy the saucer. I like to use a watering can or a long-handled watering wand with a shutoff valve. You can lay the wand down and leave it trickling on one plant while you move on to the next. The saucer should hold water for a few seconds. If the water breaks through the berm, shore it up with more dirt.

13. Apply a layer of bark mulch about 2 inches to 3 inches thick over and outside the entire saucer area, and gently pat it in place to stabilize the whole arrangement.

+ Kid Gloves

A few plants detest root disturbance and should be treated more gingerly than described on pages 64–66. For these, you should ignore the normal advice about mangling the root mass when transplanting. Just slide the plant gently out of the pot and into the prepared hole.

False indigo	*Baptisia australis*
Corydalis	*Corydalis lutea*
Bleeding heart	*Dicentra eximia*
Baby's breath	*Gypsophila paniculata*
Poppies	*Papaver*
Balloon flower	*Platycodon grandiflorus*
Globeflower	*Trollius chinensis*

AFTER YOU PLANT

Shredded bark mulch is extremely effective for retaining moisture and suppressing weeds in perennial beds. A 2-inch layer is sufficient. If you use the dark brown variety of shredded bark mulch, it is not very visible because these beds are planted very densely, and the foliage covers it up for most of the year.

If you don't like bark mulch, try compost, shredded leaves, or buckwheat hulls (though the latter are very expensive). My friend Rick Sawyer, owner of Fernwood Nursery in Swanville, Maine, gives his plants the Rolls Royce treatment with a layer of compost topped with shredded leaves.

If you do use bark mulch, it's best not to let it get mixed in with the soil, because it can tie up nitrogen as it decomposes. If you need to disturb the bed to put in a new plant or to divide an old one, pull the mulch aside first and spread it back when done.

During its first year, the new garden should be watered deeply and regularly. Watering is especially important during the first month, when you might need to do it from once a day to twice a week, depending on sun exposure, heat, and season. Stick your finger all the way down into the soil next to the root-ball to test for dryness. Ideally, new transplants should never get completely dry during the first month.

One deep watering is better than several shallow waterings, as it encourages deep root growth. One caveat: It is possible to overwater a new garden if you absolutely soak it with water every single day. The soil must be allowed to retain its little air spaces to keep the roots from rotting.

+ Smothered by Annuals

Sometimes people get impatient for blossoms during the garden's first year. It's best to resist the temptation to fill in the gaps between new perennials with annuals — they can choke a new garden and rob the perennials of light and nutrients. Remember the old gardener's adage, "The first year the plants sleep, the second they creep, and the third year they leap." If you do want to use some annuals, be sure they're not too close to the perennials — don't ever let them touch.

Buckwheat hull mulch is beautiful but much more expensive and less effective for retaining moisture than shredded pine bark mulch.

5

GETTING BULBS INTO THE GROUND

Up **until now,** we've discussed only how to plant perennials, but spring bulbs are a very important — and welcome — part of any garden. As with any kind of plant, the most important first step is to choose the right spot for your spring bulbs: They usually flourish where the snow melts first, because these spots tend to be warmer and better drained. Bulbs in foundation plantings, especially on southern exposures, often bloom at least a week earlier than those more out in the open. Variations in weather can cause bloom times to fluctuate by as much as a month from year to year.

Another consideration is how to disguise bulbs after bloom, when their dying foliage must be left to mature (see page 80). I like to choose a location such as behind daylilies, where the foliage of other plants hides the dying tulip foliage from the primary viewing angle.

October is the best time to plant fall bulbs in Maine, but you can usually get away with doing it in September or November if necessary. Check with other gardeners or at your local garden center to find out the ideal time for planting where you live. If you plant too early, you run the risk they'll sprout and put up foliage; too late and they won't have time to put down any roots before the ground freezes.

PLANTING LARGE BULBS

Long ago I discovered a good bulb-planting technique in an antique gardening book and have used it ever since. Planting them is a bit of work, though, so be prepared to get your knees dirty. This works for planting tulips and other large bulbs.

The technique requires fertilizer and sand, and I put these ingredients in separate flip-top Rubbermaid drink bottles for easy dispensing directly into the planting hole. I use granular bulb fertilizer instead of bone meal, because inhaling bone meal is suspected of causing serious health issues. Adding sand on top improves drainage and cushions the bulb from the fertilizer; the roots grow down through the sand to find the fertilizer. I use "play sand" or "sandbox sand" because it contains no silica and the dust is not hazardous to breathe. This technique is especially good with daffodils, which are so finicky about drainage.

1. Put bulb fertilizer and sand in their own shaker bottles for ease of application.

2. Use your weight to press down on the bulb planter and wiggle it into the ground right up to the handle.

3. Gently twist the bulb planter out and set it aside. It should be full of soil. Don't let soil fall back into the hole.

4. Following the package instructions, sprinkle the recommended amount of fertilizer into the hole, then pour about ½ inch of sand on top of the fertilizer.

5. Place the bulb in the hole, being sure the pointy end is pointing up. If you ever need to plant a bulb that doesn't have an obvious top and bottom, plant it on its side and it will right itself as it grows.

6. Push the soil back out of the bulb planter into the hole. It's much easier to push it out toward the handle. Gently pat the soil flat (do not pack it down).

PLANTING SMALL BULBS

For small bulbs, I have developed a planting system I rather ghoulishly refer to as the "mass grave technique." Like the previous technique, this system uses granular bulb fertilizer and sand.

1. Excavate a straight-sided (not slope-sided), flat-bottomed, oval or kidney-shaped hole about 12 inches long and several inches deep, then sprinkle granular fertilizer evenly across the bottom.

2. Top the fertilizer with ½ inch of sand.

3. Place the small bulbs at the recommended spacing on top of the sand. Gently replace the soil, being careful not to tip over the little bulbs.

6 ENSURING BLOOM IN FUTURE SPRINGS

Most bulb foliage must be allowed to mature for six weeks after blooms have faded. This is how sunlight recharges the bulb for next year's blossoms. You might be tempted to cut the unsightly foliage back too early, but this will only bring disappointment the following spring. The dilemma of the ugly foliage can be solved by placing tulips, lilies, and daffodils in the back half of a flower bed, especially behind perennials like daylilies, whose foliage provides a hiding place.

If you are growing tulips as annuals, you can simply remove the bulb and foliage when it's done flowering. Getting the whole bulb out is easier said than done, however, and any leftover annual tulip bulb will put up a lot of foliage and just an anemic little blossom the following year.

A cheery group of species tulips (*Tulipa saxatilis*) and squill (*Scilla siberica*) drink up the sun on a warm spring day.

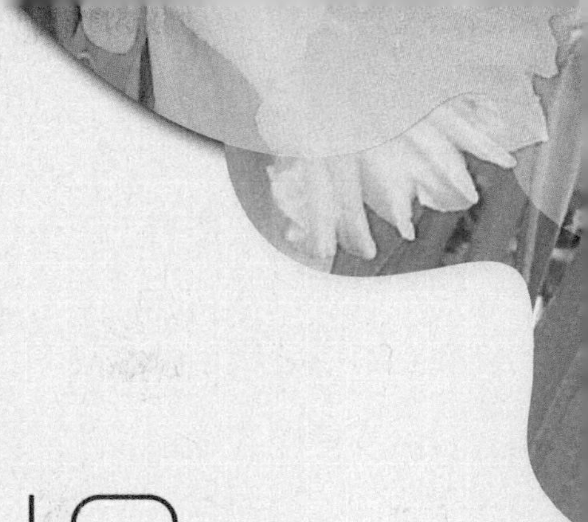

CHAPTER SEVEN

IMPROVING AN EXISTING BED

Most of us rarely have the opportunity to create a completely new bed from scratch; usually we're just trying to improve beds we've been working on for years. Luckily, the Blueprint method lends itself perfectly to assessing and improving existing beds. You can use the technique to improve a single bed or to fill in the gaps in bloom time for plantings (including flowering shrubs and trees) scattered throughout your yard by cataloging everything on a single Blueprint and checking for subseasons that need improvement. In the second instance, you might be dealing with plants that are not necessarily densely planted, and you will have a wider choice of perennials (and flowering woody perennials) than those recommended specifically in my Plant Palette. One way to approach a whole yard is to create seasonal vignettes or focal points of bloom in various parts of the yard that "turn on" and "turn off" as the seasons pass.

WORKING EXISTING PLANTS INTO YOUR BLUEPRINT

The first step for improving an existing flower bed is to catalog what you have and enter those plants into the Blueprint. Next, decide which old plants to keep and add a complementary selection of new plants to provide continuous blooms from spring to fall. Here is the procedure, step by step.

1. Measure the bed.

Start by measuring the existing bed. If you want to play with the layout on paper, draw the outline on graph paper at this point (see page 10).

2. Calculate the number of plants.

Use the method described in chapter 1 to calculate the total number of short, medium, and tall plants you need. For the purposes of this example, let's say the bed has 60 square feet with a fairly typical ratio of 30% short, 50% medium, and 20% tall plants. According to the calculations from page 198, this makes the target numbers 12 short, 20 medium, and 6 tall plants. Transfer these target quantities to the boxes at the top of a blank Blueprint (see page 217). For this example, assume the bed is in full sun to partial shade.

3. Catalog existing plants.

Now, list the names and quantities of all the plants that are already in the bed, using a regular piece of notebook paper. Don't try to put them in any order at this point. Be as specific as you can, but don't worry if you can't remember exact cultivar names. It's all right to use common names at first for your list; you can add the scientific names later by looking them up in the Index of Common Plant Names (page 207). If you're doing this cataloging step when the plants are not in bloom and you're not sure what they are, it helps to look at old photos of the bed if you have any. (I use a digital camera to record bloom time in my gardens.)

Your list should look something like this:

2 **Black-eyed Susan** (*Rudbeckia fulgida*)
3 **Sedum 'Autumn Joy'**
1 **Siberian iris** (blue; medium height) (*Iris sibirica*)
1 **Peony** (light pink) (*Paeonia*)
4 **Astilbe** (medium pink)
2 **Tall white phlox** (*Phlox paniculata*)
2 **Daylilies** (yellow) (*Hemerocallis*)
1 **Daylily** (red) (*Hemerocallis*)
3 **Delphiniums** (blue)
1 **Purple coneflower** (*Echinacea purpurea*)

4. Transfer plants to the Blueprint.

Locate the bloom month for your plants by looking them up in the Flower Catalog (page 120). In some cases you'll have to choose the closest match. In this example, I used the bloom data for *Hemerocallis* 'Hyperion' for the yellow daylilies, because that's probably a pretty close match. It's usually not a big deal if a few plants are mistakenly identified, so don't feel like you have to nail everything down exactly. Place each plant and its quantity in the proper slot on the Blueprint, but leave some extra space at the start of

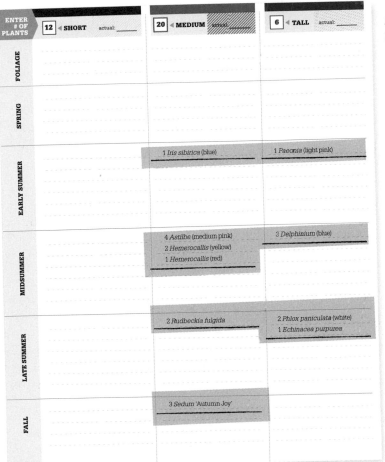

Step 4: Transfer plants to the Blueprint

Table header:

ENTER # OF PLANTS	12 ◀ SHORT actual: ____	20 ◀ MEDIUM actual: ____	6 ◀ TALL actual: ____
FOLIAGE			
SPRING			
EARLY SUMMER		1 *Iris sibirica* (blue)	1 *Paeonia* (light pink)
MIDSUMMER		4 *Astilbe* (medium pink) 2 *Hemerocallis* (yellow) 1 *Hemerocallis* (red)	3 *Delphinium* (blue)
LATE SUMMER		2 *Rudbeckia fulgida*	2 *Phlox paniculata* (white) 1 *Echinacea purpurea*
FALL		3 *Sedum* 'Autumn Joy'	

each line. After filling in all your old plants, draw a dark, fat line with a felt pen below each clump of old plants in the Blueprint to separate them from the new plants, which you add next. Another way to clearly distinguish the old plants from the new on your Blueprint is to use a highlighter to mark all the old plants.

If your garden contains perennials that are not in this book, look up their bloom information by searching on the Internet, in a reference book, or in a plant catalog. (See page 209 for recommended books and Web sites with information on perennials.

5. Choose which old plants to keep.

What color scheme do you want for your new bed? Now is the time to ruthlessly remove any plant that doesn't fit the plan. Excess plants can be given away or potted up for future use elsewhere. Mark an X to the left of any plant that will be excluded from the new bed. It's usually a mistake to try to be too frugal by "making do" with old plants that don't really fit your new design. Remember that it's taking a lot of effort to create your

continued on next page

new garden, and you don't want to dull the effect of the new bed by reusing old plants you never liked that much in the first place.

For this example, I'm choosing a color scheme that incorporates many of the existing plants: pink, purple, blue, yellow, and white. To follow this plan, I have to remove the red *Hemerocallis* in the midsummer category and the gold *Rudbeckia* in late summer, and so I've placed an X to the left of those entries to show they should be removed.

Besides the plants I want to eliminate completely, there are also some that could be reduced in number. For the size of this

bed, four pink astilbes seems like a lot (and it limits the number of new plants I can add), so I reduce the astilbes to one, writing "1" to the left of "4 Astilbe." Two clumps of *Phlox paniculata* also seems like too much, so I reduce them, too, to one. For the other plants that I am simply accepting, I copy the quantity to the left to make it easier to add up the total number of plants in each height category as I go along.

These eliminations leave me with 7 medium plants and 6 tall plants (which I write at the top right side of the medium and tall columns for reference). I still need to choose 12 short plants and 13 medium plants (20 target plants minus 7 old plants). There are already 6 tall plants in the garden, so I don't need any more of those.

Step 5: Blueprint with "Keepers"

	actual: ____	**20** ◀ **MEDIUM** actual: ____		**6** ◀ **TALL** actual: ____
		1 1 *Iris sibirica* (blue)	**1** 1 *Paeonia* (light pink)	
		1 4 *Astilbe* (medium pink)	**3** 3 *Delphinium* (blue)	
		2 2 *Hemerocallis* (yellow)		
		X 1 *Hemerocallis* (red)		
		X 2 *Rudbeckia fulgida*	**1** 2 *Phlox paniculata* (white)	
			1 1 *Echinacea purpurea*	

6. Select new plants.

Turning to the Plant Palette, start choosing complementary plants in your selected color scheme. For the sample garden here, I definitely need to add quite a few for spring, as that bloom category is completely empty in the old garden. Chapter 3 gives helpful suggestions about choosing plants for a Blueprint. You'll notice that the quantities for the bulbs (*Iris reticulata* and *Tulipa*) are listed in parentheses. This indicates they are not to be included in the plant count because they are tucked in among the perennials and don't really take up room. The exception is the *Allium schubertii,* which is a bulb but it takes up so much room it has to be counted.

7. Other notations.

I sometimes draw circles, squares, or triangles around the quantity of plants to help me remember what I'm doing. When I use circles, triangles, and squares this way, I jot a note at the top of the Blueprint to help me remember what it means. For example, it might say:
"[square] = move; [circle] = divide."

In this garden, a square around the quantity of any plant means I need to move it from its current location in the bed. Here are some examples of things I might flag for myself this way:

▶ Plants that need to be moved

▶ Plants that need division

▶ Plants available in another bed that I plan to move to the new bed (that is, plants I don't need to buy)

8. Shopping, layout, and planting.

As with a Blueprint for a new bed, you can use this one directly as a shopping list. The plants you already have are clearly separated by the thick line (or by highlighting) from the ones you need to buy. As you purchase plants you can check them off the list. If you need to make a substitution, you can easily see what qualities (height, bloom time, color) are needed.

If the existing plants do not need division and are well positioned in the bed, you can just lay out the new plants around them. For me, this is usually not the case, and I want to move things around to create a more harmonious and balanced composition. I usually dig up the plants I want to reuse and set each one loosely in an oversized plastic pot, which is easy to move around in the bed as I play with the layout. You can also use plastic grocery bags for this, although they're more floppy and it's harder to see at a glance what the plant is.

As you work your plan, be sure not to put small, new plants right up against large, overgrown established plants (which really need division), because the new plants just can't compete. Even though it's more work, it's better to dig up the big old ones, divide them, and reuse parts in the new bed.

For more helpful information about layout and planting, see chapter 5.

Step 6: Blueprint finalized

ENTER # OF PLANTS	12 ◀ SHORT actual: *12*	20 ◀ MEDIUM actual: ~~1~~ *21*	6 ◀ TALL actual: *6*
FOLIAGE		2 *Sedum* 'Purple Emperor'	
SPRING	1 *Iberis* 1 *Veronica* 'Georgia Blue' (25) *Iris reticulata* 'Harmony'	2 *Iris* 'Crimson King' (purple), (25) *Tulipa* 'Beau Monde' (pink/white Triumph)	
EARLY SUMMER	3 *Allium schubertii*	**1** 1 *Iris sibirica* (blue) 2 *Iris sibirica* 'Butter and Sugar'	**1** 1 *Paeonia* (light pink)
SUMMER	2 *Campanula* 'Blue Clips'	**1** 4 *Astilbe* (medium pink) **2** 2 *Hemerocallis* (yellow) **X** 1 *Hemerocallis* (red)	**3** 3 *Delphinium* (blue)

75

'Summer Sun' sunflower heliopsis (*Heliopsis helianthoides* 'Summer Sun') is a mainstay of the low-maintenance garden, blooming for eight weeks without deadheading.

CHAPTER EIGHT

ENJOYING AND MAINTAINING YOUR GARDEN

They say that gardeners don't sit in chairs, and remembering to pause and enjoy the garden can be hard. Weeding and deadheading (removing faded flowers) are like eating potato chips, and sometimes I have to force myself just to sit in a chair, ignoring everything that seems wrong and the impulse to fix it on the spot. It helps to remind myself that the maintenance is potentially endless, while this precious moment of leisure is very finite.

The only garden maintenance I truly like is weeding moss in my Japanese garden, which I find very restful. Otherwise, I'm afraid most garden maintenance just seems like a chore to me. If you're one of the lucky ones who loves puttering in the garden, however, your choice of plants expands, as you can include more high-maintenance plants.

Gardens designed according to the Blueprint technique described in this book tend to require less maintenance, because they are densely planted and the 200-odd recommended plants tend to be very low maintenance. It's nice to have a garden that can look good under conditions of near-total neglect, and that's been my aim. And if you do have the extra time and the inclination to take better care of it, it's just icing on the cake. I've prepared the following bare-bones maintenance tips for people who are busy or disinclined to putter (or both, like me). During its first year, the new perennial garden needs special care. The roots are undeveloped, making the plants more susceptible to dryness and invasion by weeds. In future years, it will demand less attention.

THE IMPORTANCE OF WATERING

Water the new garden regularly and deeply, in the morning if possible. Watering during the heat of the day increases loss to evaporation; watering late in the day leaves the foliage wet at night and increases the likelihood of mildew and other foliar diseases. Using an overhead sprinkler is okay during the morning hours, but the best method is to apply water with a watering wand directly to the crown of each plant (underneath the foliage).

To test for dryness, stick your finger all the way down into the soil next to the crown of several plants — the soil should be moist but not waterlogged. Be sure to water deeply, as shallow watering prevents the new plants from growing the deep roots that sustain them and hold them in the ground during spring freezing and thawing.

SUGGESTED WATERING SCHEDULE

This schedule for newly planted perennials assumes that there is no natural rain; reduce watering if substantial rain occurs.

▶ **Week 1.** Water every other day.

▶ **Week 2.** Water two or three times.

▶ **Rest of first season.** Water twice a week.

▶ **Fall.** Continue watering occasionally in the fall until the ground begins to freeze.

+ Mortality: What's Normal?

It is unusual for every single perennial to survive. It's normal to lose about 5 percent or so of new plants during the first year due to weather, diseases, pests, and accidental damage. In densely planted beds, the remaining plants should fill in to cover the gaps, so there is usually no need to replace them unless they constitute a key element in the bloom scheme.

Purple coneflower (*Echinacea purpurea* 'Magnus') needs no deadheading and serves up bright blossoms for two months or more.

WEEDING NEEDS

Planting densely and applying bark mulch immediately after transplanting greatly reduces the number of weeds, but you should still check for them every couple of weeks. If you are unsure what is a weed, consult a professional or a book. One trick for identifying weeds is to look at the plants in uncultivated areas near the garden and match them to the suspected weeds. Some weeds are more damaging than others. Here are some common notorious ones:

▶ **Field bindweed** (a morning glory relative) can quickly strangle new perennials, and it reproduces rapidly if allowed to drop seed.

▶ **Vetch** (another twining, vining weed) has pretty purple flowers and flat rows of small leaves lining each tendril. If allowed to go to seed it can be hard to eradicate.

▶ **Dandelions** are best pulled promptly on a moist day when the whole root comes up easily. Leftover root tips produce octopus-like monsters that are very hard to remove. If a dandelion growing in the crown of a perennial gets big, it's virtually impossible to get out without disturbing or even killing the plant.

▶ **Oxalis** (whose leaves resemble clover but which has yellow flowers) is worth nipping in the bud because it will plague you for years if allowed to set seed.

▶ **Goutweed.** If you are unlucky enough to have this nuisance in your garden, you will have to weed constantly just to keep it under control enough to prevent it from killing everything.

FLOWERS AND DEADHEADING

Although you'll see blossoms on perennials the first year, their numbers increase dramatically during the second and third years. Of course, this assumes you've started with high-quality plants and planted them carefully. Perennials benefit from having their dead or declining flower heads snipped off when they are done blooming. This allows the plant to put its energy into root and foliage growth instead of producing seeds, which takes an enormous amount of the plant's energy. Most perennials are best deadheaded by cutting the stem just above the highest leaf. You can always cut off just the blossom itself instead, but that often leaves an unsightly stem.

Some perennials, like 'Kobold' blanketflower (*Gaillardia* 'Kobold', also sold as *G.* 'Goblin'), stop blooming pre-

maturely if left alone, but they bloom for months on end if deadheaded. With plants like this, your maintenance effort will be handsomely rewarded if you have the time. Another example of this type of perennial is lanceleaf coreopsis (*Coreopsis lanceolata).*

Other flowers should not be deadheaded because they self-seed, thus increasing your plants. When you have self-seeders in your garden, "edit" out any that sprout in the wrong place, like near the crown of another plant. Some examples of self-seeders are:

▶ Columbine   *Aquilegia*

▶ Rose campion   *Lychnis coronaria*

▶ Hollyhock   *Alcea rosea*

▶ Lady's mantle *Alchemilla mollis*

▶ Lungwort   *Pulmonaria*

A few special perennials don't care if they're not deadheaded and go on to produce attractive or inconspicuous seed heads. 'Purple Rain' sage (*Salvia verticillata* 'Purple Rain') (which I think is one of the very best plants) often develops attractive, grayish purple seed heads. 'Moonbeam' threadleaf coreopsis (*Coreopsis verticillata* 'Moonbeam') continues to bloom without deadheading and produces inconspicuous seed heads.

Tall asters, such as 'Alma Pötschke' New England aster (*Aster novae-angliae* 'Alma Pötschke'), develop dead, brown leaves on their stalks just when the flowers are blooming and your attention is drawn to the plant. You can easily remove the dead leaves simply by sliding your (gloved) hand up each stem from bottom to top. The leaves flutter down to the base where they are inconspicuous, leaving clean stems topped with beautiful flowers.

AFTER-BLOOM TULIP AND OTHER BULB FOLIAGE

Tulips and other bulbs need to keep their foliage for six weeks after bloom in order to recharge the bulb for next year's blossoms. Removing their dead or browning foli-

This 'Purple Rain' sage (*Salvia verticillata* 'Purple Rain') still looks good in September in Maine because the seed heads are attractive.

age too early results in poor blooms the following year. For this reason, bulbs should be planted behind perennials with foliage that can hide the browning bulb foliage. After the six-week period is over, you may snip off or gently pull off the browned foliage.

MANAGING SPREADING PLANTS

Some plants, such as soapwort (*Saponaria ocymoides*) and wall rock cress (*Arabis*), are meant to spread and drape over the edges of the bed, and they should be allowed to expand this way. On the other hand, some plants spread too far if left unchecked. Some examples are peachleaf bellflower (*Campanula persicifolia*) and 'Valerie Finnis' wormwood (*Artemisia ludoviciana* 'Valerie Finnis'). These plants should be pulled back from their neighbors each spring, if necessary, by pulling or cutting off some of their side shoots, leaving a neat clump. You might like to pot up or replant these shoots elsewhere.

If spreading plants are encroaching on sensitive neighbors, they should be pulled back later in the season. The Lancaster geranium (*Geranium sanguineum* var. *striatum*) shown below, left, is being pulled back from a pair of 'Purple Dome' New England asters (*Aster novae-angliae* 'Purple Dome'). The asters, which are still pretty short in midsummer, require full sun and would be choked and smothered by the geraniums without help.

Plants such as grapeleaf anemone (*Anemone tomentosa* 'Robustissima') that resent being crowded should be given extra room or placed on the edge of the bed where they're not so boxed in. If their neighbors encroach too much, they should be thinned back or cut back away from the anemone. Plants that spread and need to be pulled back regularly are also best placed on the edges where they can easily be controlled.

Pull back the perennial geraniums (A) from the asters (B) in midsummer.

The gray-foliaged 'Valerie Finnis' wormwood (*Artemisia ludoviciana* 'Valerie Finnis') on the left can be thinned back regularly to keep it from overwhelming its neighbors.

PREPARING FOR WINTER

The garden requires special treatment the first winter, and although it's optional in future winters, it can be beneficial then as well. In fall when foliage is in decline, it can be cut back to about 4 inches tall. You can cut back the unattractive foliage of early bloomers to neaten the bed's appearance when fall plants are still in bloom. Do not, however, cut back lavender or other woody perennials such as Montauk daisy (*Nipponanthemum nipponicum*) or tree peony (*Paeonia suffruticosa*).

COVER UPS

After the ground freezes (usually after Thanksgiving in Maine), cover the bed with a layer of fir boughs placed upside down so they won't blow away so easily. The main purpose of these boughs is to prevent damage due to wide variations of temperature in the spring. When plants are not well rooted, they are more susceptible to popping out of the ground in the spring, exposing the roots and often killing the plant. Do not do this too early in the fall, as placing boughs on the garden before the ground has frozen can cause the plants to rot.

Fir boughs laid upside down on a new garden protect it from alternating freezing and thawing during the spring.

Fifty pounds of boughs will cover an area 10 feet square. Spruce boughs are also acceptable, but don't use hemlock because the needles fall off. Fir boughs (called "banking boughs" or "brush") can be purchased at local nurseries in Maine in the fall. (Living fir trees need three nights of below-freezing temperatures to "set" their needles so they won't fall off when the branches are cut. Sometimes unscrupulous brush cutters harvest too early and sell you brush that falls apart right away.) You can cut up your Christmas tree and use the branches for banking boughs. After the first year, covering the garden with boughs in the winter is optional (but recommended).

+ Cutting Back

▲ To neaten the garden by cutting back Siberian iris foliage, hold the foliage back with one hand and shear it off a few inches from the ground.

▲ Trimming all the leaves to the same height produces a clean mound that lets you appreciate nearby blooming plants.

Make blunt cuts on tough-stemmed perennials ▲ like garden phlox (*Phlox paniculata*) to make spring cleanup less painful. Avoid angled cuts, which create sharp, painful spears that can poke you later on.

5 ONGOING CARE

Remove banking boughs gradually over the course of about a week in the spring when growth is showing on the plants. Do not remove the boughs too early or all at once as this can shock the plants.

The first spring (during April, if possible), top-dress plants with a 50-50 mixture of good compost and good composted manure ("good" means containing no peat). Spread a small shovelful of compost/manure mixture around (not on) the crown of the plant. Do not top-dress lavender, bearded irises, or other plants that require poor, dry soil. In future years, top-dressing is more discretionary, but recommended at least every few years.

MULCH KNOW-HOW

The bark mulch will need to be renewed every few years. If the bark mulch is too thin, the bed will get weedy and need watering more often. It's best not to mix the bark mulch into the soil when adding plants, as it can draw nitrogen away from the plants as it decomposes. If the bark mulch develops a silvery, moldy appearance it should be removed and replaced with fresh mulch.

LIVE AND LET LIVE

I like to garden organically and have almost never found it necessary to use broad-spectrum herbicides and pesticides. I prefer to discourage bad bugs through good cultural practices rather than by killing them, especially since most pesticides kill beneficial insects along with the pests. These days there are more and more good choices in the organic and narrow-spectrum pesticide category, too.

As far as animal pests go, my own belief is that no plant is worth killing an animal for, but I don't expect everyone to agree with me on that. Using nontoxic deterrents (see below) seems like a good way to save favorite plants in a nonviolent way. The Internet and your local Cooperative Extension Office are good sources of information on low-impact garden solutions.

As a general philosophy, I like to think of my garden as a place to coexist with other creatures, even if it means losing a plant once in a while or putting up with a little chewed foliage. When a plant gets eaten up in my garden, I take it as a clue to try a different plant, not as an invitation to wage war. The garden is purely a luxury to me. By practicing a little tolerance, I can make it a source of peaceful relaxation rather than a place of contention and conflict.

OH, DEER!

Choosing plants distasteful to deer is one foolproof way to avoid damage from deer. But if you must have tulips, which are tender, tasty treats to deer, Tree Guard (a nontoxic, bitter spray available at garden centers) repels both deer and rodents. Tree Guard is waterproof, but it does become slightly weaker as the plant grows. A good application regime is once when the bud first emerges and again when the plant is about 6 inches tall. Doing this for two years in my deer-intensive yard permanently trained the deer to steer clear of the tulips.

Tree Guard also keeps deer, squirrels, and chipmunks from helping themselves to tasty perennial foliage such as daylily leaves. I've applied it to all sorts of herbaceous and woody plants over the course of the past 10 or so years without a single problem. Don't use it on vegetables or fruit plants because it will make the fruit bitter for you, too. Be sure to wash out the sprayer assembly thoroughly with soapy water after each use or the mechanism will seize up.

DETERRING RODENTS

I've had luck discouraging rodents (and deer) with a product called Deervik, which is a thick, stinky goo. The label says to place Deervik-dipped sticks around the garden, but it's less hazardous to absentminded gardeners (who have sometimes been horrified to discover it in their hair) to put it in little vented containers. Those green plastic tubes with rubber tops that florists use for cut flowers make ideal Deervik receptacles. Just cut the opening in the rubber top a bit larger to allow more odor to escape, insert a bit of Deervik with a stick, and replace the rubber top. Snipping off the bottom tip of the tube allows any rainwater to drain out so the odor is not weakened. Sink the capsules in the soil at an angle, leaving the rubber cap exposed, several feet apart in the bed.

PART TWO
SUCCESSFUL CONTINUOUSLY BLOOMING GARDENS:
FIVE CASE STUDIES

The five "real" gardens in the pages that follow are gardens that I designed for busy clients (and one for myself), some (especially mine) receiving little maintenance. They are designed to look good with almost no effort, although they look even better if there's time for a bit of weeding and staking. I never have as much time as I expect, so I'm glad for the minimal-maintenance option.

Each garden was designed to suit certain color and plant preferences and to fit a particular site. I've included the actual Blueprint for each, along with detailed comments about the garden, including special challenges and ideas for improvements. The photos show each garden as it looks through the seasons.

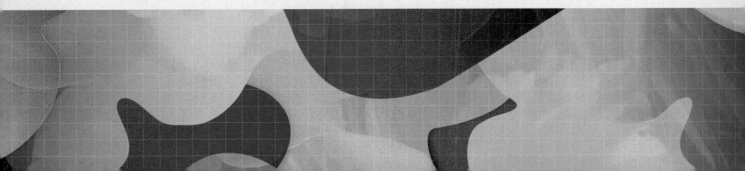

1

Garden One:
SOOTHING BLUE FOR SUMMER COOL

MAY 13 (SPRING) ▶ See Blueprint on p.88 for key

This very floriferous raised bed is boomerang shaped and edged with a low stone wall. The client is a professional woman who visits this oceanside summer house sporadically in spring, summer, and fall. A small amount of maintenance is done by the client and, occasionally, by a gardening professional, but because the owner's primary residence is out of state, it was important that the garden be low maintenance. The site is sunny and sheltered from major winds.

The client and I decided on a raised bed of weathered fieldstone to make the flowers more visible from the kitchen and dining room, which are slightly elevated. The raised bed also eliminates the need for edging, as would have been necessary for a bed surrounded by lawn. The slightly irregular boomerang shape creates a sense of enclosure between the bed and the house. The bed is viewed from one end when leaving the parking area and walking downhill toward the house, then the view gradually shifts to a broadside angle when you step up on an entry deck. The broad side of the garden is also visible from the kitchen and dining room.

Planted a year before most of the photos here were taken, the garden features a color scheme of purple, white, blue, lavender, and violet, with a touch of yellow. The cool colors of this palette are soothing in the summer sun. The client is especially fond of delphiniums,

columbine, and peonies, and she was willing to do the extra work to stake tall delphiniums.

The size is 110 square feet, which I calculated by adding all the whole squares and half the partial squares enclosed in the drawing (on facing page). I chose a fairly standard height ratio of 20% short, 55% medium, and 25% tall. Too many tall plants would make this bed top-heavy for its size; too many small plants would be lost at the standard viewing distance of 10 to 20 feet.

Right away you might notice the rather vast discrepancy between the target numbers and the actual numbers of plants for this particular garden. There are two reasons for this, one good and one bad. The bad one is that I had proposed a slightly larger bed than I actually built, but I never adjusted my plan accordingly. The good reason is that tall delphiniums (of which there are seven) and Culver's root (*Veronicastrum viginicum*, of which there are five) don't take up as much room as most tall plants, so I knew I had some extra space. Another reason I got away with packing so many plants in this garden is the large number of draping rock garden plants, such as the *Veronicas*, soapwort (*Saponaria ocymoides*), and the wonderful *Aster* 'Schneegitter', which could be planted right next to the stone retaining edge, effectively increasing the plantable space. The result is a very densely planted bed with very little

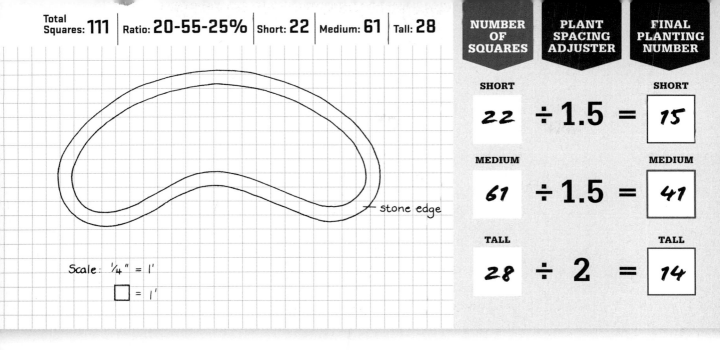

| Total Squares: **111** | Ratio: **20-55-25%** | Short: **22** | Medium: **61** | Tall: **28** |

NUMBER OF SQUARES	PLANT SPACING ADJUSTER	FINAL PLANTING NUMBER
SHORT		**SHORT**
22 ÷ **1.5** =		*15*
MEDIUM		**MEDIUM**
61 ÷ **1.5** =		*41*
TALL		**TALL**
28 ÷ **2** =		*14*

stone edge

Scale: ¼" = 1'

☐ = 1'

The 'Snowcap' wall rock cress (*Arabis caucasica* 'Snowcap') drapes over the edge of the bed.

room for weeds and a few more casualties than usual from plants getting squeezed out.

Many of the tallest plants, such as the purple smokebush (*Cotinus coggygria* 'Royal Purple') and azure monkshood (*Aconitum carmichaelii* 'Arendsii'), are clustered at the far end of the bed (beyond which hardly anyone ventures), creating a backdrop and anchoring the bed. The other tall items (the delphiniums and the *Veronicastrum*) are scattered in clumps throughout the back two-thirds of the rest of the bed.

My favorite thing about this garden is the subtle intermingling of sages (*Salvia*), catmint (*Nepeta*), balloonflower (*Platycodon*), self heal (*Prunella grandiflora*), and *Clematis* in shades of purple, blue, and pink in midsummer. The biggest problem with this garden is that the two catmint plants stand ready to wipe out everything within reach if they are not cut back drastically or otherwise contained (by tying up with twine) during the summer. This adds to required maintenance and also results in a temporary sore spot in the bed while the catmint puts out a new flush of foliage.

During the first year I lost the aster 'Wood's Purple' (*Aster* 'Wood's Purple') (probably due to overcrowding or shading), the 'Honorine Jobert' anemone (*Anemone* × *hybrida* 'Honorine Jobert') (which I no longer use because of 100% mortality to date), and the 'Bicolor' monkshood (*Aconitum cammarum* 'Bicolor') (ditto). The Montauk daisy (*Nipponanthemum nipponicum*) failed to bloom during the garden's second year, possibly because of crowding, but did at least contribute lovely foliage all season. The 'David' phlox (*Phlox* 'David') and the 'Little Spire' Russian sage (*Perovskia atriplicifolia* 'Little Spire') were nearly crushed by a catmint (*Nepeta* 'Walker's Low'), but rescued just in time. The mortality was within the acceptable 5–10% range, however, so I still consider it a success.

This garden could be improved through the addition of a couple of purple coneflowers (*Echinacea purpurea* 'Magnus') to add more color in late summer. Otherwise, I was happy with the timing, quantity, and distribution of blossoms through the season.

ENTER # OF PLANTS	15 ◀ **SHORT** actual: _25_	41 ◀ **MEDIUM** actual: _44_	14 ◀ **TALL** actual: _28_
FOLIAGE	3 *Heuchera* 'Amethyst Myst'	2 *Artemisia ludoviciana* 'Valerie Finnis' ⑧ 2 *Sedum* 'Purple Emperor' ⑬	1 *Cotinus coggygria* ⑯
SPRING	2 *Veronica umbrosa* 'Georgia Blue' 2 *Arabis caucasia* 'Snowcap' ⑭ (25) *Muscari armeniacum* ② 2 *Iberis sempervirens*	3 *Iris* 'Crimson King' (60) Darwin Hybrid Tulips 20 'Cream Jewel' 10 'Golden Parade' 30 'Big Chief' ① (30) *Tulipa batalinii* 'Apricot Jewel'	
EARLY SUMMER	2 *Geranium sanguineum* 'Album' ⑦ 3 *Myosotis sylvatica* 'Victoria Blue' 2 *Saponaria ocymoides*	3 *Aquilegia alpina* (25) *Allium caeruleum* 1 *Clematis integrifolia* 'Rosea' 2 *Iris sibirica* 'Butter and Sugar' 2 *Iris sibirica* 'Dreaming Spires' 2 *Papaver* 'Springtime' 2 *Veronica austriaca* 'Crater Lake Blue'	1 *Baptista australis* ⑤ 1 *Iris sibirica* 'Caesar's Brother' ③ 1 *Paeonia* 'Miss America' ④ 1 *Paeonia* 'Martha Bulloch'
MIDSUMMER	2 *Campanula carpatica* 'Blue Clips' ⑨	(25) *Allium sphaerocephalon* 2 *Nepeta* 'Walker's Low' 2 *Hemerocallis* 'Little Grapette' 3 *Salvia verticilliata* 'Purple Rain' ⑪ 3 *Salvia nemerosa* 'May Night' ⑥	1 *Leucanthemum vulgare* 'Becky' ⑩ 3 *Delphinium* 'Black Knight' 2 *Delphinium* 'Galahad' 2 *Delphinium* 'Summer Skies' 2 *Aconitum napellus* 1 *Aquilegia chrysantha*
LATE SUMMER	2 *Limonium latifolium* 1 *Prunella grandiflora* 'Pink Loveliness'	1 *Perovskia atriplicifolia* 'Little Spire' 2 *Gypsophila paniculata* 3 *Hemerocallis* 'Ice Carnival' 2 *Platycodon grandiflorus* 'Florist Blue' 2 *Platycodon grandiflorus* 'Florist White'	2 *Aconitum cammarum* 'Bicolor' 1 *Phlox* 'David' 5 *Veronicastrum virginicum* ⑫ 1 *Hemerocallis* 'Autumn Minaret'
FALL	2 *Aster* 'Schneegitter' ⑱ 2 *Aster* 'Wood's Purple'	2 *Aster novae-angliae* 'Purple Dome' ⑰ 2 *Anemone × hybrida* 'Honorine Jobert' 1 *Nipponanthemum nipponicum*	3 *Aconitum carmichaelii* 'Arendsii' ⑮

Throughout the Seasons

See Blueprint (on opposite page) for plant labels.

June 20 (Early Summer)

July 24 (Midsummer)

August 25 (Late Summer)

October 18 (Fall)

Garden Two:
AN EXUBERANT WELCOME AT THE FRONT DOOR

AUGUST 7 (MIDSUMMER) ▶   **See Blueprint on p.92 for key**

At this site, the bland gravel driveway used to come right up to the front door and the side of the house. I wanted to create a focal point beside the main entrance that would provide color and lead the eye to the front door and away from another door (formerly the main entrance) which could be mistaken for it. I built an irregular oblong-shaped raised bed out of round, weathered stones, less than a foot from the wall of the house. A custom-built cast-iron trellis allows a clematis planted in the bed to reach over and climb the wall. The clients, who are away much of the year, especially love purple and pink, and the bed has to look good up close and approaching it from a distance of about 30 feet. In full sun to part shade, the 49-square-foot garden is low maintenance. The photos shown here were mostly taken when the garden was two years old.

This raised stone bed solves several problems. An addition put on by the present owners had the unintended effect of creating an unfortunate intersection of an awkwardly sloped gravel area and an ornate entry door placed oddly off center on the edge of an old patio. The new raised bed draws attention away from the odd arrangement of elements and also provides a level surface to settle the eye.

For a small bed there is a lot going on here, most of it pretty successfully. Spring bulbs give way to Siberian irises and an unknown dark pink peony that was transplanted from another area. Asiatic hybrid lilies and 'Purple Rain' sage (*Salvia verticillata* 'Purple Rain') put on a show, followed by daylilies and the extremely dramatic Culver's root (*Veronicastrum virginicum*) and Oriental hybrid lilies. The end of the season is more sedate, as the 'Robustissima' anemone, which should steal the show for six or more weeks, failed to bloom (possibly due to overcrowding by the *Salvia*, which was not cut back) during the garden's second year.

During the second year a few plants died or were accidentally weeded out: the *Saponaria*, *Gypsophila*, *Dicentra*, and *Salvia nemerosa* 'Rose Queen'. The *Phlox subulata*, which was added later by someone else, has filled in the vacancies and is actually looking pretty good. (I am prejudiced against this phlox, mainly because its foliage tends to be unattractive after bloom.)

The garden could be improved by cutting neighboring plants away from the anemone throughout the season to encourage it to bloom. If the anemone still refuses to bloom, I will try replacing it with a 'Clara Curtis' mum (*Chrysanthemum* 'Clara Curtis').

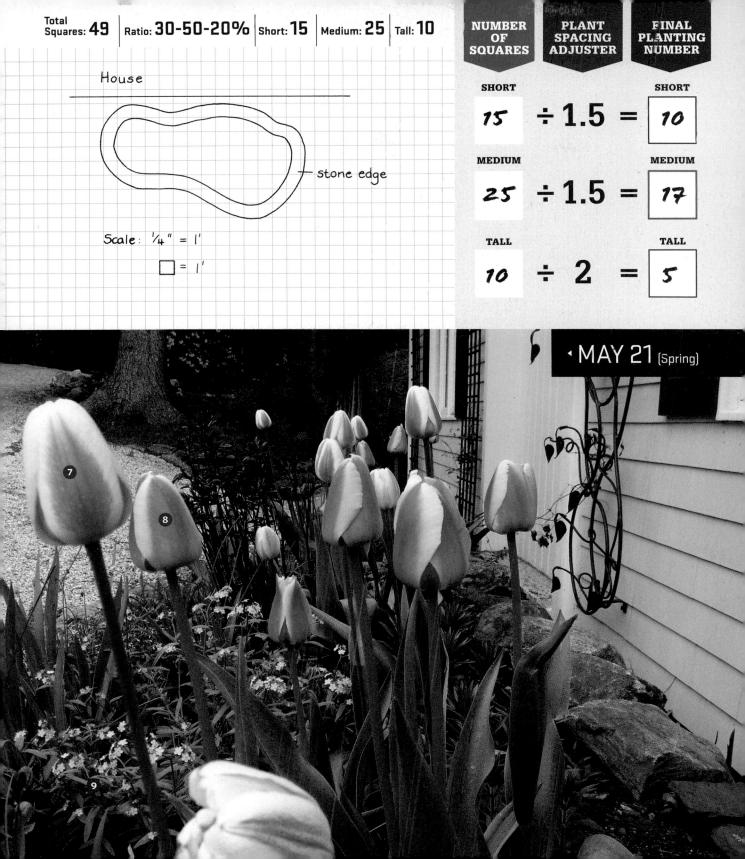

Total Squares: **49** | Ratio: **30-50-20%** | Short: **15** | Medium: **25** | Tall: **10**

House

stone edge

Scale: $\frac{1}{4}'' = 1'$

□ = 1'

NUMBER OF SQUARES	PLANT SPACING ADJUSTER	FINAL PLANTING NUMBER
SHORT		**SHORT**
15 ÷ **1.5** =		*10*
MEDIUM		**MEDIUM**
25 ÷ **1.5** =		*17*
TALL		**TALL**
10 ÷ **2** =		*5*

‹ MAY 21 (Spring)

ENTER # OF PLANTS	10 ◀ SHORT actual: *12*	17 ◀ MEDIUM actual: *19*	5 ◀ TALL actual: *6*
FOLIAGE		1 *Sedum* 'Purple Emperor'	

SPRING	(15) *Chionodoxa*
	(25) *Iris reticulata* 'Gordon'
	(15) *Muscari armeniacum*
	3 *Phlox subulata* (light pink: unknown cultivar)
		2 *Iris* 'Crimson King'
		(20) Darwin Hybrid and Triumph Tulips
		   10 'Ollioules' **8**
		   10 'Beau Monde' **7**	

EARLY SUMMER	1 *Geranium sanguineum* var. striatum **13** 3 *Myosotis sylvatica* 'Victoria Blue' **9** 1 *Saponaria ocymoides* 1 *Gypsophila repens* 'Rosea'	1 *Iris sibirica* 'Pink Haze' **12** (15) *Allium caeruleum* 1 *Dicentra* 'Zestful'	1 *Paeonia* (unknown cultivar) **10** 1 *Iris sibirica* 'Caesar's Brother' **11**
MIDSUMMER	1 *Heuchera* 'Mount St. Helens' 1 *Campanula carpatica* 'Blue Clips'	3 *Lilium* 'Lollypop' **14** (15) *Allium sphaerocephalon* 1 *Salvia verticillata* 'Purple Rain' **4** 1 *Salvia nemerosa* 'Rose Queen'	1 *Clematis jackmanii* **1**
LATE SUMMER		2 *Hemerocallis* 'Siloam Irving Hepner' **3** 1 *Lilium* 'Mona Lisa' **6** 2 *Lilium* 'Casa Blanca' **15** 2 *Hemerocallis* 'Catherine Woodbury' **5**	3 *Veronicastrum virginicum* **2**
FALL	1 *Aster* 'Wood's Pink'	1 *Aster novae-angliae* 'Purple Dome' **16** 1 *Anemone tomentosa* 'Robustissima'	

Throughout the Seasons

See Blueprint (on opposite page) for plant labels.

June 25 (Early Summer)

July 16 (Midsummer)

August 25 (Late Summer)

October 11 (Fall)

Garden Three:
AN OASIS OF COLOR (IN A SEA OF ASPHALT)

JUNE 23 (EARLY SUMMER) ▶   See Blueprint on p.96 for key

This small garden was created for a business in a small city — a beauty parlor in full, baking sun all day. It was my first continually blooming garden. It is bordered on two sides by established evergreen shrubs and a side of the building (including a small deck) and on the other two by an asphalt curb and driveway. Low maintenance, it features drought-tolerant plantings. It was designed with high-impact colors and flowers, as the garden is viewed primarily by people driving by on a busy highway and rarely is viewed up close. The garden pictured here is 12 years old; it has had several add-ons through the present, and it is professionally maintained. The planting area is 260 square feet.

Notice that this garden does not fit the density formula I now use. It is less densely planted (the target number of plants is much more than the actual number). Instead, the perennials were allowed to develop to maximum spread. I made this garden before I had fully developed the Blueprint system, and I drew up the Blueprint that appears here later. In the early days, I used quite a few annuals to fill the gaps between plants in this garden. A dozen years later, the tall plants have developed mature girth and the spreading plants have filled in all the gaps so there is no longer any room for annuals. The densely planted gardens I usually design now appear mature much more quickly than this one did.

A large percentage of the perennials are of short and medium height because I had to keep the sign visible from all angles. I tried to arrange the plantings to draw the eye to the sign. Seven large stepping stones were added in a V pointing at the sign to make it a focal point, to improve access for maintenance, and to create an intimate feeling in the spring, which is the only time the stones are not concealed by foliage.

This garden is surrounded by asphalt and exposed to searing sun from the east and the south, so I used only drought-tolerant plants to minimize maintenance. A thick (3-inch) layer of bark mulch is added every spring to hold the moisture and to keep the garden looking neat. It usually needs watering only a few times, in the heat of summer. The hot, dry conditions prevent the hydrangea from blooming, but its foliage is still an asset, especially in the fall when it provides lovely texture and color in front of the 'Alma Pötschke' New England aster (*Aster novae-angliae* 'Alma Pötschke').

Everybody wants to know what kind of poppies these are. The blood-red 'Rembrandt' poppies (*Papaver* 'Rembrandt') have 8-inch blossoms on 4- to 5-foot self-supporting stems, and they can really stop traffic.

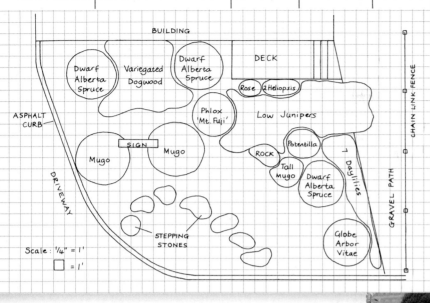

Total Squares: **260** | Ratio: **20-30-50%** | Short: **130** | Medium: **78** | Tall: **52**

NUMBER OF SQUARES	PLANT SPACING ADJUSTER	FINAL PLANTING NUMBER
SHORT		**SHORT**
130	÷ 1.5 =	87
MEDIUM		**MEDIUM**
78	÷ 1.5 =	52
TALL		**TALL**
52	÷ 2 =	26

‹ JUNE 21 (Early Summer)

Unlike most poppies, they are also good as cut flowers. When I planted them, I had no idea they were anything special, but I've since found the are very rare in the commercial trade in the United States. A similar type is *Papaver bracteatum*, available by seed from Thompson & Morgan.

The voluptuous 'Festiva Maxima' peony (*Paeonia* 'Festiva Maxima') is huge and incredibly floriferous, but there's a tradeoff, as this cultivar has very weak stems and requires a virtual forest of bamboo stakes and twine to keep up the heavy flower heads during bloom. Forget about a plain old peony ring! It needs deadheading several times during bloom or it will bury its cowering neighbors with browning petals. That said, I think it's a spectacular focal point and well worth all the trouble.

ENTER # OF PLANTS ▸	**87** ◂ SHORT actual: *60*	**52** ◂ MEDIUM actual: *38*	**26** ◂ TALL actual: *15*
FOLIAGE	1 *Artemisia schmidtiana*	1 *Hydrangea macrophylla* 'Blue Wave' 1 *Hosta* (variegated; unknown cultivar)	
SPRING	(40) *Crocus* (unknown varieties) (25) *Muscari armeniacum* ⑨ (50) *Narcissus* 'Hawera' ⑪ (50) *Tulipa* Kaufmanniana hybrids (John Scheepers 'Peacock Tulip Mixture') ⑧ (10) *Tulipa batalinii* 'Bright Gem' 4 *Aurinia* 'Compacta' 2 *Arabis* × *sturii*	6 *Iris* 'Crimson King' ⑩ 1 *Euphorbia polychroma*	
EARLY SUMMER	5 *Alchemilla alpina* 12 *Geranium sanguineum* var. *striatum* ④ 3 *Thymus praecox* 3 *Gypsophila repens* 'Rosea'	1 *Penstemon digitalis* 'Husker's Red'	3 *Papaver* 'Rembrandt' ⑦ 1 *Paeonia* 'Festiva Maxima' ②
MIDSUMMER	6 *Heuchera* (unknown cultivar) 5 *Sedum spurium* 'Tricolor' 6 *Campanula poscharskyana* ③ 1 *Campanula carpatica* 'White Clips' 2 *Scabiosa columbaria* 'Butterfly Blue' ⑤	(25) *Allium sphaerocephalon* ⑭ 1 *Anthemis tinctoria* 'Susanna Mitchell' 12 *Hemerocallis* (unknown varieties) ⑯ 1 *Knautia macedonica* ① 1 *Coreopsis lanceolata* 3 *Lilium* 'Montreux' (Asiatic Hybrid) 2 *Lilium* 'Navona' (Asiatic Hybrid)	2 *Leucanthemum vulgare* 'Marconi' ⑮ 1 *Rosa* 'New Dawn' ⑰
LATE SUMMER	3 *Gaillardia* 'Kobold' ⑥	2 *Rudbeckia* 'Goldsturm' ⑬ 2 *Platycodon grandiflorus* (blue; unknown cultivar) ⑫	2 *Heliopsis helianthoides* 'Summer Sun' 1 *Phlox* 'Fujiyama' 1 *Echinacea purpurea* 'Ruby Star'
FALL	4 *Aster novi-belgii* 'Professor Kippenberg' 3 *Sedum* 'Bertram Anderson'	2 *Sedum* 'Autumn Joy' 2 *Aster novae-angliae* 'Purple Dome'	1 *Solidago rugosa* 'Fireworks' ⑲ 2 *Aconitum carmichaelii* 'Arendsii' 1 *Aster novae-angliae* 'Alma Pötschke' ⑱

Throughout the Seasons

See Blueprint (on opposite page) for plant labels.

May 7 (Spring)

May 22 (Spring)

July 28 (Midsummer)

October 5 (Fall)

4

SPLASHES OF COLOR ADORN THE DOORYARD

JUNE 22 (EARLY SUMMER) ▶ See Blueprint on p.100 for key

This small entry garden flanks both sides of our front door and everything in it is highly visible. It has to look good from a distance of about 20 feet (when you first catch sight of it from the driveway), then it has to keep looking good as you draw closer to enter the door. It's a bed where I've trialed plants (including *Geranium* 'Midnight Reiter' and *Euphorbia griffithii*), and it has gradually evolved into a fairly attractive garden. Like all of the gardens at my house, it receives almost no maintenance. (When I'm being generous with myself, I claim this is because I'm testing the drought-tolerance and low-maintenance qualifications of the plants, but it's probably just because I'm a lazy gardener at heart.) The garden is bordered by the house on the back side and by a large arborvitae (*Thuja occidentalis*), natural stone steps, a small area of a stone-enclosed raised bed to the right of the steps, stone dust paths, and a brick apron on the sides and front. It is in partial shade (it faces west) and exposed to bitter winter wind. Originally planted six years before these photos were taken, it has had add-ons through the present. The perennial planting area is 67 square feet.

This garden is kind of a moving target since I'm always sticking things in to trial, and it has a few gaps right now. One empty spot is the top tier of the small raised stone bed to the right of the steps. I gradually killed a 'Moonbeam' threadleaf coreopsis (*Coreopsis verticillata* 'Moonbeam'), which hung on in that inhospitable spot for several years. It's a tricky corner because it's very dry (elevated in a tiny raised bed and under the roof overhang) and it receives very little sun, as it faces west and is shaded by the taller bee balm (*Monarda*) on its south side. This would probably be a great spot for 'Autumn Bride' hairy alumroot (*Heuchera villosa* 'Autumn Bride'), an underappreciated plant that thrives in dry shade or partial shade. Other good candidates would be dead nettle (*Lamium maculatum*), bugloss (*Brunnera*), a small hosta, or foamflower (*Tiarella cordifolia*). All these plants look good throughout the season, an important quality for a doorside garden.

The peony-flowered poppies (*Papaver somniferum paeoniflorum*) arrived uninvited from another garden. Once you have one of these poppies in your garden, the seeds end up everywhere and you'll have an endless supply. (The seeds are illegal in some places, as they are a form of opium poppy.) They are only hardy in Zones 8–10, but that doesn't affect their successful and constant self-seeding in Zone 5. When finished blooming they should be yanked promptly as they quickly become a shabby mess.

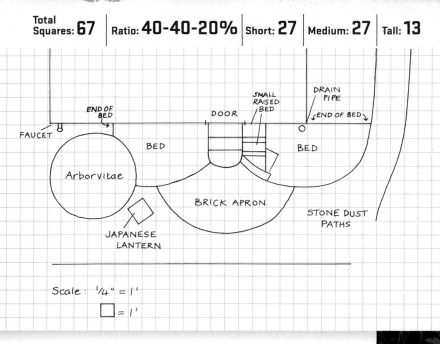

Total Squares: **67** | Ratio: **40-40-20%** | Short: **27** | Medium: **27** | Tall: **13**

FAUCET · END OF BED · Arborvitae · JAPANESE LANTERN · BED · DOOR · SMALL RAISED BED · BRICK APRON · DRAIN PIPE · END OF BED · BED · STONE DUST PATHS

Scale : 1/4" = 1'

☐ = 1'

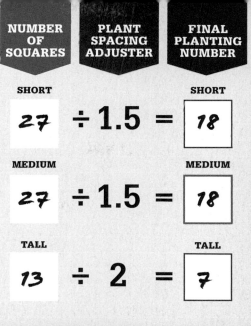

NUMBER OF SQUARES	PLANT SPACING ADJUSTER	FINAL PLANTING NUMBER
SHORT		**SHORT**
27 ÷	1.5 =	18
MEDIUM		**MEDIUM**
27 ÷	1.5 =	18
TALL		**TALL**
13 ÷	2 =	7

The original *Allium schubertii* rotted in a wet spring five years after the garden went in (along with all the rest of them in Knox County that year), and I replaced them the following fall. At the same time, I added 'Night Beacon' daylily (*Hemerocallis* 'Night Beacon') and 'Magnus' purple coneflower (*Echinacea purpurea* 'Magnus'). This planting of 'Gateway' Joe-Pye weed (*Eupatorium maculatum* 'Gateway'), facing west and half-wedged behind a huge arborvitae, has become proof to me that this cultivar can bloom and thrive in partial shade (contrary to most catalog descriptions). Besides testing for drought tolerance, one of the things I'm frequently looking for in my trial plantings is how far I can push the sun or shade tolerance of specific plants.

The most important plant here is the grapeleaf anemone (*Anemone tomentosa* 'Robustissima'), which graces the garden with excellent foliage all season then cranks out blossoms for two full months in the fall. I don't deadhead it. The gorgeous (mostly white) 'Black Dragon' lily (*Lilium* 'Black Dragon') obligingly supports itself on the foliage of the anemones and 'Gateway', thus eliminating the need to stake it and causing the blossoms to appear down at the 24-inch level.

ENTER # OF PLANTS	18 ◀ SHORT actual: *17*	18 ◀ MEDIUM actual: *15*	7 ◀ TALL actual: *7*
FOLIAGE			
SPRING	2 *Veronica umbrosa* 'Georgia Blue' **7** 1 *Dicentra formosa* (15) *Scilla siberica* (10) *Tulipa batalinii* 'Apricot Jewel' **6** (20) *Tulipa saxatilis* (20 *Iris reticulata* 'Gordon' (20) *Tulipa humilis Violacea* group (15) *Chionodoxa luciliae* 'Alba' (10) *Tulipa vvedenski* 'Tangerine Beauty' **5**	1 *Euphorbia griffithii* **3**	
EARLY SUMMER	5 *Allium schubertii* **1** 3 *Viola tricolor* **4** 1 *Gypsophila repens* 3 *Myosotis* (unknown cultivar)	(20) *Allium caeruleum*	1 *Paeonia* 'Karl Rosenfield' **2** 1 *Baptisia australis*
MIDSUMMER	1 *Geranium* 'Midnight Reiter'	1 *Campanula* 'Kent Belle' 1 *Hemerocallis* 'Night Beacon' 5 *Papaver somniferum paeoniflorum* **9** (20) *Allium sphaerocephalon*	2 *Lilium* 'Black Dragon' 1 *Monarda* 'Jacob Cline' **8**
LATE SUMMER	1 *Sedum* 'Rosy Glow' **10**	3 *Rudbeckia fulgida* (self-seeded) **13** 1 *Hemerocallis* 'White Temptation'	1 *Eupatorium maculatum* 'Gateway' **11** 1 *Echinacea purpurea* 'Magnus'
FALL		3 *Anemone tomentosa* 'Robustissima' **12**	

Throughout the Seasons

See Blueprint (on opposite page) for plant labels.

May 20 (Spring)

July 25 (Midsummer)

August 19 (Late Summer)

September 25 (Fall)

5

Garden Five:
A ROCK GARDEN WITH PIZZAZZ

JULY 30 (MIDSUMMER) ▶   **See Blueprint on p.104 for key**

I uncovered **large areas** of ledge at this windy, sunny oceanside garden, removing scruffy weeds and overgrown shrubs and trees to reveal the natural beauty of the underlying rock. In a few natural pockets, I built shallow raised beds edged with native stone and added some topsoil. These spots were naturally suited for rock garden plants. Shallow beds surrounded by ledge heat up more than regular beds because of the heat absorbed by the rock and transferred to the soil. Such beds are always unsuitable for plants like delphiniums that need cool, moist soil, regardless of how much they are watered. I designed this one using the client's favorite colors: purples, blues, and some pink. The 19-square-foot garden, planted two years before these photos were taken, is very low maintenance.

This tiny garden adds up to more than the sum of its parts because the changing color combinations are lovely and because so many of the plants provide interest both in color and in form. The tall sedums have wonderful buds before bloom and seed heads after, the sea lavender (*Limonium latifolium*) adds an airy texture that lends a lavender blush when it blooms, and the 'Munstead' and 'Hidcote' lavenders (*Lavandula angustifolia* 'Munstead' and 'Hidcote') contribute their woolly gray foliage and fantastic little drumstick blossoms. 'Purple

Rain' sage (*Salvia verticillata* 'Purple Rain') works its magic both in dramatic, swirling, purple blossoms and with its slightly purple-tinted seed heads. The speedwell (*Veronica pectinata*) makes a neat mat of crisp foliage when it's not in bloom, and the 'Angelina' stonecrop (*Sedum reflexum* 'Angelina') provides an orange-yellow accent of wonderful texture that lasts all season long. Meanwhile, the low, mat-forming stonecrops (*Sedum spurium* 'John Creech' and 'Fuldaglut') lay down a swath of foliage color and blossoms.

As usual, I exceeded the target number of plants, but I knew I could fit in some extras since most of the plants are small and will spill over rocks. If I had more space I would add soapwort (*Saponaria ocymoides*) or dwarf lady's mantle (*Alchemilla alpina*) to augment the color in June. Only one plant was lost — *Sedum* 'Vera Jameson', which I've had trouble with in other plantings.

ROCKS & SHRUBS

STONE EDGE

BIRDBATH

Scale: 1/4" = 1'

▢ = 1'

PATH

NUMBER OF SQUARES	PLANT SPACING ADJUSTER	FINAL PLANTING NUMBER
SHORT		SHORT
11	÷ 1.5 =	8
MEDIUM		MEDIUM
8	÷ 1.5 =	6
TALL		TALL
0	÷ 2 =	0

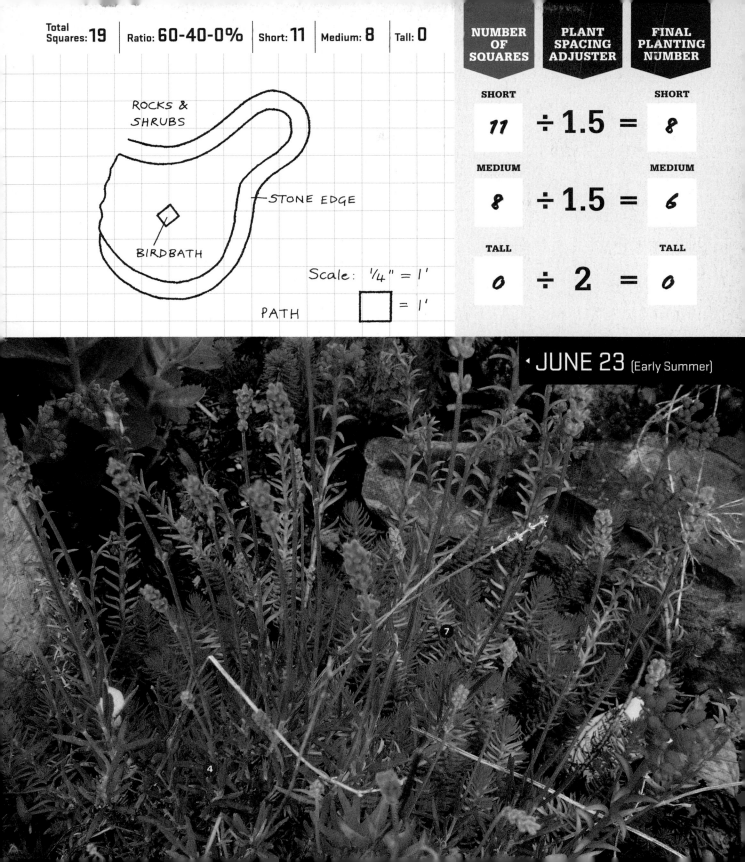

◄ JUNE 23 (Early Summer)

ENTER # OF PLANTS	8 ◀ SHORT actual: _13_	6 ◀ MEDIUM actual: _6_	0 ◀ TALL actual: _0_
FOLIAGE	1 *Sedum reflexum* 'Angelina' **7**	1 *Sedum* 'Purple Emperor' **11**	
SPRING	2 *Arabis* × *sturii* **8**		
EARLY SUMMER	1 *Veronica pectinata* **9**	1 *Lupine* (wild; volunteer)	
MIDSUMMER	1 *Sedum* 'John Creech' **5** 1 *Sedum spurium* 'Fuldaglut' **10** 1 *Lavandula angustifolia* 'Munstead' **4** 1 *Lavandula angustifolia* 'Hidcote'	1 *Salvia verticillata* 'Purple Rain' **1**	
LATE SUMMER	1 *Limonium latifolium* **12** 1 *Sedum* 'Rosy Glow'		
FALL	1 *Sedum* 'Bertram Anderson' **6** 1 *Sedum sieboldii* 1 *Sedum* 'Vera Jameson'	1 *Sedum* 'Autumn Joy' **13** 1 *Sedum spectabile* 'Brilliant' **2** 1 *Sedum* 'Matrona' **3**	

Throughout the Seasons

See Blueprint (on opposite page) for plant labels.

May 22 (Spring)

July 9 (Midsummer)

August 21 (Late Summer)

October 15 (Fall)

PART THREE

The Plant Palette gives you at-a-glance access to all the specially recommended plants that grow in each season. On facing pages, you'll find all the plants that bloom in a single season, so you don't have to flip pages to find choices for that slot in your Blueprint. The page for each season is divided into columns for short, medium, and tall plants, just like the Blueprint. I use the Plant Palette to choose the plants for my Blueprint every time I design a garden, and I find it very helpful to have all the information summarized and organized in this way.

THE PLANT PALETTE

If you need more information or if you want to see a photo of a plant, look it up in the alphabetically arranged Flower Catalog in the next section. Much of the same information (and exactly the same plants) is featured in both places, but the plants are organized differently: by subseason in the Plant Palette and alphabetically (and more extensively) in the Flower Catalog. The information in the Plant Palette is kept concise so all the choices for a particular subseason fit on facing pages for easy reference.

A thrilling mix of foliage forms and hues electrifies the garden in mid-October. Shown here are 'Purple Emperor' stonecrop (*Sedum* 'Purple Emperor'), the golden stems of 'Florist White' balloonflower (*Platycodon grandiflorus* 'Florist White') and the gray-green leaves of 'Walker's Low' catmint (*Nepeta* 'Walker's Low').

	Spring	Early Summer	Midsummer	Late Summer	Fall

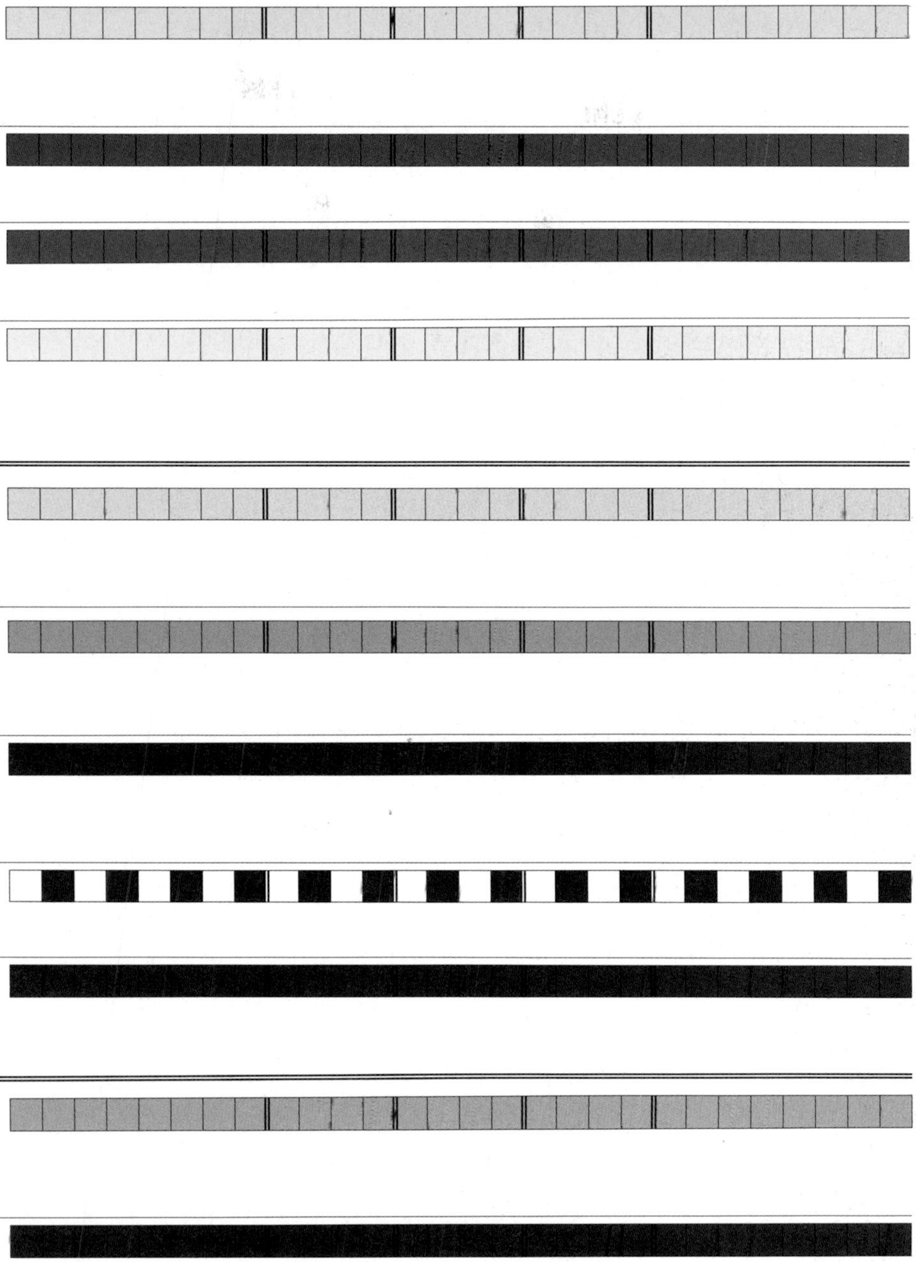

SHORT (UP TO 12")

Artemisia schmidtiana 'Silver Mound'
▸ **10–18"** | Z 5–8 | ☼

Heuchera 'Amethyst Mist'
▸ **8–18"** | Z 4–8 | ☼ ◉

Heuchera 'Stormy Seas'
▸ **8–18"** | Z 4–8 | ☼ ◉

Lamium maculatum 'White Nancy'
▸ **6–8"** | Z 3–8 | ☼ ◉

MEDIUM (12"–30")

Artemisia ludoviciana 'Valerie Finnis'
▸ **18–24"** | Z 4–9 | ☼

Eupatorium rugosum 'Chocolate'
▸ **24–48"** | Z 4–7 | ☼ ◉

Euphorbia dulcis 'Chameleon'
▸ **12–18"** | Z 4–7 | ☼ ◉

Hosta 'Patriot'
▸ **12–24"** | Z 3–8 | ◉

Sedum 'Purple Emperor'
▸ **12–18"** | Z 3–7 | ☼

TALL (OVER 30")

Cotinus coggygria 'Royal Purple'
▸ **48–72"** | Z 4–8 | ☼

Physocarpus opulifolius 'Diabolo'
▸ **48–72"** | Z 3–7 | ☼

KEY | Full sun ☼ | Part shade ◉ | Shade ●

Spring Plant Palette

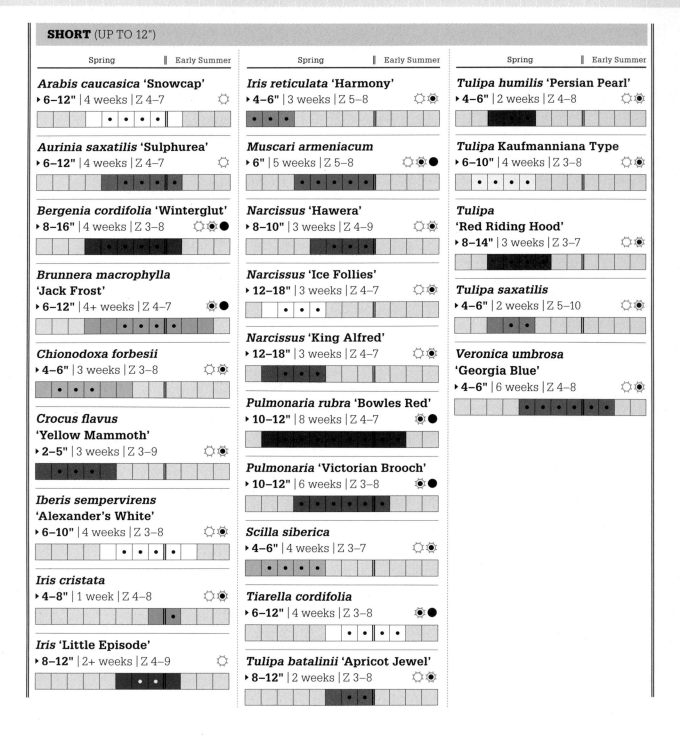

SHORT (UP TO 12")

	Spring	Early Summer

Arabis caucasica 'Snowcap'
▸ **6–12"** | 4 weeks | Z 4–7

Aurinia saxatilis 'Sulphurea'
▸ **6–12"** | 4 weeks | Z 4–7

Bergenia cordifolia 'Winterglut'
▸ **8–16"** | 4 weeks | Z 3–8

Brunnera macrophylla 'Jack Frost'
▸ **6–12"** | 4+ weeks | Z 4–7

Chionodoxa forbesii
▸ **4–6"** | 3 weeks | Z 3–8

Crocus flavus 'Yellow Mammoth'
▸ **2–5"** | 3 weeks | Z 3–9

Iberis sempervirens 'Alexander's White'
▸ **6–10"** | 4 weeks | Z 3–8

Iris cristata
▸ **4–8"** | 1 week | Z 4–8

Iris 'Little Episode'
▸ **8–12"** | 2+ weeks | Z 4–9

Iris reticulata 'Harmony'
▸ **4–6"** | 3 weeks | Z 5–8

Muscari armeniacum
▸ **6"** | 5 weeks | Z 5–8

Narcissus 'Hawera'
▸ **8–10"** | 3 weeks | Z 4–9

Narcissus 'Ice Follies'
▸ **12–18"** | 3 weeks | Z 4–7

Narcissus 'King Alfred'
▸ **12–18"** | 3 weeks | Z 4–7

Pulmonaria rubra 'Bowles Red'
▸ **10–12"** | 8 weeks | Z 4–7

Pulmonaria 'Victorian Brooch'
▸ **10–12"** | 6 weeks | Z 3–8

Scilla siberica
▸ **4–6"** | 4 weeks | Z 3–7

Tiarella cordifolia
▸ **6–12"** | 4 weeks | Z 3–8

Tulipa batalinii 'Apricot Jewel'
▸ **8–12"** | 2 weeks | Z 3–8

Tulipa humilis 'Persian Pearl'
▸ **4–6"** | 2 weeks | Z 4–8

Tulipa Kaufmanniana Type
▸ **6–10"** | 4 weeks | Z 3–8

Tulipa 'Red Riding Hood'
▸ **8–14"** | 3 weeks | Z 3–7

Tulipa saxatilis
▸ **4–6"** | 2 weeks | Z 5–10

Veronica umbrosa 'Georgia Blue'
▸ **4–6"** | 6 weeks | Z 4–8

MEDIUM (12"–30")

| | Spring ‖ Early Summer |

Euphorbia polychroma
▸ **12–18"** | 5 weeks | Z 4–7   ☼

Iris
'Crimson King'
▸ **12–22"** | 2+ weeks | Z 4–9   ☼

Stylophorum diphyllum
▸ **12–18"** | 8 weeks | Z 4–8   ◉

Tulipa 'Apeldoorn'
▸ **20–24"** | 3 weeks | Z 3–7   ☼ ◉

Tulipa 'Flaming Purissima'
▸ **16–18"** | 3 weeks | Z 3–8   ☼ ◉

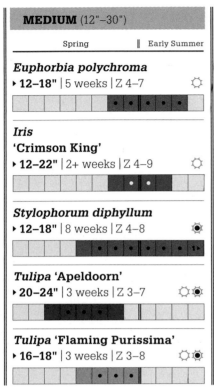

TALL (OVER 30")

| | Spring ‖ Early Summer |

NONE

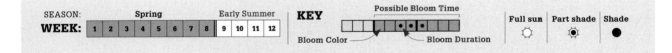

| SEASON: | Spring | | Early Summer | KEY | | Possible Bloom Time | Full sun | Part shade | Shade |
| WEEK: | 1 2 3 4 5 6 7 8 | 9 10 11 12 | | | | | ☼ | ◉ | ● |

Bloom Color ⎯ ⎯ Bloom Duration

Early Summer Plant Palette

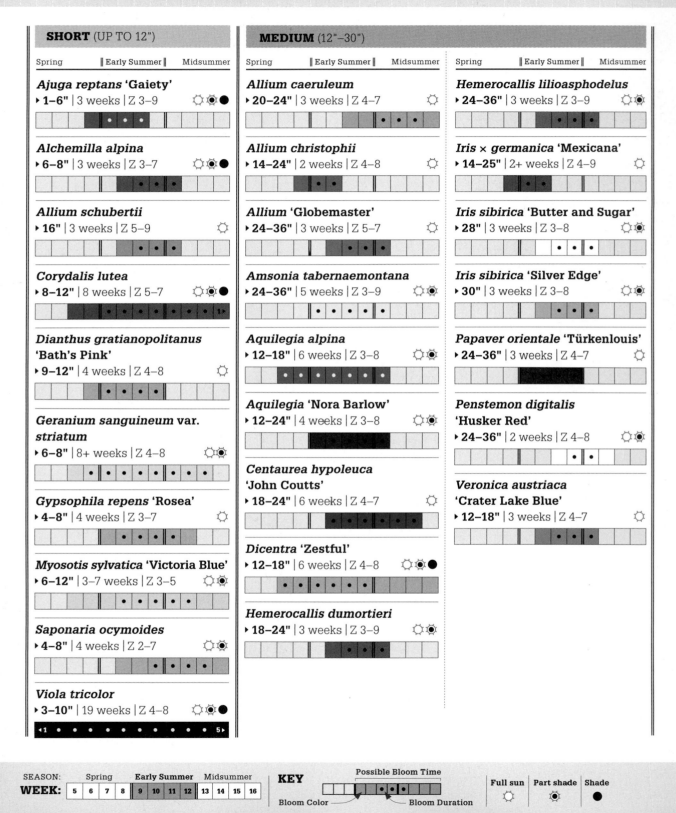

SHORT (UP TO 12")

Spring · ‖ Early Summer ‖ · Midsummer

Ajuga reptans 'Gaiety'
▸ 1–6" | 3 weeks | Z 3–9

Alchemilla alpina
▸ 6–8" | 3 weeks | Z 3–7

Allium schubertii
▸ 16" | 3 weeks | Z 5–9

Corydalis lutea
▸ 8–12" | 8 weeks | Z 5–7

Dianthus gratianopolitanus 'Bath's Pink'
▸ 9–12" | 4 weeks | Z 4–8

Geranium sanguineum var. striatum
▸ 6–8" | 8+ weeks | Z 4–8

Gypsophila repens 'Rosea'
▸ 4–8" | 4 weeks | Z 3–7

Myosotis sylvatica 'Victoria Blue'
▸ 6–12" | 3–7 weeks | Z 3–5

Saponaria ocymoides
▸ 4–8" | 4 weeks | Z 2–7

Viola tricolor
▸ 3–10" | 19 weeks | Z 4–8

MEDIUM (12"–30")

Spring · ‖ Early Summer ‖ · Midsummer

Allium caeruleum
▸ 20–24" | 3 weeks | Z 4–7

Allium christophii
▸ 14–24" | 2 weeks | Z 4–8

Allium 'Globemaster'
▸ 24–36" | 3 weeks | Z 5–7

Amsonia tabernaemontana
▸ 24–36" | 5 weeks | Z 3–9

Aquilegia alpina
▸ 12–18" | 6 weeks | Z 3–8

Aquilegia 'Nora Barlow'
▸ 12–24" | 4 weeks | Z 3–8

Centaurea hypoleuca 'John Coutts'
▸ 18–24" | 6 weeks | Z 4–7

Dicentra 'Zestful'
▸ 12–18" | 6 weeks | Z 4–8

Hemerocallis dumortieri
▸ 18–24" | 3 weeks | Z 3–9

Hemerocallis lilioasphodelus
▸ 24–36" | 3 weeks | Z 3–9

Iris × germanica 'Mexicana'
▸ 14–25" | 2+ weeks | Z 4–9

Iris sibirica 'Butter and Sugar'
▸ 28" | 3 weeks | Z 3–8

Iris sibirica 'Silver Edge'
▸ 30" | 3 weeks | Z 3–8

Papaver orientale 'Türkenlouis'
▸ 24–36" | 3 weeks | Z 4–7

Penstemon digitalis 'Husker Red'
▸ 24–36" | 2 weeks | Z 4–8

Veronica austriaca 'Crater Lake Blue'
▸ 12–18" | 3 weeks | Z 4–7

SEASON: Spring · Early Summer · Midsummer
WEEK: 5 6 7 8 | 9 10 11 12 | 13 14 15 16

KEY — Possible Bloom Time / Bloom Color / Bloom Duration

Full sun · Part shade · Shade

TALL (OVER 30")		
Spring	‖ Early Summer ‖	Midsummer

Baptisia australis
▸ **24–48"** | 3 weeks | Z 3–8 ☼ ◉

Iris 'Pride of Ireland'
▸ **24–38"** | 2+ weeks | Z 3–8 ☼ ◉

Iris sibirica 'Caesar's Brother'
▸ **36"** | 3 weeks | Z 3–8 ☼ ◉

Paeonia 'Karl Rosenfield'
▸ **30–36"** | 2 weeks | Z 3–8 ☼ ◉

Paeonia 'Miss America'
▸ **30–36"** | 2 weeks | Z 3–8 ☼ ◉

Paeonia 'Reine Hortense'
▸ **36–38"** | 2 weeks | Z 3–8 ☼ ◉

Paeonia suffruticosa
▸ **36–48"** | 2 weeks | Z 4–8 ☼ ◉

Midsummer Plant Palette

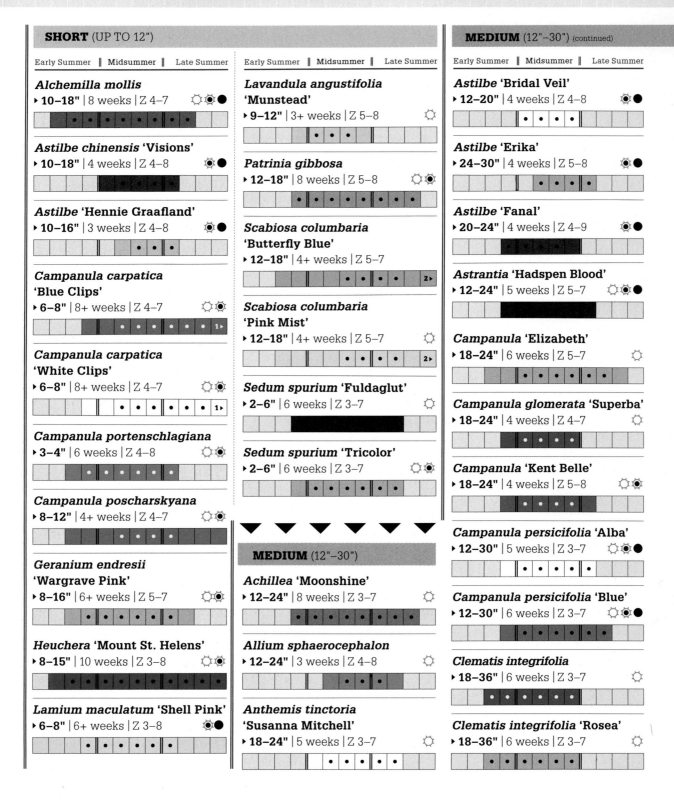

SHORT (UP TO 12")

| Early Summer ‖ Midsummer ‖ Late Summer |

Alchemilla mollis
▸ **10–18"** | 8 weeks | Z 4–7

Astilbe chinensis 'Visions'
▸ **10–18"** | 4 weeks | Z 4–8

Astilbe 'Hennie Graafland'
▸ **10–16"** | 3 weeks | Z 4–8

Campanula carpatica 'Blue Clips'
▸ **6–8"** | 8+ weeks | Z 4–7

Campanula carpatica 'White Clips'
▸ **6–8"** | 8+ weeks | Z 4–7

Campanula portenschlagiana
▸ **3–4"** | 6 weeks | Z 4–8

Campanula poscharskyana
▸ **8–12"** | 4+ weeks | Z 4–7

Geranium endresii 'Wargrave Pink'
▸ **8–16"** | 6+ weeks | Z 5–7

Heuchera 'Mount St. Helens'
▸ **8–15"** | 10 weeks | Z 3–8

Lamium maculatum 'Shell Pink'
▸ **6–8"** | 6+ weeks | Z 3–8

| Early Summer ‖ Midsummer ‖ Late Summer |

Lavandula angustifolia 'Munstead'
▸ **9–12"** | 3+ weeks | Z 5–8

Patrinia gibbosa
▸ **12–18"** | 8 weeks | Z 5–8

Scabiosa columbaria 'Butterfly Blue'
▸ **12–18"** | 4+ weeks | Z 5–7

Scabiosa columbaria 'Pink Mist'
▸ **12–18"** | 4+ weeks | Z 5–7

Sedum spurium 'Fuldaglut'
▸ **2–6"** | 6 weeks | Z 3–7

Sedum spurium 'Tricolor'
▸ **2–6"** | 6 weeks | Z 3–7

MEDIUM (12"–30")

Achillea 'Moonshine'
▸ **12–24"** | 8 weeks | Z 3–7

Allium sphaerocephalon
▸ **12–24"** | 3 weeks | Z 4–8

Anthemis tinctoria 'Susanna Mitchell'
▸ **18–24"** | 5 weeks | Z 3–7

MEDIUM (12"–30") (continued)

| Early Summer ‖ Midsummer ‖ Late Summer |

Astilbe 'Bridal Veil'
▸ **12–20"** | 4 weeks | Z 4–8

Astilbe 'Erika'
▸ **24–30"** | 4 weeks | Z 5–8

Astilbe 'Fanal'
▸ **20–24"** | 4 weeks | Z 4–9

Astrantia 'Hadspen Blood'
▸ **12–24"** | 5 weeks | Z 5–7

Campanula 'Elizabeth'
▸ **18–24"** | 6 weeks | Z 5–7

Campanula glomerata 'Superba'
▸ **18–24"** | 4 weeks | Z 4–7

Campanula 'Kent Belle'
▸ **18–24"** | 4 weeks | Z 5–8

Campanula persicifolia 'Alba'
▸ **12–30"** | 5 weeks | Z 3–7

Campanula persicifolia 'Blue'
▸ **12–30"** | 6 weeks | Z 3–7

Clematis integrifolia
▸ **18–36"** | 6 weeks | Z 3–7

Clematis integrifolia 'Rosea'
▸ **18–36"** | 6 weeks | Z 3–7

TALL (OVER 30")

Coreopsis lanceolata
▸ **18–36"** | 6+ weeks | Z 4–8

Coreopsis verticillata 'Moonbeam'
▸ **12–18"** | 8+ weeks | Z 5–9

Digitalis grandiflora
▸ **24–30"** | 4 weeks | Z 3–8

Hemerocallis 'Happy Returns'
▸ **10–18"** | 6 weeks | Z 3–9

Hemerocallis 'Hyperion'
▸ **24–36"** | 5 weeks | Z 3–9

Hemerocallis 'Little Grapette'
▸ **14–20"** | 4 weeks | Z 3–9

Hemerocallis 'Red Magic'
▸ **24–36"** | 4 weeks | Z 3–9

Iris ensata 'Mount Fuji'
▸ **24–36"** | 2 weeks | Z 4–9

Iris ensata 'Royal Robe'
▸ **27–36"** | 3 weeks | Z 4–9

Knautia macedonica
▸ **12–30"** | 6+ weeks | Z 5–7

Liatris spicata 'Kobold'
▸ **24–30"** | 3 weeks | Z 4–9

Lilium 'Lollypop'
▸ **18–24"** | 3 weeks | Z 4–8

Lilium 'Spirit'
▸ **18–24"** | 3 weeks | Z 4–8

Lychnis chalcedonica
▸ **24–36"** | 5 weeks | Z 3–7

Lychnis coronaria
▸ **24–30"** | 3 weeks | Z 4–7

Nepeta 'Walker's Low'
▸ **15–24"** | 5 weeks | Z 4–7

Oenothera fruticosa
▸ **12–20"** | 4 weeks | Z 4–8

Phlox carolina 'Miss Lingard'
▸ **24–36"** | 4 weeks | Z 5–8

Salvia nemerosa 'May Night'
▸ **18–28"** | 4+ weeks | Z 5–7

Salvia verticillata 'Purple Rain'
▸ **12–18"** | 5 weeks | Z 5–7

Trollius chinensis 'Golden Queen'
▸ **24–36"** | 4 weeks | Z 5–7

Achillea 'Coronation Gold'
▸ **24–36"** | 9 weeks | Z 3–9

Aconitum napellus
▸ **36–48"** | 4 weeks | Z 3–6

Aquilegia chrysantha
▸ **30–36"** | 4 weeks | Z 4–8

Aruncus dioicus
▸ **48–72"** | 3 weeks | Z 3–7

Delphinium Belladonna Group
▸ **36–48"** | 4 weeks | Z 3–7

Delphinium 'Black Knight'
▸ **48–84"** | 4 weeks | Z 3–7

Filipendula rubra 'Venusta'
▸ **48–72"** | 3 weeks | Z 3–7

Helenium 'Moerheim Beauty'
▸ **36–48"** | 4+ weeks | Z 3–8

Leucanthemum vulgare 'Becky'
▸ **10–36"** | 8 weeks | Z 4–7

Monarda 'Jacob Cline'
▸ **24–42"** | 7 weeks | Z 4–7

Nepeta sibirica 'Souvenir d'André Chaudron'
▸ **24–48"** | 8 weeks | Z 3–7

Late Summer Plant Palette

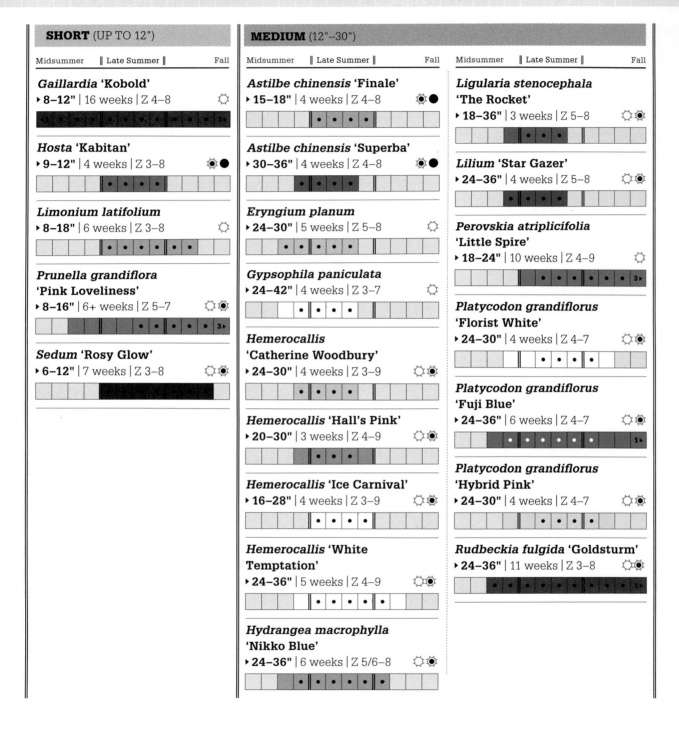

SHORT (UP TO 12")

Midsummer ‖ Late Summer ‖ Fall

Gaillardia **'Kobold'**
▸ **8–12"** | 16 weeks | Z 4–8 ☼

Hosta **'Kabitan'**
▸ **9–12"** | 4 weeks | Z 3–8 ☀ ●

Limonium latifolium
▸ **8–18"** | 6 weeks | Z 3–8 ☼

Prunella grandiflora **'Pink Loveliness'**
▸ **8–16"** | 6+ weeks | Z 5–7 ☼ ☀

Sedum **'Rosy Glow'**
▸ **6–12"** | 7 weeks | Z 3–8 ☼ ☀

MEDIUM (12"–30")

Midsummer ‖ Late Summer ‖ Fall

Astilbe chinensis **'Finale'**
▸ **15–18"** | 4 weeks | Z 4–8 ☀ ●

Astilbe chinensis **'Superba'**
▸ **30–36"** | 4 weeks | Z 4–8 ☀ ●

Eryngium planum
▸ **24–30"** | 5 weeks | Z 5–8 ☼

Gypsophila paniculata
▸ **24–42"** | 4 weeks | Z 3–7 ☼

Hemerocallis **'Catherine Woodbury'**
▸ **24–30"** | 4 weeks | Z 3–9 ☼ ☀

Hemerocallis **'Hall's Pink'**
▸ **20–30"** | 3 weeks | Z 4–9 ☼ ☀

Hemerocallis **'Ice Carnival'**
▸ **16–28"** | 4 weeks | Z 3–9 ☼ ☀

Hemerocallis **'White Temptation'**
▸ **24–36"** | 5 weeks | Z 4–9 ☼ ☀

Hydrangea macrophylla **'Nikko Blue'**
▸ **24–36"** | 6 weeks | Z 5/6–8 ☼ ☀

Midsummer ‖ Late Summer ‖ Fall

Ligularia stenocephala **'The Rocket'**
▸ **18–36"** | 3 weeks | Z 5–8 ☼ ☀

Lilium **'Star Gazer'**
▸ **24–36"** | 4 weeks | Z 5–8 ☼ ☀

Perovskia atriplicifolia **'Little Spire'**
▸ **18–24"** | 10 weeks | Z 4–9 ☼

Platycodon grandiflorus **'Florist White'**
▸ **24–30"** | 4 weeks | Z 4–7 ☼ ☀

Platycodon grandiflorus **'Fuji Blue'**
▸ **24–36"** | 6 weeks | Z 4–7 ☼ ☀

Platycodon grandiflorus **'Hybrid Pink'**
▸ **24–30"** | 4 weeks | Z 4–7 ☼ ☀

Rudbeckia fulgida **'Goldsturm'**
▸ **24–36"** | 11 weeks | Z 3–8 ☼ ☀

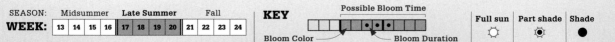

SEASON: Midsummer **Late Summer** Fall
WEEK: 13 14 15 16 | 17 18 19 20 | 21 22 23 24

KEY
Possible Bloom Time
Bloom Color ⎯ ⎯ Bloom Duration

Full sun ☼ | Part shade ☀ | Shade ●

TALL (OVER 30")

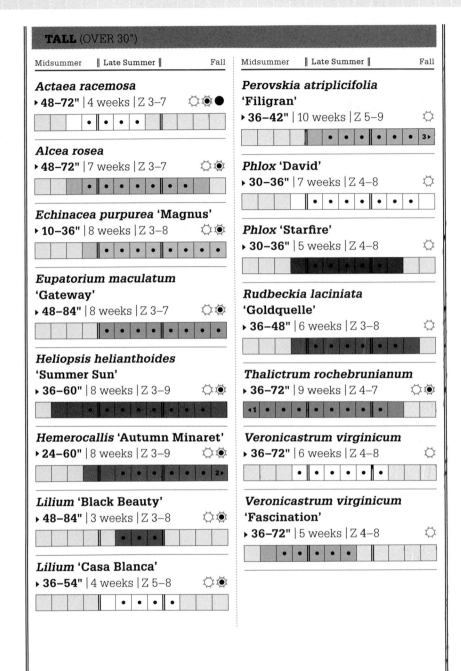

Midsummer	‖ Late Summer ‖	Fall

Actaea racemosa
▸ **48–72"** | 4 weeks | Z 3–7

Alcea rosea
▸ **48–72"** | 7 weeks | Z 3–7

Echinacea purpurea 'Magnus'
▸ **10–36"** | 8 weeks | Z 3–8

Eupatorium maculatum 'Gateway'
▸ **48–84"** | 8 weeks | Z 3–7

Heliopsis helianthoides 'Summer Sun'
▸ **36–60"** | 8 weeks | Z 3–9

Hemerocallis 'Autumn Minaret'
▸ **24–60"** | 8 weeks | Z 3–9

Lilium 'Black Beauty'
▸ **48–84"** | 3 weeks | Z 3–8

Lilium 'Casa Blanca'
▸ **36–54"** | 4 weeks | Z 5–8

Midsummer	‖ Late Summer ‖	Fall

Perovskia atriplicifolia 'Filigran'
▸ **36–42"** | 10 weeks | Z 5–9

Phlox 'David'
▸ **30–36"** | 7 weeks | Z 4–8

Phlox 'Starfire'
▸ **30–36"** | 5 weeks | Z 4–8

Rudbeckia laciniata 'Goldquelle'
▸ **36–48"** | 6 weeks | Z 3–8

Thalictrum rochebrunianum
▸ **36–72"** | 9 weeks | Z 4–7

Veronicastrum virginicum
▸ **36–72"** | 6 weeks | Z 4–8

Veronicastrum virginicum 'Fascination'
▸ **36–72"** | 5 weeks | Z 4–8

Fall Plant Palette

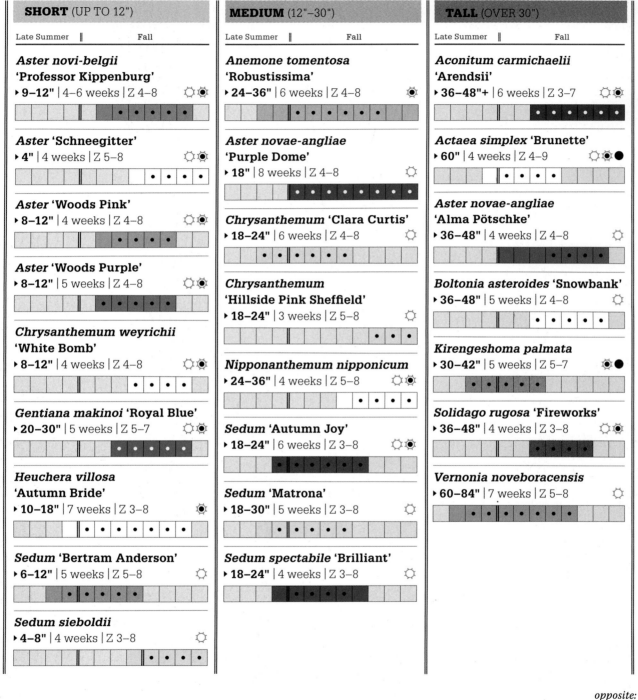

SHORT (UP TO 12")

Late Summer ‖ Fall

Aster novi-belgii 'Professor Kippenburg'
▸ **9–12"** | 4–6 weeks | Z 4–8 ☼◉

Aster 'Schneegitter'
▸ **4"** | 4 weeks | Z 5–8 ☼◉

Aster 'Woods Pink'
▸ **8–12"** | 4 weeks | Z 4–8 ☼◉

Aster 'Woods Purple'
▸ **8–12"** | 5 weeks | Z 4–8 ☼◉

Chrysanthemum weyrichii 'White Bomb'
▸ **8–12"** | 4 weeks | Z 4–8 ☼◉

Gentiana makinoi 'Royal Blue'
▸ **20–30"** | 5 weeks | Z 5–7 ☼◉

Heuchera villosa 'Autumn Bride'
▸ **10–18"** | 7 weeks | Z 3–8 ◉

Sedum 'Bertram Anderson'
▸ **6–12"** | 5 weeks | Z 5–8 ☼

Sedum sieboldii
▸ **4–8"** | 4 weeks | Z 3–8 ☼

MEDIUM (12"–30")

Late Summer ‖ Fall

Anemone tomentosa 'Robustissima'
▸ **24–36"** | 6 weeks | Z 4–8 ◉

Aster novae-angliae 'Purple Dome'
▸ **18"** | 8 weeks | Z 4–8 ☼

Chrysanthemum 'Clara Curtis'
▸ **18–24"** | 6 weeks | Z 4–8 ☼

Chrysanthemum 'Hillside Pink Sheffield'
▸ **18–24"** | 3 weeks | Z 5–8 ☼

Nipponanthemum nipponicum
▸ **24–36"** | 4 weeks | Z 5–8 ☼◉

Sedum 'Autumn Joy'
▸ **18–24"** | 6 weeks | Z 3–8 ☼◉

Sedum 'Matrona'
▸ **18–30"** | 5 weeks | Z 3–8 ☼

Sedum spectabile 'Brilliant'
▸ **18–24"** | 4 weeks | Z 3–8 ☼

TALL (OVER 30")

Late Summer ‖ Fall

Aconitum carmichaelii 'Arendsii'
▸ **36–48"+** | 6 weeks | Z 3–7 ☼◉

Actaea simplex 'Brunette'
▸ **60"** | 4 weeks | Z 4–9 ☼◉●

Aster novae-angliae 'Alma Pötschke'
▸ **36–48"** | 4 weeks | Z 4–8 ☼

Boltonia asteroides 'Snowbank'
▸ **36–48"** | 5 weeks | Z 4–8 ☼

Kirengeshoma palmata
▸ **30–42"** | 5 weeks | Z 5–7 ◉●

Solidago rugosa 'Fireworks'
▸ **36–48"** | 4 weeks | Z 3–8 ☼◉

Vernonia noveboracensis
▸ **60–84"** | 7 weeks | Z 5–8 ☼

opposite:
Sedum 'Autumn Joy'

SEASON: Late Summer — Fall
WEEK: 17 18 19 20 21 22 23 24 25 26 27 28

KEY

Possible Bloom Time
Bloom Color ⟶ ⟵ Bloom Duration

Full sun ☼ | Part shade ◉ | Shade ●

PART FOUR

FLOWER
CATALOG

+ Criteria for Inclusion

The plants on the following pages have been carefully selected and tested over many years. Obviously, only a few plants meet *all* these criteria (those I refer to as "the very best plants"), so I created this list weighing a lot of pros and cons.

▶ Attractive flower

▶ Hardy at least to Zone 5 or lower

▶ Long-lived plant

▶ Good foliage (or foliage that can easily be hidden if unattractive)

▶ Long bloom time

▶ Ability to survive close planting

▶ Readily available at retail

▶ Adapted to sun or part-sun conditions

▶ Grows well in ordinary garden soil and moisture conditions

▶ Not invasive

KEY TO FLOWER CATALOG

Scientific name. Most gardeners are not eager to delve into the realm of scientific names, and it's easy to see why. (If you're still awake at the end of this paragraph you should reward yourself by splurging on a nice plant with a fancy name.) Plant names usually look foreign, seem impossible to pronounce, and — perhaps worst of all — are not universally accepted or consistent. However, I would encourage you to try to familiarize yourself (maybe gradually) with them as they are the only sure way to positively identify a particular plant you might want. Most scientific plant names follow this formula: They have a genus name (which is capitalized and italicized) followed by a species name (which is italicized but not capitalized) and/or a cultivar name (which is listed in single quotation marks, capitalized, and not italicized). We have, for example, *Aconitum carmichaelii* 'Arendsii': *Aconitum* is the genus, *carmichaelii* is the species, and

Photo **Scientific name** **Pronunciation** **Comments**

Common name

Trollius chinensis 'Golden Queen' TRO-lee-us
'Golden Queen' globeflower | vivid yellow-orange ◀— **Flower Color**

The long root makes this difficult to transplant and it dislikes sitting in a pot. Tolerates heavy clay soil, but needs good moisture to thrive. Color is luminous and mixes well. Prefers a somewhat shady, moist site. Flowers are a bit small for a rather large plant with long stems, but the color is a knockout. 'Lemon Queen' is light yellow and easy to blend.

Sun	Height	Possible Bloom Time	Zone	Bloom group	Habit Type
☼ ◉	Medium (24–36")	3–4 weeks	5–7	Midsummer	

Spring	Early Summer	Midsummer	Late Summer	Fall

'Arendsii' is the specific cultivar. In some cases, it is common practice to list the specific cultivar name without a species name, so you might see a perennial listed in one place as *Aster ericoides* 'Schneegitter' and somewhere else simply as *Aster* 'Schneegitter'. Certain international organizations try to keep track of plant names and to recommend a particular name when more than one exists. This book follows the recommendations of the two most widely accepted authorities, Naamlist and RHS (Royal Horticultural Society). You can look up these resources on the Internet to research and check plant names yourself.

Common name. Many different plants have the same common name, which is why we have to pay attention to scientific names. Again, I have based the common names in this book largely on Allan Armitage's book, listed below.

Pronunciation (accented syllable in uppercase). Pronunciation of scientific names is not always intuitive, and again, certain authorities have established themselves on this point. For the most part, I've used the pronunciations given by Allan Armitage in his definitive book *Herbaceous Perennial Plants: A Treatise on Their Identification, Culture, and Garden Attributes.*

Flower color. Naming colors is very subjective but I've done my best, often borrowing from various published sources, as well as drawing on my own experience.

Comments. This category provides pertinent details not covered in the other sections. Especially important is the information about whether other similar plants may be substituted with good results.

Height category and minimum and maximum height. Height information is based primarily on data from Van Berkum Nursery, Allan Armitage's books, and my own experience. Height classification is generally based on short (up to 12"), medium (12"–30"), and tall (over 30"); but sometimes a plant is classed differently if it is best suited for another category. This could happen, for example, if a plant has very short foliage that should not be shaded too much but has tall flowers — such a plant might be classed as "short" because it should be planted with other short plants.

Light requirements

Height category (minimum and maximum height)

Hardiness Zone

Bloom group

Plant habit

Trollius chinensis 'Golden Queen' TRO-lee-us
'Golden Queen' globeflower | vivid yellow-orange
The long root makes this difficult to transplant and it dislikes sitting in a pot. Tolerates heavy clay soil, but needs good moisture to thrive. Color is luminous and mixes well. Prefers a somewhat shady, moist site. Flowers are a bit small for a rather large plant with long stems, but the color is a knockout. 'Lemon Queen' is light yellow and easy to blend.

Sun ☼ ☀	Height **Medium** (24–36")	Possible Bloom Time **3–4 weeks**	Zone **5–7**	Bloom group **Midsummer**	Habit Type

Spring | Early Summer | Midsummer | Late Summer | Fall

Bloom Groups
Each Bloom group is divided into quadrants

Possible Bloom Time
Colored cells indicate the time during each season when the bloom might occur

Bloom Duration
Dotted cells indicate the actual number of weeks you can expect the plant to bloom (4 weeks in this instance).

Plant habit. Each plant is classified as one of twelve basic types. Identifying types, rather than illustrating each plant habit individually, allows you to scan the illustrations quickly for a particular type. (See page 54 for further information on plant habit.)

Light requirements. Expressed in symbols standing for sun ☼, part sun ◉, and shade ●. These are based on data collected at Van Berkum Nursery and my own observations and those of Debby Smith, another very experienced gardener in midcoast Maine. If you live in a more southern climate, you might need to provide more afternoon shade than we do here in Maine. Here again, Allan Armitage's book *Herbaceous Perennial Plants: A Treatise on their Identification, Culture, and Garden Attributes* provides a lot of helpful detail for you as he lives in Zone 7 Georgia and makes many specific comments about growing particular perennial cultivars there.

Hardiness zone. Lower limits were taken primarily from the Van Berkum Nursery (located in New Hampshire) catalog; upper limits primarily from Allan Armitage's *Herbaceous Perennial Plants* (he's in Zone 7 in Georgia and also has a lot of experience in Michigan and Canada). Conflicting zone information was generally resolved in the conservative direction.

Bloom group. I live in Zone 5 in Maine, but talking about what month things bloom here will not help someone living in another part of the United States. To make this book more useful for people "from away" (as people say here in Maine), I have used a system of seasons divided into quarters (instead of months divided into weeks). Each plant is classified with one group or season: spring, early summer, midsummer, late summer, or fall, plus "foliage," which is an important part of the garden for reasons other than bloom. Each season is divided into four quarters, roughly corresponding to weeks. (For instance, in Maine, spring is April/May,

early summer is June, midsummer is July, late summer is August, and fall is September/October. Spring and fall each include the equivalent of two months because the weather vastly impacts their potential length in any particular year. That is, you can't necessarily count on anything blooming in April or October.) The description of each plant includes information about both "bloom time" and "bloom duration."

Possible bloom time. These are the times during each season when the bloom might occur. For example, a plant might bloom early one year and a quarter or two later another year because of weather. The "bloom time" shows all the parts of each season during which it might be in bloom. These bloom times are based primarily on my observations over many years in coastal Maine, Zone 5. You can adjust them for your zone. For example, spring usually arrives in New York City a week or two before Maine. In midsummer we're probably having about the same things in bloom, then fall usually comes a little later and lasts a little longer in New York. You can evaluate the relevancy of my bloom times to your own locale by comparing my bloom data with your own for a plant you already have growing in your garden or in your neighborhood. (Or just move to Maine, where the state motto is "The Way Life Should Be"!)

Some plants have bloom times that defy easy classification. Plants with very long bloom times are generally classified in the first full season when they start blooming or in their best season of bloom. Plants that start blooming halfway through a season and end halfway through another are generally classed with the first season.

Bloom duration. This is the actual number of weeks you can expect the plant to be in bloom. "Bloom length" is always the same as or shorter than the "bloom time" (above).

Achillea 'Coronation Gold' a-kil-LEE-a
'Coronation Gold' yarrow | gold

Grayish, feathery foliage looks good all season. Gets leggy in shade. Generally do not substitute, except the shorter *A.* 'Moonshine' (below) and *A.* 'Anthea' (18–20" tall), which has lighter yellow flowers. I avoid pink/red/rust-colored achilleas (*A. millefolium* cultivars) because their foliage deteriorates after bloom and is then hard to hide. Gold can be hard to blend, but long bloom time and good foliage make this plant valuable.

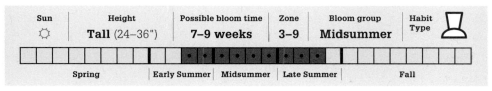

Sun	Height	Possible bloom time	Zone	Bloom group	Habit Type
☼	**Tall** (24–36")	**7–9 weeks**	3–9	**Midsummer**	

| | | | Spring | | | Early Summer | Midsummer | Late Summer | | | Fall | | |

Achillea 'Moonshine' a-kil-LEE-a
'Moonshine' yarrow | light canary yellow

Grayish, feathery foliage looks good all season. Generally do not substitute, except the taller *A.* 'Coronation Gold' (above) and *A.* 'Anthea' (18–20" tall), which has lighter yellow flowers. See note above about pink/red/rust achilleas. Tends to be short-lived.

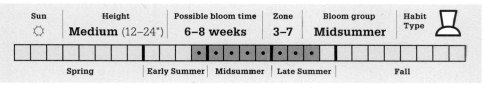

Sun	Height	Possible bloom time	Zone	Bloom group	Habit Type
☼	**Medium** (12–24")	**6–8 weeks**	3–7	**Midsummer**	

| | | | Spring | | | Early Summer | Midsummer | Late Summer | | | Fall | | |

Aconitum carmichaelii 'Arendsii' a-ko-NY-tum
Azure monkshood | deep purplish blue

Blooms much later and has foliage far superior to *A. napellus*. Several other cultivars exist, but I think 'Arendsii' is the best. Foliage looks terrific all season; forms a tall, dark mass and sometimes turns golden while plant is still in bloom. Spectacular, and one of the very best plants. In ideal conditions it can reach 72" tall. Best planted in a cluster of three or more plants. Self-supporting. Poisonous.

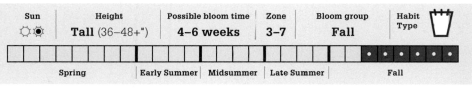

Sun	Height	Possible bloom time	Zone	Bloom group	Habit Type
☼◐	**Tall** (36–48+")	**4–6 weeks**	3–7	**Fall**	

| | | | Spring | | | Early Summer | Midsummer | Late Summer | | | Fall | | |

HABIT TYPES low mound | low mound, blossoms above | tall stems | fan-shaped foliage | low mound, dense mass above | mingled vertical mass | stems form vertical mass | blossoms top vertical mass | matlike foliage | intertwining stems | vase-shaped stemmed blossoms | basal foliage huge blossom

Aconitum napellus a-ko-NY-tum

Common monkshood | dark purplish blue

Each plant produces voluminous foliage that is frillier than *A. carmichaelii* 'Arendsii' (page 125). Unfortunately, it usually becomes stringy and blackened after bloom; keeping plant moist helps prevent this. Needs 24" or more of space. You'll probably want to cut it back completely after bloom, so plan for a big gap. Usually self-supporting. Shorter bloom time in part shade. Poisonous.

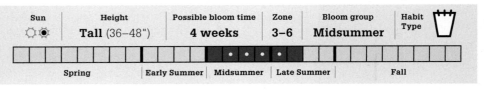

Sun	Height	Possible bloom time	Zone	Bloom group	Habit Type
☼ ◉	**Tall** (36–48")	**4 weeks**	**3–6**	**Midsummer**	

Spring · Early Summer | Midsummer | Late Summer · Fall

Actaea racemosa ak-TAY-a

Bugbane, Snakeroot | white

Previously known as *Cimicifuga,* this dramatic, architectural plant puts up a profusion of curvy, white spires. Usually self-supporting with a tiny bit of help (such as planting along a fence or next to other tall plants); unsupported stems usually bend but don't break. Seed heads continue to provide interest after bloom. Native.

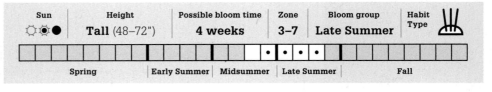

Sun	Height	Possible bloom time	Zone	Bloom group	Habit Type
☼ ◉ ●	**Tall** (48–72")	**4 weeks**	**3–7**	**Late Summer**	

Spring · Early Summer | Midsummer | Late Summer · Fall

Actaea simplex 'Brunette' ak-TAY-a

'Brunette' bugbane or snakeroot | white

Deep purple foliage and dramatic bottlebrush blossoms on tall stems make this a knockout. Blossoms start out white and become pinker. Previously known as *Cimicifuga.* Other purple-leaved varieties also good (for example, 'Hillside Black Beauty'). Self-supporting. Foliage can suffer in dry weather. Fragrant.

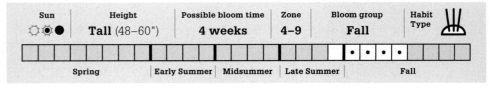

Sun	Height	Possible bloom time	Zone	Bloom group	Habit Type
☼ ◉ ●	**Tall** (48–60")	**4 weeks**	**4–9**	**Fall**	

Spring · Early Summer | Midsummer | Late Summer · Fall

KEY

No growth | Possible bloom time | No growth

Bloom color — Bloom duration

Full sun ☼ | Part shade ◉ | Shade ●

Ajuga reptans 'Gaiety' a-JEW-ga

'Gaiety' bugleweed | violet-blue

Many nice varieties, including variegated and purple-leaved types. Spreads quickly by runners for edging or as a groundcover for large areas. Thin to a reasonable clump in spring if necessary. Foliage usually looks terrific all season. Spreads into adjacent lawn if not contained.

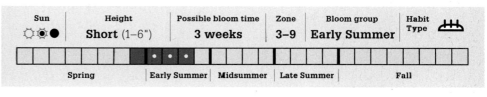

Sun	Height	Possible bloom time	Zone	Bloom group	Habit Type
☼◉●	**Short** (1–6")	**3 weeks**	**3–9**	**Early Summer**	

Spring | Early Summer | Midsummer | Late Summer | Fall

Alcea rosea al-SAY-a

Hollyhock | pink, white, yellow, or dark maroon and combinations

Extremely tall and wide; requires extra space. Good in a mass to fill a corner. Long-blooming, short-lived perennial. Self-seeds. Available in doubles and singles. Bloom time shown does not reflect scattered rebloom through fall, which is common. *A. ficifolia* is also very nice. Both types are susceptible to rust. Self supporting.

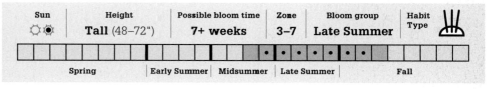

Sun	Height	Possible bloom time	Zone	Bloom group	Habit Type
☼◉	**Tall** (48–72")	**7+ weeks**	**3–7**	**Late Summer**	

Spring | Early Summer | Midsummer | Late Summer | Fall

Alchemilla alpina al-keh-MILL-a

Dwarf lady's mantle | chartreuse

Forms neat mounds of long-lasting, silver-edged pleated foliage. Flowers less conspicuous than *A. mollis*. This plant doesn't elbow its neighbors or need to have its foliage cut back like *A. mollis*. I grow this primarily for its wonderful, subtle foliage, but the blossoms also contribute and blend easily.

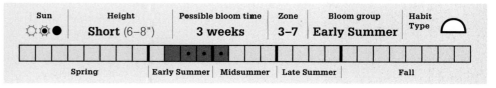

Sun	Height	Possible bloom time	Zone	Bloom group	Habit Type
☼◉●	**Short** (6–8")	**3 weeks**	**3–7**	**Early Summer**	

Spring | Early Summer | Midsummer | Late Summer | Fall

HABIT TYPES   low mound   low mound, blossoms above   tall stems   fan-shaped foliage   low mound, dense mass above   mingled vertical mass   stems form vertical mass   blossoms top vertical mass   matlike foliage   intertwining stems   vase-shaped stemmed blossoms   basal foliage huge blossom

Alchemilla mollis al-kem-ILL-a
Lady's mantle | chartreuse

Lovely pleated foliage in June and July, but both foliage and flowers usually deteriorate and need to be cut back drastically in midsummer to encourage a fresh flush of foliage. Self-seeds unless you cut off the spent flower heads before seeds form. The biggest drawback is that it will totally smother neighboring plants if not controlled by cutting back the foliage or leaving it a really big space in the layout.

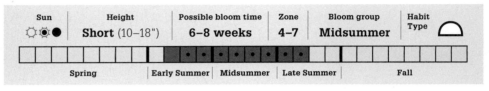

Sun	Height	Possible bloom time	Zone	Bloom group	Habit Type
☼ ◉ ●	Short (10–18")	6–8 weeks	4–7	Midsummer	

Spring | Early Summer | Midsummer | Late Summer | Fall

Allium caeruleum AL-ium
Azure allium | light steel blue

Often sold as *A. azureum*. This small allium is excellent planted in masses of five to nine around short and medium-height perennials. Beautiful, easy, inexpensive bulb; less well-known than its cousin *A. sphaerocephalon* (drumstick allium), which follows with another three weeks of blooms. Do not surround with taller plants or this allium will die away.

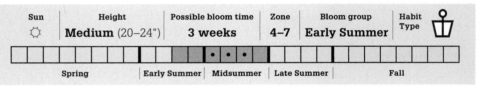

Sun	Height	Possible bloom time	Zone	Bloom group	Habit Type
☼	Medium (20–24")	3 weeks	4–7	Early Summer	

Spring | Early Summer | Midsummer | Late Summer | Fall

Allium christophii AL-ium
Star of Persia | amethyst-violet

A vividly colored, medium-sized allium for those times when you want more impact than *A. caeruleum* or *A. sphaerocephalon* but you're not quite ready to commit to something as flamboyant as 'Globemaster'. Also sold as *A. albopilosum*.

Sun	Height	Possible bloom time	Zone	Bloom group	Habit Type
☼	Medium (14–24")	2 weeks	4–8	Early Summer	

Spring | Early Summer | Midsummer | Late Summer | Fall

KEY

No growth | Possible bloom time | No growth

Bloom color ← → Bloom duration

Full sun ☼ | Part shade ◉ | Shade ●

Allium 'Globemaster'   AL-ium

'Globemaster' allium | violet

Big alliums spell drama, and 'Globemaster' is a good cultivar with foliage that emerges early and stays green. Not for shy gardeners. Seed heads look attractive enough to leave all season. Unlike most bulbs, these are included in the plant count because they occupy a lot of space and both seed heads and foliage remain attractive.

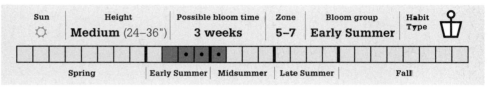

Sun	Height	Possible bloom time	Zone	Bloom group	Habit Type
☼	**Medium** (24–36")	**3 weeks**	**5–7**	**Early Summer**	

Spring | Early Summer | Midsummer | Late Summer | Fall

Allium schubertii   AL-ium

Allium | rose-purple

Speaking of drama, this unique allium sports flowers 10"+ in diameter on plants only 16" tall. The bulbs are susceptible to rotting in a wet spring, but they're so spectacular it's worth losing and replacing them once in a while. Seed heads (shown in photo) are as interesting as blooms and last throughout the season. Classed as "short" because the whole plant must be seen. Unlike most other bulbs, these are included in the plant count because they occupy a lot of space and the seed heads are just as good as the bloom.

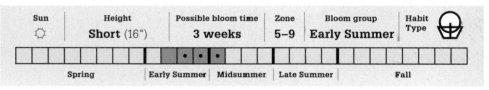

Sun	Height	Possible bloom time	Zone	Bloom group	Habit Type
☼	**Short** (16")	**3 weeks**	**5–9**	**Early Summer**	

Spring | Early Summer | Midsummer | Late Summer | Fall

Allium sphaerocephalon   AL-ium

Drumstick allium | lavender

Excellent planted in small masses around short- and medium-height perennials. Follows the three-week bloom of *A. caeruleum*. Do not surround with taller plants or these alliums will die away. Blossoms become shaggy from top down as they age, giving an impression of "hat hair." Easy and inexpensive bulb. Also known as *A. sphaerocephalum*.

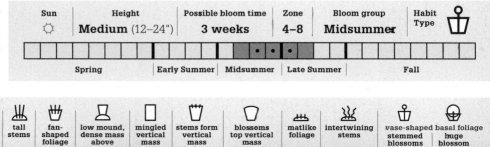

Sun	Height	Possible bloom time	Zone	Bloom group	Habit Type
☼	**Medium** (12–24")	**3 weeks**	**4–8**	**Midsummer**	

Spring | Early Summer | Midsummer | Late Summer | Fall

HABIT TYPES   low mound | low mound, blossoms above | tall stems | fan-shaped foliage | low mound, dense mass above | mingled vertical mass | stems form vertical mass | blossoms top vertical mass | matlike foliage | intertwining stems | vase-shaped stemmed blossoms | basal foliage huge blossom

Amsonia tabernaemontana am-SO-nee-a

Blue star flower | pale blue

It took me a while to appreciate this plant, as the flowers are rather subtle. Foliage is nice all season and turns bright yellow in the fall, producing a good foil for fall-blooming asters and monkshood. Allow 24–30" space for each plant so you can appreciate its lovely vase-shaped structure. This plant does a good job of tying together strong colors that might otherwise be discordant.

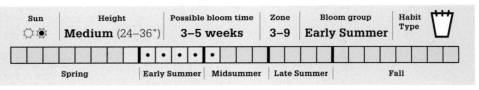

Sun	Height	Possible bloom time	Zone	Bloom group	Habit Type
☼◉	Medium (24–36")	3–5 weeks	3–9	Early Summer	

Spring | Early Summer | Midsummer | Late Summer | Fall

Anemone tomentosa 'Robustissima' a-NEM-o-nee

Grapeleaf anemone | medium pink

'Robustissima' blooms long and late and offers large, irregularly shaped, dark green foliage throughout the season. One of the very best plants, but do not crowd it or it will die or fail to bloom. Seed heads are attractive little buttons. Self-seeding can be a problem. I wish I could include *A.* × *hybrida* 'Honorine Jobert' (an elegant white cultivar) in this list, but I have managed to kill every single one I have planted. My guess is the climate here is not quite right for it, or perhaps the zone assignment is too optimistic.

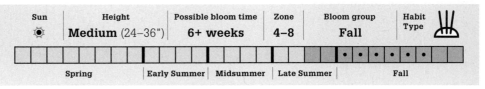

Sun	Height	Possible bloom time	Zone	Bloom group	Habit Type
◉	Medium (24–36")	6+ weeks	4–8	Fall	

Spring | Early Summer | Midsummer | Late Summer | Fall

Anthemis tinctoria 'Susanna Mitchell' AN-them-is

'Susanna Mitchell' golden marguerite | white with large yellow center

Anthemis needs frequent division, rots in wet springs, and is often short-lived, but these drawbacks are worth enduring for its cheerful and abundant little daisylike flowers on twining grayish stems. Other cultivars are also good; some are yellow such as the bright 'Kelway's Variety'. Looks great intermingled with campanulas and other low-growing flowers.

Sun	Height	Possible bloom time	Zone	Bloom group	Habit Type
☼	Medium (18–24")	3–5 weeks	3–7	Midsummer	

Spring | Early Summer | Midsummer | Late Summer | Fall

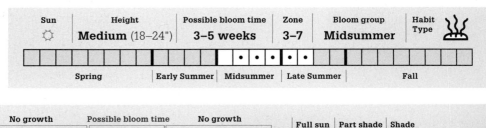

KEY

No growth | Possible bloom time | No growth

Bloom color — Bloom duration

Full sun ☼ | Part shade ◉ | Shade ●

Aquilegia alpina ak-will-EE-ja
Alpine columbine | bluish purple

An old-fashioned favorite, *A. alpina* offers relatively early bloom time. Self-seeds and hybridizes with other columbines. Many commercially bred hybrid columbines are available in bright, often two-toned colors, but I prefer the more subtle, easily blended color of *A. alpina*. Native *A. canadensis* is also nice, but the grayish red and yellow blossoms are difficult to blend with other colors.

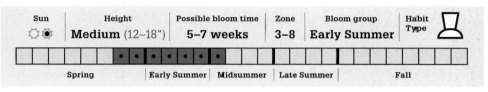

Sun	Height	Possible bloom time	Zone	Bloom group	Habit Type
☼◉	**Medium** (12–18")	**5–7 weeks**	**3–8**	**Early Summer**	

Spring · Early Summer · Midsummer · Late Summer · Fall

Aquilegia chrysantha ak-will-EE-ja
Golden columbine | sulfur yellow

This plant has been available since Victorian times but is usually hard to find because it dislikes being in a pot. Long-blooming and very dramatic, it is much larger than other columbines and has long, exotic spurs. Nice mixed up with purple foliage if you're into that kind of thing.

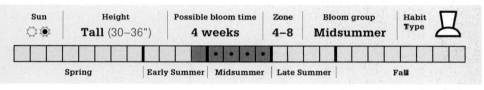

Sun	Height	Possible bloom time	Zone	Bloom group	Habit Type
☼◉	**Tall** (30–36")	**4 weeks**	**4–8**	**Midsummer**	

Spring · Early Summer · Midsummer · Late Summer · Fall

Aquilegia 'Nora Barlow' ak-will-EE-ja
'Nora Barlow' columbine | deep pink/white

Nora Barlow was a granddaughter of Charles Darwin, but this columbine existed centuries before it was so named. The fluffy double pink and white blossoms dangle irresistibly from tall stems. Produces wonderful, natural hybrids in double deep purples and whites when planted in the same bed with *A. alpina*.

Sun	Height	Possible bloom time	Zone	Bloom group	Habit Type
☼◉	**Medium** (12–24")	**3–4 weeks**	**3–8**	**Early Summer**	

Spring · Early Summer · Midsummer · Late Summer · Fall

HABIT TYPES low mound | low mound, blossoms above | tall stems | fan-shaped foliage | low mound, dense mass above | mingled vertical mass | stems form vertical mass | blossoms top vertical mass | matlike foliage | intertwining stems | vase-shaped stemmed blossoms | basal foliage huge blossom

Arabis caucasica 'Snowcap' AR-a-bis

'Snowcap' wall rock cress | white

Indispensible as an edging plant to drape out of raised beds, the soft grayish foliage forms a neat, dense mat that puts on reddish autumn tones in fall. Do not crowd; requires full sun. Shear off spent blossoms to neaten after bloom. *A. × sturii* is a cousin with small, mouse-ear-shaped green foliage that is also useful (see its listing under Sunny Groundcovers, page 194).

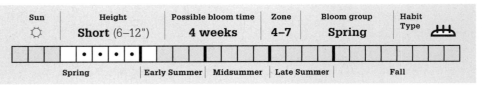

Sun	Height	Possible bloom time	Zone	Bloom group	Habit Type
☼	**Short** (6–12")	**4 weeks**	**4–7**	**Spring**	

Spring Early Summer | Midsummer | Late Summer Fall

Artemisia ludoviciana 'Valerie Finnis' are-ti-MEEZ-ee-a

'Valerie Finnis' wormwood | gray foliage

Light gray, felty foliage softens any planting. This is the only tall artemisia I've had any luck with in these tight plantings, and it still tends to reach a stage where it looks ragged and needs to be cut back in the fall. Takes some light shade. Cut off unsightly yellowish blossoms. Spreads, but not unbearably; in spring pull back shoots to a manageable clump. Will not infest the entire neighborhood like *A.* 'Silver King'. Some local gardeners have had luck with it in partial shade.

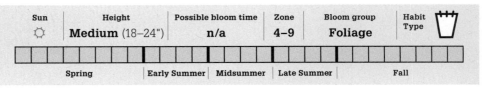

Sun	Height	Possible bloom time	Zone	Bloom group	Habit Type
☼	**Medium** (18–24")	**n/a**	**4–9**	**Foliage**	

Spring Early Summer | Midsummer | Late Summer Fall

Artemisia schmidtiana are-ti-MEEZ-ee-a

Silver Mound artemisia | gray foliage

These frilly gray mounds are most useful in low plantings since they require full sun and cannot withstand crowding. Shear off the rather unattractive flower buds as they appear or shear after bloom. Also known as *A. schmidtiana* 'Nana'. Some people have luck growing this in some shade.

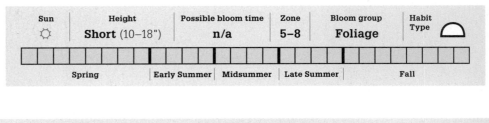

Sun	Height	Possible bloom time	Zone	Bloom group	Habit Type
☼	**Short** (10–18")	**n/a**	**5–8**	**Foliage**	

Spring Early Summer | Midsummer | Late Summer Fall

Aruncus dioicus ah-RUN-kus
Goat's beard | cream

Goatsbeard is best in a mass or row by itself or at the back of a border. Needs a 24–30" space. Foliage can suffer in dry weather and dry soil. Seed heads are relatively interesting and can be left on. *A. aethusifolius* (dwarf goat's beard) is a very short, dense, mounding version that can take full shade. Self supporting.

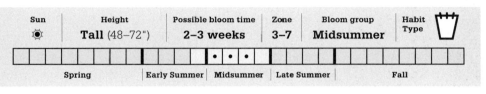

Sun	Height	Possible bloom time	Zone	Bloom group	Habit Type
☀	**Tall** (48–72")	**2–3 weeks**	**3–7**	**Midsummer**	

Spring | Early Summer | Midsummer | Late Summer | Fall

Aster novae-angliae 'Alma Pötschke' ASS-ter
'Alma Pötschke' New England aster | magenta-pink

One of my very favorite plants, and not just because of the irresistible name. Its color blends wonderfully and is not harsh as you might think from the description. In part shade it still blooms, although the stems flop. Strip dead leaves off tall stems with a swipe of the fingers to neaten this terrific plant at bloom time. Self supporting.

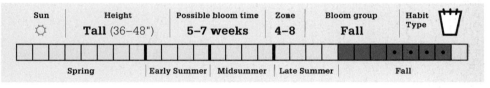

Sun	Height	Possible bloom time	Zone	Bloom group	Habit Type
☀	**Tall** (36–48")	**5–7 weeks**	**4–8**	**Fall**	

Spring | Early Summer | Midsummer | Late Summer | Fall

Aster novae-angliae 'Purple Dome' ASS-ter
'Purple Dome' New England aster | deep purple

Great shorter companion for 'Alma Pötschke'. Do not allow surrounding plants to smother it. Totally reliable and easy to blend, 'Purple Dome' provides a long-lasting swath of color when many gardens are already done for the year.

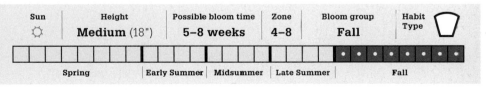

Sun	Height	Possible bloom time	Zone	Bloom group	Habit Type
☀	**Medium** (18")	**5–8 weeks**	**4–8**	**Fall**	

Spring | Early Summer | Midsummer | Late Summer | Fall

HABIT TYPES — low mound | low mound, blossoms above | tall stems | fan-shaped foliage | low mound, dense mass above | mingled vertical mass | stems form vertical mass | blossoms top vertical mass | matlike foliage | intertwining stems | vase-shaped stemmed blossoms | basal foliage huge blossom

Aster novi-belgii 'Professor Kippenberg' ASS-ter
'Professor Kippenberg' aster | lavender

Another wonderfully named aster, this short one spreads into an irregularly shaped mass. Bloom is more sporadic and patchier than *A. novae-angliae* cultivars. Best in a mingled planting with other flowers of similar height. Tolerates only very light shade.

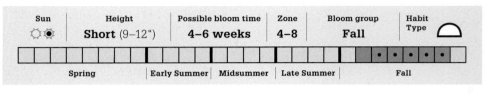

Sun	Height	Possible bloom time	Zone	Bloom group	Habit Type
☼◉	**Short** (9–12")	**4–6 weeks**	**4–8**	**Fall**	⌒

Spring | Early Summer | Midsummer | Late Summer | Fall

Aster 'Schneegitter' ASS-ter
'Schneegitter' aster | white

Forms an attractive, low mound of foliage resembling Japanese garden juniper (*Juniperus procumbens* 'Nana') that looks great all season, then rewards you with a blanket of tiny white flowers in late September. Drapes over rock walls and doesn't get all bent out of shape if its neighbors shade it a little bit. Looks a little cruddy when flowers are just gone by, but it's impossible to deadhead and the ugly stage doesn't last long. Also sold as *Aster ericoides* 'Schneegitter'.

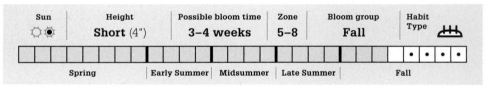

Sun	Height	Possible bloom time	Zone	Bloom group	Habit Type
☼◉	**Short** (4")	**3–4 weeks**	**5–8**	**Fall**	⊞

Spring | Early Summer | Midsummer | Late Summer | Fall

Aster 'Wood's Pink' ASS-ter
'Wood's Pink' aster | violet-tinged pink

'Woods Pink' is a soft, easily blended color. Bloom is more sporadic and patchier than *A. novae-angliae* cultivars. Best in a mingled planting with other flowers of similar height. Tolerates only very light shade.

Sun	Height	Possible bloom time	Zone	Bloom group	Habit Type
☼◉	**Short** (8–12")	**3–4 weeks**	**4–8**	**Fall**	⌒

Spring | Early Summer | Midsummer | Late Summer | Fall

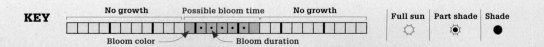

KEY No growth | Possible bloom time | No growth Bloom color — Bloom duration Full sun ☼ | Part shade ◉ | Shade ●

Aster 'Wood's Purple' ASS-ter

'Wood's Purple' aster | violet-purple

'Wood's Purple' is a soft, easily blended color. Bloom is more sporadic and patchier than *A. novae-angliae* cultivars. Best in a mingled planting with other flowers of similar height. Tolerates only very light shade.

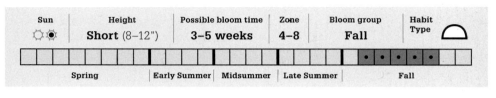

Sun	Height	Possible bloom time	Zone	Bloom group	Habit Type
☼◉	Short (8–12")	3–5 weeks	4–8	Fall	

Spring | Early Summer | Midsummer | Late Summer | Fall

Astilbe 'Bridal Veil' as-TIL-bee

'Bridal Veil' astilbe | white

'Bridal Veil' is a lovely, long-blooming astilbe with good foliage. Even its white buds are nice. All white astilbes go through an unattractive brown phase when the flowers have just gone by, but if you can live with it for a week or so, the seed heads are quite attractive and can be kept until frost.

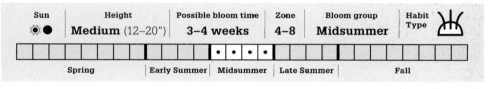

Sun	Height	Possible bloom time	Zone	Bloom group	Habit Type
◉●	Medium (12–20")	3–4 weeks	4–8	Midsummer	

Spring | Early Summer | Midsummer | Late Summer | Fall

Astilbe chinensis 'Finale' as-TIL-bee

'Finale' astilbe | light pink

Aptly named, as it is the latest blooming astilbe, 'Finale' is attractive and useful for extending bloom time. Astilbes all bloom from bottom to top. Though this one looks less appealing during the half-open and half-gone-by stages than *A.* 'Erika', 'Fanal', 'Hennie Graafland', and 'Vision', it is still especially useful because of its late bloom time.

Sun	Height	Possible bloom time	Zone	Bloom group	Habit Type
◉●	Medium (15–18")	3–4 weeks	4–8	Late Summer	

Spring | Early Summer | Midsummer | Late Summer | Fall

HABIT TYPES

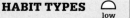

low mound | low mound, blossoms above | tall stems | fan-shaped foliage | low mound, dense mass above | mingled vertical mass | stems form vertical mass | blossoms top vertical mass | matlike foliage | intertwining stems | vase-shaped stemmed blossoms | basal foliage huge blossom

Astilbe chinensis 'Superba' as-TIL-bee
'Superba' astilbe | dark rose

'Superba' offers dramatic stature and a color that's easy to blend. Classified as medium height because its foliage is much shorter than its blossoms. As with 'Finale', it looks less attractive during half-open and half-gone-by stages.

Sun	Height	Possible bloom time	Zone	Bloom group	Habit Type
☀●︎	**Medium** (30–36")	**3–4 weeks**	4–8	**Late Summer**	

Spring   Early Summer   Midsummer   Late Summer   Fall

Astilbe chinensis 'Visions' as-TIL-bee
'Visions' astilbe | rich purple-pink

A stunning, show-stopping color in a fluffy blossom that resembles cotton candy. 'Visions in Pink' and 'Visions in Red' are also good cultivars. Looks great throughout bloom period.

Sun	Height	Possible bloom time	Zone	Bloom group	Habit Type
☀●︎	**Short** (10–15")	**4 weeks**	4–8	**Midsummer**	

Spring   Early Summer   Midsummer   Late Summer   Fall

Astilbe 'Erika' as-TIL-bee
'Erika' astilbe | medium pink

Looks attractive throughout bloom period, unlike some of the other pink astilbes. Easy color to blend.

Sun	Height	Possible bloom time	Zone	Bloom group	Habit Type
☀●︎	**Medium** (24–30")	**3–4 weeks**	5–8	**Midsummer**	

Spring   Early Summer   Midsummer   Late Summer   Fall

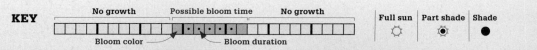
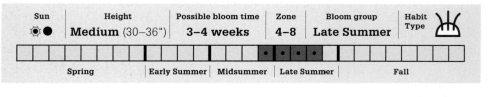

Astilbe 'Fanal'   as-TIL-bee

'Fanal' astilbe | ruby red

One of the earliest blooming astilbes, 'Fanal' looks good throughout its bloom period (including during the bud stage) and all season long, even as the red blossoms turn brown. 'Red Sentinel' is very similar but starts blooming about a week later.

Sun	Height	Possible bloom time	Zone	Bloom group	Habit Type
◉●	**Medium** (20–24")	**4 weeks**	4–9	**Midsummer**	

Spring   Early Summer   Midsummer   Late Summer   Fall

Astilbe 'Hennie Graafland'   as-TIL-bee

'Hennie Graafland' astilbe | rosy pink

Excellent massed, with crisp, dark foliage that looks great all season. Looks attractive throughout bloom period.

Sun	Height	Possible bloom time	Zone	Bloom group	Habit Type
◉●	**Short** (10–16")	**3 weeks**	4–8	**Midsummer**	

Spring   Early Summer   Midsummer   Late Summer   Fall

Astrantia 'Hadspen Blood'   a-STRAN-tee-a

'Hadspen Blood' masterwort | dark red

Astrantia offers good foliage and unusual, coin-sized, spiky blossoms. The other varieties are all good and come in various shades of pale to medium pink. Seed heads add interest after bloom, but you might want to deadhead to prevent their enthusiastic self-seeding. Self-seeding is greatly curtailed in dense plantings utilizing bark mulch.

Sun	Height	Possible bloom time	Zone	Bloom group	Habit Type
○◉●	**Medium** (12–24")	**3–5 weeks**	5–7	**Midsummer**	

Spring   Early Summer   Midsummer   Late Summer   Fall

HABIT TYPES   low mound | low mound, blossoms above | tall stems | fan-shaped foliage | low mound, dense mass above | mingled vertical mass | stems form vertical mass | blossoms top vertical mass | matlike foliage | intertwining stems | vase-shaped stemmed blossoms | basal foliage huge blossom

Aurinia saxatilis 'Sulphurea' aw-RI-nee-a

'Sulphurea' basket of gold | sulfur yellow

You can't beat *Aurinia* for an early spring splash of color. Gray-green foliage forms a mat and looks fantastic all season. Will drape over stone edges. 'Compacta' is another excellent cultivar with much brighter, canary yellow blossoms. Cut back into fleshy stems after bloom to stimulate new growth if it becomes too leggy.

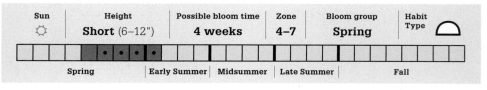

Sun	Height	Possible bloom time	Zone	Bloom group	Habit Type
☼	**Short** (6–12")	**4 weeks**	**4–7**	**Spring**	

Spring | Early Summer | Midsummer | Late Summer | Fall

Baptisia australis bap-TIZ-i-a

False indigo | indigo blue

Vivid green, pealike foliage. The main contribution of this plant is its crisp, healthy, shrublike presence throughout the season and beyond fall frost. One of the best plants. Dislikes transplanting and dividing, so be sure you locate it well the first time. Will occupy a space 30" wide. 'Purple Smoke' is an exceptionally good cultivar with smoky purple flowers and grayish stems.

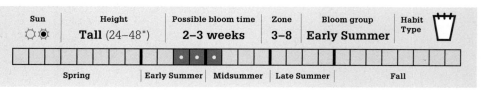

Sun	Height	Possible bloom time	Zone	Bloom group	Habit Type
☼◉	**Tall** (24–48")	**2–3 weeks**	**3–8**	**Early Summer**	

Spring | Early Summer | Midsummer | Late Summer | Fall

Bergenia cordifolia 'Winterglut' ber-GEN-i-a

'Winterglut' pigsqueak | bright red

Leathery, evergreen foliage turns red-purple in winter. Other cultivars are also good. Leaf margins are susceptible to notching by chewing insects. Do not crowd or overshadow with taller plants. Blossoms arrive with the Darwin hybrid tulips and *Tulipa batalinii*.

Sun	Height	Possible bloom time	Zone	Bloom group	Habit Type
☼◉●	**Short** (8–16")	**4 weeks**	**3–8**	**Spring**	

Spring | Early Summer | Midsummer | Late Summer | Fall

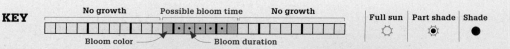

Boltonia asteroides 'Snowbank' bol-TOE-nee-a

'Snowbank' Bolton's aster | white

Boltonia takes a little extra room (it needs at least a 30" wide space), but it compensates with its profusion of daisylike blossoms at season's end. Mildew-resistant. Self supporting.

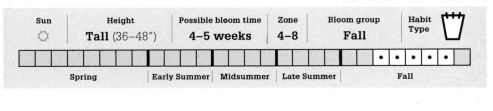

Sun	Height	Possible bloom time	Zone	Bloom group	Habit Type
☼	**Tall** (36–48")	**4–5 weeks**	**4–8**	**Fall**	

Spring | Early Summer | Midsummer | Late Summer | Fall

Brunnera macrophylla 'Jack Frost' BRUN-er-a

'Jack Frost' Siberian bugloss | French blue

'Jack Frost' offers a one-two punch with long-blooming flowers that resemble forget-me-nots and large, heart-shaped, variegated leaves of lasting quality. 'Variegata' is a similar cultivar. Ordinary *B. macrophylla* is also very nice when you want plain instead of variegated foliage.

Sun	Height	Possible bloom time	Zone	Bloom group	Habit Type
◑ ●	**Short** (6–12")	**4+ weeks**	**4–7**	**Spring**	

Spring | Early Summer | Midsummer | Late Summer | Fall

Campanula carpatica 'Blue Clips' kam-PAN-you-la

'Blue Clips' Carpathian harebell | purplish blue

A long-blooming workhorse in the continuously blooming garden. Other cultivars are also good; 'Blue Star' is more lax in habit. Some cultivars self-seed, even sprouting from cracks in stone retaining beds. Deadheading prolongs bloom but can be tedious as flowers must be snipped individually (do not shear). Foliage stays crisp and compact all season.

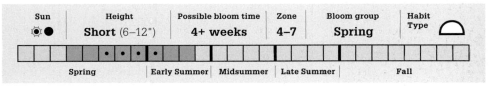

Sun	Height	Possible bloom time	Zone	Bloom group	Habit Type
☼ ◑	**Short** (6–8")	**8+ weeks**	**4–7**	**Midsummer**	

Spring | Early Summer | Midsummer | Late Summer | Fall

HABIT TYPES — low mound | low mound, blossoms above | tall stems | fan-shaped foliage | low mound, dense mass above | mingled vertical mass | stems form vertical mass | blossoms top vertical mass | matlike foliage | intertwining stems | vase-shaped stemmed blossoms | basal foliage huge blossom

Campanula carpatica 'White Clips'   kam-PAN-you-la

'White Clips' Carpathian harebell | white

Bloom time can be somewhat shorter than 'Blue Clips'. Other cultivars are also good; 'White Star' is more lax in habit. Some cultivars self-seed, even sprouting from cracks in stone retaining beds. Deadheading prolongs bloom but can be tedious as flowers must be snipped individually (do not shear). Foliage stays crisp and compact all season.

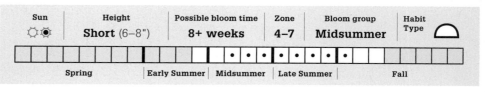

Sun	Height	Possible bloom time	Zone	Bloom group	Habit Type
☼◉	Short (6–8")	8+ weeks	4–7	Midsummer	

Spring — Early Summer | Midsummer | Late Summer — Fall

Campanula 'Elizabeth'   kam-PAN-you-la

'Elizabeth' bellflower | striped pink

A profusion of large, elongated, medium and light pink striped or mottled blossoms make this worth putting up with its habit of self-seeding like crazy. Rather lax, sprawling habit. Reblooms. Best in an area where it can fill in empty spaces without killing off other plants. Using bark mulch will help reduce self-seeding.

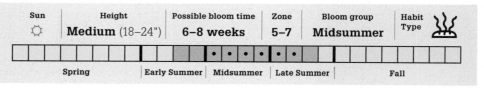

Sun	Height	Possible bloom time	Zone	Bloom group	Habit Type
☼	Medium (18–24")	6–8 weeks	5–7	Midsummer	

Spring — Early Summer | Midsummer | Late Summer — Fall

Campanula glomerata 'Superba'   kam-PAN-you-la

'Superba' clustered bellflower | violet-blue

Yet another variation on the bellflower theme, *C. glomerata* offers clusters of flowers on stem ends. 'Joan Elliot' is slightly more compact and is also good. White cultivars are also nice.

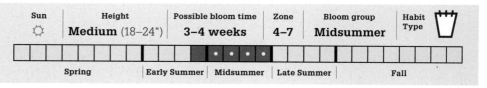

Sun	Height	Possible bloom time	Zone	Bloom group	Habit Type
☼	Medium (18–24")	3–4 weeks	4–7	Midsummer	

Spring — Early Summer | Midsummer | Late Summer — Fall

KEY

No growth — Possible bloom time — No growth

Bloom color — Bloom duration

Full sun ☼ | Part shade ◉ | Shade ●

Campanula 'Kent Belle'   kam-PAN-you-la

'Kent Belle' bellflower | violet-purple

With its draping stems and profuse, elongated, purple blossoms 'Kent Belle' conveys a romantic cottage garden feel. Reblooms and self-seeds some, but not as much as *C.* 'Elizabeth'.

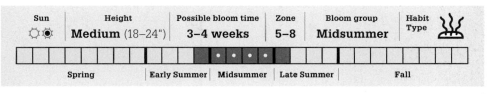

Sun	Height	Possible bloom time	Zone	Bloom group	Habit Type
☼◉◉	Medium (18–24")	3–4 weeks	5–8	Midsummer	

Spring | Early Summer | Midsummer | Late Summer | Fall

Campanula persicifolia 'Alba'   kam-PAN-you-la

'Alba' peachleaf bellflower | white

C. persicifolia is indispensible as a trouble-free, highly adaptable blossom-producer in the continuously blooming garden. It spreads, but you can easily manage it with a little spring thinning. As with most campanulas, the white form can bloom somewhat less than the purple. Deadheading extends bloom.

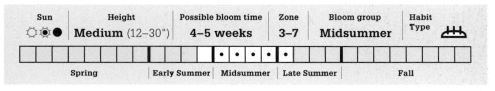

Sun	Height	Possible bloom time	Zone	Bloom group	Habit Type
☼◉●	Medium (12–30")	4–5 weeks	3–7	Midsummer	

Spring | Early Summer | Midsummer | Late Summer | Fall

Campanula persicifolia 'Blue'   kam-PAN-you-la

'Blue' Peachleaf bellflower | purplish blue

Like its white-flowered sister above, this is one of the most useful plants. Spreads, but manageable. Pull back from its neighbors in spring if it's taking up too much space. A real workhorse, especially if you deadhead for improved rebloom.

Sun	Height	Possible bloom time	Zone	Bloom group	Habit Type
☼◉●	Medium (12–30")	4–6 weeks	3–7	Midsummer	

Spring | Early Summer | Midsummer | Late Summer | Fall

HABIT TYPES low mound | low mound, blossoms above | tall stems | fan-shaped foliage | low mound, dense mass above | mingled vertical mass | stems form vertical mass | blossoms top vertical mass | matlike foliage | intertwining stems | vase-shaped stemmed blossoms | basal foliage huge blossom

Campanula portenschlagiana kam-PAN-you-la

Dalmatian bellflower | violet-blue

Offers very neat foliage and gorgeous, easily blended color. 'Birch Hybrid' is an excellent cultivar. More compact and cleaner than *C. poscharskyana*, but shorter-blooming.

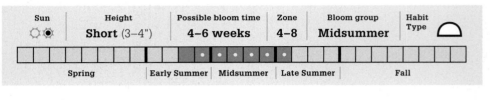

Sun	Height	Possible bloom time	Zone	Bloom group	Habit Type
☼◉	Short (3–4")	4–6 weeks	4–8	Midsummer	

Spring | Early Summer | Midsummer | Late Summer | Fall

Campanula poscharskyana kam-PAN-you-la

Serbian bellflower | medium violet-blue

Blooms much longer than *C. portenschlagiana* but has a more rangy, messy habit. Staggered bloom through August. Usually reaches a point before end of bloom when messy (and too numerous to cut individually) spent flowers necessitate cutting back. Totally adaptable and uncomplaining under all conditions, although in some climates it may spread more rapidly than you want.

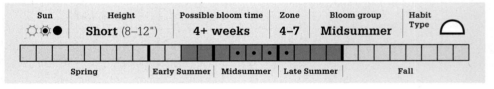

Sun	Height	Possible bloom time	Zone	Bloom group	Habit Type
☼◉●	Short (8–12")	4+ weeks	4–7	Midsummer	

Spring | Early Summer | Midsummer | Late Summer | Fall

Centaurea hypoleuca 'John Coutts' sen-TOR-ee-a

'John Coutts' knapweed | magenta-pink

Fantastic, deeply cut foliage makes a nicely textured mass topped with vivid thistlelike (but soft) flowers. Spreads; takes some shade. I find its blue cousin, *C. montana* (bachelor's buttons), disappointing, although some gardeners love it. 'John Coutts' will fill any available empty spaces and will require pulling back in the spring when it encroaches on its neighbors in a densely planted bed, but the great foliage and flowers are worth the extra trouble.

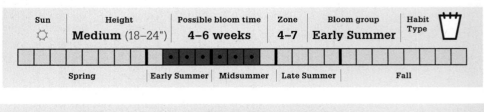

Sun	Height	Possible bloom time	Zone	Bloom group	Habit Type
☼	Medium (18–24")	4–6 weeks	4–7	Early Summer	

Spring | Early Summer | Midsummer | Late Summer | Fall

KEY

No growth | Possible bloom time | No growth

Bloom color ← → Bloom duration

Full sun ☼ | Part shade ◉ | Shade ●

Chionodoxa forbesii   ky-on-o-DOX-a

Glory of the snow | sky blue

One of the earliest of the spring bulbs, *Chionodoxa*'s cheerful blue is a welcome sight at winter's end. Other species (such as *C. luciliae*) and varieties are also good. Plant in small masses in spots that drain well in the spring. Deer-resistant. Dislikes having the foliage or flowers of other plants touching it while it's trying to bloom.

Sun	Height	Possible bloom time	Zone	Bloom group	Habit Type
☼◉	**Short** (4–6")	**2–3 weeks**	**3–8**	**Spring**	

Spring   Early Summer   Midsummer   Late Summer   Fall

Chrysanthemum 'Clara Curtis'   kris-AN-the-mum

'Clara Curtis' single mum | rose-pink

This hardy mum produces a well-shaped bouquet of blossoms at season's end. There are other good similar varieties such as the pale yellow 'Mary Stoker' and the light copper 'Paul Boissier'. Mums sold as annuals in the fall (also known as "florist mums") do not usually come back year after year.

Sun	Height	Possible bloom time	Zone	Bloom group	Habit Type
☼	**Medium** (18–24")	**4–6 weeks**	**4–8**	**Fall**	

Spring   Early Summer   Midsummer   Late Summer   Fall

Chrysanthemum 'Hillside Pink Sheffield'   kris-AN-the-mum

'Hillside Pink Sheffield' single mum | pale smoky pink

In my garden, this mum picks up a couple of weeks after 'Clara Curtis' leaves off and plugs away through frosts into November. Extremely valuable for end-of-season bloom. Mums sold as annuals (also called "florist mums") in the fall do not usually come back year after year.

Sun	Height	Possible bloom time	Zone	Bloom group	Habit Type
☼	**Medium** (18–24")	**4+ weeks**	**5–8**	**Fall**	

Spring   Early Summer   Midsummer   Late Summer   Fall

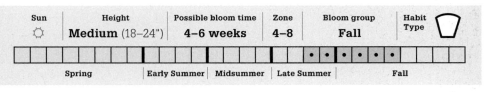

HABIT TYPES   low mound | low mound, blossoms above | tall stems | fan-shaped foliage | low mound, dense mass above | mingled vertical mass | stems form vertical mass | blossoms top vertical mass | matlike foliage | intertwining stems | vase-shaped stemmed blossoms | basal foliage huge blossom

Chrysanthemum weyrichii 'White Bomb' kris-AN-the-mum

'White Bomb' single mum | white

A cautious person might hesitate to buy a plant with this name, but it's not hard to thin 'White Bomb' back to a reasonable clump each spring. Crisp, dark green foliage mat looks fantastic all season, and clean, daisylike flowers appear in late fall. Formerly known as *Dendranthema*.

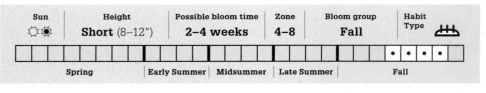

Sun	Height	Possible bloom time	Zone	Bloom group	Habit Type
☼☀	**Short** (8–12")	**2–4 weeks**	**4–8**	**Fall**	

Spring | Early Summer | Midsummer | Late Summer | Fall

Clematis integrifolia CLEM-ah-tis

Solitary clematis | violet-blue

A recent discovery for me, I wish I had tried this plant years ago. One of the very best plants and a true team player. Twines and sprawls affectionately about its neighbors without smothering. Flowers are subtle inverted whirligigs that turn into nice fuzzy seed heads. Does not climb and is much shorter than the more familiar vining clematis.

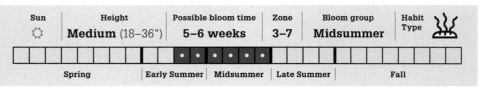

Sun	Height	Possible bloom time	Zone	Bloom group	Habit Type
☼	**Medium** (18–36")	**5–6 weeks**	**3–7**	**Midsummer**	

Spring | Early Summer | Midsummer | Late Summer | Fall

Clematis integrifolia 'Rosea' CLEM-ah-tis

'Rosea' solitary clematis | pink/white

This cousin of the plant above is so special it gets its own listing. Same habit as *C. integrifolia* (snuggles affectionately with its neighbors) but in a bicolor pink and white color scheme. Other cultivars are also desirable.

Sun	Height	Possible bloom time	Zone	Bloom group	Habit Type
☼	**Medium** (18–36")	**5–6 weeks**	**3–7**	**Midsummer**	

Spring | Early Summer | Midsummer | Late Summer | Fall

KEY

No growth | Possible bloom time | No growth

Bloom color ← → Bloom duration

Full sun ☼ | Part shade ☼ | Shade ●

Coreopsis lanceolata ko-ree-OP-sis
Lanceleaf coreopsis | golden yellow

One of longest-blooming perennials, but the gold color can be hard to blend. Deadheaded plants bloom until frost; bloom time shown is for nondeadheaded plants. Can rot in a very wet spring. Established plants tend to sprawl or lean over a bit, but the flower stalks form an attractive, upright spray.

Sun	Height	Possible bloom time	Zone	Bloom group	Habit Type
☼	Medium (18–36")	6+ weeks	4–8	Midsummer	〰

Spring | Early Summer | Midsummer | Late Summer | Fall

Coreopsis verticillata 'Moonbeam' ko-ree-OP-sis
'Moonbeam' threadleaf coreopsis | soft yellow

An extremely long-blooming, floriferous plant. Bloom time shown is without deadheading (very difficult to deadhead). Best if not crowded. 'Zagreb' is another good cultivar, but its golden yellow color is harder to blend.

Sun	Height	Possible bloom time	Zone	Bloom group	Habit Type
☼◉	Medium (12–18")	8+ weeks	5–9	Midsummer	⌒

Spring | Early Summer | Midsummer | Late Summer | Fall

Corydalis lutea ko-RI-dal-is
Corydalis | bright yellow

Foliage looks great from season's start to end, and plants have an abundance of lovely flowers. Difficult to transplant, and dislikes being in a pot. Requires good drainage. Reblooms continually after primary bloom time, and foliage stays mounded and beautiful until heavy frost. Self-seeds, sometimes seeding into the side of stone walls. Excessive seedlings can be unwelcome, but they are very easy to remove. Its cousin, the blue-flowered *C. flexuosa*, is too polite to survive in a crowded bed.

Sun	Height	Possible bloom time	Zone	Bloom group	Habit Type
☼◉●	Short (8–12")	6–8 weeks	5–7	Early Summer	⌒

Spring | Early Summer | Midsummer | Late Summer | Fall

HABIT TYPES — low mound | low mound, blossoms above | tall stems | fan-shaped foliage | low mound, dense mass above | mingled vertical mass | stems form vertical mass | blossoms top vertical mass | matlike foliage | intertwining stems | vase-shaped stemmed blossoms | basal foliage huge blossom

Cotinus coggygria 'Royal Purple' ko-TY-nus

'Royal Purple' purple smokebush | smoky plum foliage

Small shrub with deep purple leaves; cut back hard in spring to encourage new, dark purple growth. Well-behaved and a great foil for almost any flower. Adds structure to middle or back of bed. Produces puffs of smoky blooms and seed heads from midsummer through fall if not cut back in the spring. Grows too rampantly in warmer climates to use this way in mixed perennial borders.

Sun	Height	Possible bloom time	Zone	Bloom group	Habit Type
☼	**Tall** (48–72")	**n/a**	**4–8**	**Foliage**	

Spring | Early Summer | Midsummer | Late Summer | Fall

Crocus flavus 'Yellow Mammoth' KRO-kus

'Yellow Mammoth' crocus | luminous golden yellow

Bloom depends on weather: can be early or late spring (can bloom throughout March in Maine in a warm spring). Crocuses come in many, many attractive varieties, sizes, and colors. Choose light colors to stand out against dark, damp spring soil. Plant in groups of 5 to 15 bulbs. This one is also sold as *C. luteus* 'Yellow Mammoth'.

Sun	Height	Possible bloom time	Zone	Bloom group	Habit Type
☼◉	**Short** (2–5")	**3 weeks**	**3–9**	**Spring**	

Spring | Early Summer | Midsummer | Late Summer | Fall

Delphinium Belladonna Group del-FIN-ee-um

Belladonna delphinium | light blue

Shorter than Pacific Hybrid delphiniums and often requires no staking, making it a good choice for a super-low-maintenance bed or for a windy site. 'Bellamosum' is a deeper blue. Reblooms. For shorter delphiniums, some gardeners also recommend *D. grandiflorum* 'Blue Mirror'.

Sun	Height	Possible bloom time	Zone	Bloom group	Habit Type
☼	**Tall** (36–48")	**3–4 weeks**	**3–7**	**Midsummer**	

Spring | Early Summer | Midsummer | Late Summer | Fall

KEY

No growth — Possible bloom time — No growth

Bloom color → ← Bloom duration

Full sun | Part shade | Shade
☼ | ◉ | ●

Delphinium 'Black Knight' del-FIN-ee-um

'Black Knight' delphinium | vivid deep purple

One of the many excellent Pacific Hybrid delphiniums. Must be staked unless interplanted with tall, supporting plants and/or a fence. Often reblooms if cut back after first bloom. Other favorites are 'Astolat' (lavender pink), 'Galahad' (white), and 'Summer Skies' (light blue). Usually short-lived; I like to add a couple of new plants every year.

Sun	Height	Possible bloom time	Zone	Bloom group	Habit Type
☼	**Tall** (48–84")	**3–4 weeks**	**3–7**	**Midsummer**	

Spring | Early Summer | Midsummer | Late Summer | Fall

Dianthus gratianopolitanus 'Bath's Pink' dy-AN-thus

Bath's pink | light pink

Attractive, grayish, mounding foliage; good for edges. Needs frequent division and good drainage. Other varieties are also good. 'Tiny Rubies' is good, but extremely short for use in a mixed bed, since it requires full sun and is easily overshadowed.

Sun	Height	Possible bloom time	Zone	Bloom group	Habit Type
☼	**Short** (9–12")	**3–4 weeks**	**4–8**	**Early Summer**	

Spring | Early Summer | Midsummer | Late Summer | Fall

Dicentra 'Zestful' dy-SEN-tra

'Zestful' fringed bleeding heart | medium pink

Very long bloom and good foliage, in contrast to old-fashioned bleeding heart (*D. spectabilis*), which is more fussy about needing shade and goes dormant after bloom. 'Zestful' is much longer-blooming and more vigorous than other varieties of *D. eximia*. Attractive grayish foliage. Requires good drainage.

Sun	Height	Possible bloom time	Zone	Bloom group	Habit Type
☼◐●	**Medium** (12–18")	**4–8 weeks**	**4–8**	**Early Summer**	

Spring | Early Summer | Midsummer | Late Summer | Fall

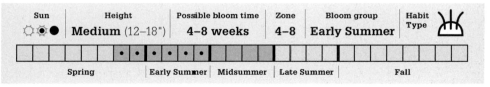

HABIT TYPES low mound | low mound, blossoms above | tall stems | fan-shaped foliage | low mound, dense mass above | mingled vertical mass | stems form vertical mass | blossoms top vertical mass | matlike foliage | intertwining stems | vase-shaped stemmed blossoms | basal foliage huge blossom

Digitalis grandiflora dij-i-TAH-lis
Yellow foxglove | soft yellow

Yellow foxglove is a true perennial, unlike *D. purpurea* and its hybrids, which are biennial and harder to grow in a typical mixed perennial bed. Soft yellow flowers are easy to blend.

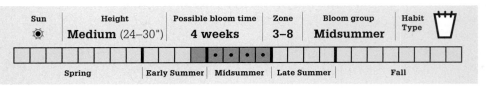

Sun	Height	Possible bloom time	Zone	Bloom group	Habit Type
☀	Medium (24–30")	4 weeks	3–8	Midsummer	

Spring | Early Summer | Midsummer | Late Summer | Fall

Echinacea purpurea 'Magnus' ek-in-AY-see-a
Purple coneflower | rose-pink

One of the very best plants, with good form, long bloom time, and nice seed heads after bloom. Do not crowd excessively. There are many other good varieties, especially 'Ruby Star' (carmine red) and 'Bravado' (similar to 'Magnus' but slightly shorter and harder to find). 'Sunrise' and 'Sundown' are also good, but avoid the Meadowbrite line ('Orange Meadowbrite', 'Mango Meadowbrite'), which seem more anemic.

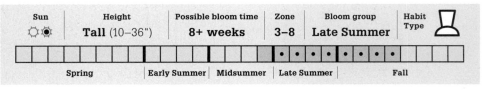

Sun	Height	Possible bloom time	Zone	Bloom group	Habit Type
☼ ☀	Tall (10–36")	8+ weeks	3–8	Late Summer	

Spring | Early Summer | Midsummer | Late Summer | Fall

Eryngium planum e-RIN-ji-um
Sea holly | steel blue

This plant barely made the list because of its unruly reseeding habit. Bluish foliage and spiky, bluish flower heads; blooms in August when few things do. People either love it or hate it. Be sure to dig up all the zillions of seedlings in the spring, or they'll overwhelm everything else in the garden. Use with caution and keep a close eye on it. Makes a wonderful cut flower.

Sun	Height	Possible bloom time	Zone	Bloom group	Habit Type
☼	Medium (24–30")	4–6 weeks	5–8	Late Summer	

Spring | Early Summer | Midsummer | Late Summer | Fall

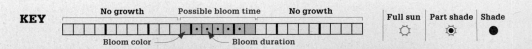

KEY

No growth | Possible bloom time | No growth

Bloom color ⟶ ⟵ Bloom duration

Full sun ☼ | Part shade ☀ | Shade ●

Eupatorium maculatum 'Gateway'   yew-pa-TOR-ee-um
'Gateway' Joe-Pye weed | lavender-pink

Super tall, yet requiring no staking, this butterfly attractant has good foliage all season long. Still looks good during seedhead stage in fall. Even after frost, stems are wine-colored and leaves sometimes turn golden when planted in full sun (foliage in partial shade tends just to shrivel up). Needs at least a 30" space. Site carefully as it's difficult to move once established.

Sun ☼◉	Height **Tall** (48–84")	Possible bloom time **6–8 weeks**	Zone **3–7**	Bloom group **Late Summer**	Habit Type

Spring | Early Summer | Midsummer | Late Summer | Fall

Eupatorium rugosum 'Chocolate'   yew-pa-TOR-ee-um
'Chocolate' white snakeroot | dusty purple foliage

Purple foliage. Tends to be short-lived, or possibly less hardy. If it does survive, it turns into a shrubby plant as it ages with a profusion of small white blossoms in fall. Quite variable in color and size.

Sun ☼◉	Height **Medium** (24–48")	Possible bloom time **n/a**	Zone **4–7**	Bloom group **Foliage**	Habit Type

Spring | Early Summer | Midsummer | Late Summer | Fall

Euphorbia dulcis 'Chameleon'   yew-FOR-bee-a
'Chameleon' spurge | burgundy-purple foliage

Be prepared to pull out seedlings all over the place, but it's worth it for this purple-foliaged, nicely textured plant. Can easily engulf its neighbors if not kept in check. Produces rather inconspicuous chartreuse-yellow flowers from spring to midsummer. This is a plant people notice and rave about.

Sun ☼◉	Height **Medium** (12–18")	Possible bloom time **n/a**	Zone **4–7**	Bloom group **Foliage**	Habit Type

Spring | Early Summer | Midsummer | Late Summer | Fall

HABIT TYPES   low mound   low mound, blossoms above   tall stems   fan-shaped foliage   low mound, dense mass above   mingled vertical mass   stems form vertical mass   blossoms top vertical mass   matlike foliage   intertwining stems   vase-shaped stemmed blossoms   basal foliage huge blossom

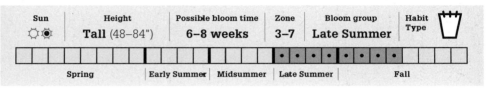

Euphorbia polychroma yew-FOR-bee-a
Cushion spurge | chartreuse-yellow

Offering early and long-lasting color, this super-easy plant also has red fall foliage. Foliage has nice structure and looks good all season. What appear to be flowers are actually colored bracts. Formerly known as *E. epithymoides*. Reseeds. Another nice relative is *E. griffithii*, which is slightly larger and more shrubby with redder bracts.

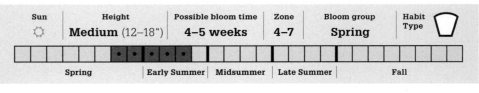

Sun	Height	Possible bloom time	Zone	Bloom group	Habit Type
☼	**Medium** (12–18")	**4–5 weeks**	**4–7**	**Spring**	

Spring　　Early Summer　Midsummer　Late Summer　　Fall

Filipendula rubra 'Venusta' fil-i-PEN-dew-la
'Venusta' queen of the prairie | light pink

Tall and stately, but requiring no staking, with its fluffy panicles of cotton-candylike blossoms. This plant will spread, but not uncontrollably. Just pull some of the spreading roots away from around the edges of the clump to leave a manageable sized plant each spring. Foliage can suffer in dry weather.

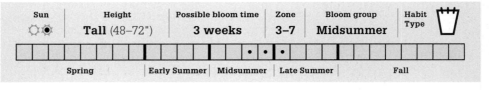

Sun	Height	Possible bloom time	Zone	Bloom group	Habit Type
☼◉	**Tall** (48–72")	**3 weeks**	**3–7**	**Midsummer**	

Spring　　Early Summer　Midsummer　Late Summer　　Fall

Gaillardia 'Kobold' gay-LAR-dee-a
'Kobold' blanketflower | red/yellow

Probably the longest-blooming perennial I've used, although it must be deadheaded to perpetuate bloom. Spent blossoms become attractive, fuzzy red balls, so it's hard to cut them off. Other varieties (such as 'Dazzler') are more leggy and not nearly as floriferous or long-blooming. Can be short-lived. Bloom time shown is with deadheading. Placed in August bloom category because there are fewer good choices then. Also sold as *G.* 'Goblin'.

Sun	Height	Possible bloom time	Zone	Bloom group	Habit Type
☼	**Short** (8–12")	**8–16 weeks**	**4–8**	**Late Summer**	

Spring　　Early Summer　Midsummer　Late Summer　　Fall

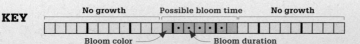

KEY　No growth　Possible bloom time　No growth　　Full sun ☼　Part shade ◉　Shade ●

Bloom color　　Bloom duration

Gentiana makinoi 'Royal Blue' jen-she-AN-uh

'Royal Blue' gentian | royal violet-blue

The lateness and incredibly vivid color of this flower more than compensate for its meandering, drapey habit. Other cultivars and varieties of gentian and other colors in the 'Royal' group are also nice. Classed as "short" because of lax habit. Intermingles well with short and medium plants.

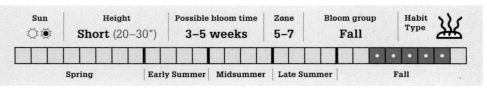

Sun	Height	Possible bloom time	Zone	Bloom group	Habit Type
☼	**Short** (20–30")	**3–5 weeks**	5–7	**Fall**	

Spring | Early Summer | Midsummer | Late Summer | Fall

Geranium endresii 'Wargrave Pink' jer-AYE-nee-um

'Wargrave Pink' hardy cranesbill | medium pink

This workhorse cranesbill provides a long bloom time and smothers encroaching grass. Excellent for borders. You can actually cut it back with a lawnmower when it gets overgrown and unattractive. Self-seeds. Languishes in too much shade. Like many perennial geraniums, it hates to be in a pot, so get it in the ground as soon as you can. Another fantastic geranium is the recent purple-flowered introduction *G. wallichianum* 'Rozanne'.

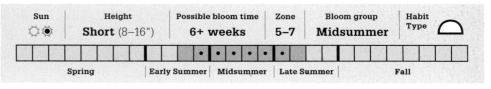

Sun	Height	Possible bloom time	Zone	Bloom group	Habit Type
☼	**Short** (8–16")	**6+ weeks**	5–7	**Midsummer**	

Spring | Early Summer | Midsummer | Late Summer | Fall

Geranium sanguineum var. *striatum* jer-AYE-nee-um

Lancaster geranium | soft pink

One of the most useful plants I've found, this geranium is very tough and attractive, producing billowing masses of flowery foliage. Extremely drought-tolerant, it features foliage that turns red after bloom in a hot, sunny location. Reblooms lightly after main bloom time. Pull back periodically from other short neighbors such as asters to prevent smothering. Also sold as *G.* 'Lancastriense' and *G.* 'Prostratum'. *G. sanguineum* 'Album' is also nice, but a little less of a fighter.

Sun	Height	Possible bloom time	Zone	Bloom group	Habit Type
☼	**Short** (6–8")	**6–8+ weeks**	4–8	**Early Summer**	

Spring | Early Summer | Midsummer | Late Summer | Fall

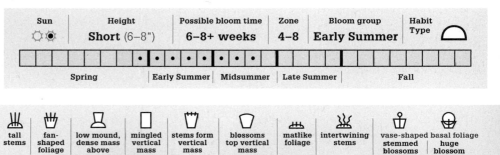

HABIT TYPES low mound | low mound, blossoms above | tall stems | fan-shaped foliage | low mound, dense mass above | mingled vertical mass | stems form vertical mass | blossoms top vertical mass | matlike foliage | intertwining stems | vase-shaped stemmed blossoms | basal foliage huge blossom

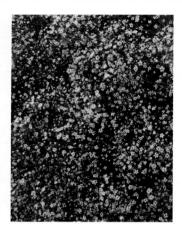

Gypsophila paniculata jip-SOF-fill-a
Baby's breath | white

Plant this anywhere in the bed for a cloud of tiny white flowers in midsummer. Elbows its way around lanky neighbors. Gypsophila prefers an alkaline (limey) soil. Taproot makes transplanting difficult; dislikes sitting in a pot. Another nice species, *G. pacifica*, has pale pink flowers, broader leaves, and slightly later bloom but is much less voluminous. Classed as medium height because best in middle of bed.

Sun	Height	Possible bloom time	Zone	Bloom group	Habit Type
☼	**Medium** (24–42")	**3–4 weeks**	**3–7**	**Late Summer**	

Spring | Early Summer | Midsummer | Late Summer | Fall

Gypsophila repens 'Rosea' jip-SOF-fill-a
'Rosea' creeping baby's breath | pale pink

Drapes over the edge of a sunny path or raised bed. Prefers alkaline (limey) soil. The plain white species, *Gypsophila repens,* is also good. Taproot makes transplanting difficult; dislikes sitting in a pot. Often reblooms. Takes a tiny bit of shade but definitely prefers full sun.

Sun	Height	Possible bloom time	Zone	Bloom group	Habit Type
☼	**Short** (4–8")	**3–4 weeks**	**3–7**	**Early Summer**	

Spring | Early Summer | Midsummer | Late Summer | Fall

Helenium 'Moerheim Beauty' hel-LEE-ni-um
'Moerheim Beauty' sneezeweed | brick red

A terrific, colorful plant that stands up to the summer heat. Long bloom starts out brick red and gradually fades to an attractive bittersweet. 'Riverton Beauty' (goldish yellow) is also a good plant but seems rather hard to find. The plain yellow species *H. autumnale* is 60" tall, gangly, and much less useful. Self supporting.

Sun	Height	Possible bloom time	Zone	Bloom group	Habit Type
☼ ◉	**Tall** (36–48")	**4+ weeks**	**3–8**	**Midsummer**	

Spring | Early Summer | Midsummer | Late Summer | Fall

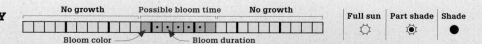

KEY

No growth | Possible bloom time | No growth

Bloom color ⟶ ⟵ Bloom duration

Full sun	Part shade	Shade
☼	◉	●

Heliopsis helianthoides 'Summer Sun'   hee-lee-OP-sis
'Summer Sun' sunflower heliopsis | gold

Many sources list this as 36" tall, but it's more like 48–60" in my experience. Excellent dark green foliage, long bloom, and optional deadheading (that is, it blooms abundantly even without deadheading). Needs at least 24" spacing. Don't confuse with *Helianthus*, which is much taller and spreads too much. Self supporting.

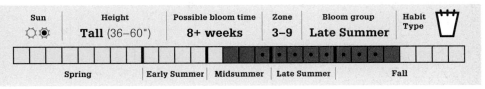

Sun	Height	Possible bloom time	Zone	Bloom group	Habit Type
☼☀	Tall (36–60")	8+ weeks	3–9	Late Summer	

Spring | Early Summer | Midsummer | Late Summer | Fall

Hemerocallis 'Autumn Minaret'   hem-er-o-KAL-is
'Autumn Minaret' daylily | luminous peachy yellow

My all-time favorite, this long- and late-blooming daylily produces a steady stream of small, elegant blossoms on 5' stems. Its rather frowsy foliage (not its best feature) is 24" tall. 'Autumn Daffodil' is similar, but with daffodil-yellow blossoms. These tall daylilies can be planted at the front of a bed, where they provide interesting height variety without blocking the plants behind. Self supporting.

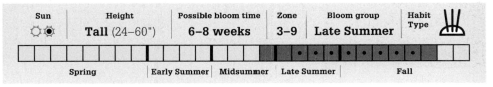

Sun	Height	Possible bloom time	Zone	Bloom group	Habit Type
☼☀	Tall (24–60")	6–8 weeks	3–9	Late Summer	

Spring | Early Summer | Midsummer | Late Summer | Fall

Hemerocallis 'Catherine Woodbury'   hem-er-o-KAL-is
'Catherine Woodbury' daylily | orchid-pink

The soft color of this daylily makes it easy to blend and beautiful at close range. Exceptional flowers and good foliage, steady succession of large, individual blossoms. My favorite midseason daylily.

Sun	Height	Possible bloom time	Zone	Bloom group	Habit Type
☼☀	Medium (24–30")	2–4 weeks	3–9	Late Summer	

Spring | Early Summer | Midsummer | Late Summer | Fall

HABIT TYPES low mound   low mound, blossoms above   tall stems   fan-shaped foliage   low mound, dense mass above   mingled vertical mass   stems form vertical mass   blossoms top vertical mass   matlike foliage   intertwining stems   vase-shaped stemmed blossoms   basal foliage huge blossom

Hemerocallis dumortieri hem-er-o-KAL-is

Early daylily | golden yellow with brown stripes

One of a tiny handful of species daylilies still in production, *H. dumortieri* has good blending color and good foliage, and it blooms very early. Brownish bronze stripes on petal backs soften the color and improve blending properties. Fragrant. This plant can be hard to find but it's well worth the effort.

Sun	Height	Possible bloom time	Zone	Bloom group	Habit Type
☼	Medium (18–24")	2–3 weeks	3–9	Early Summer	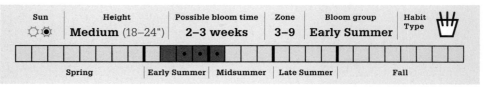

Spring | Early Summer | Midsummer | Late Summer | Fall

Hemerocallis 'Hall's Pink' hem-er-o-KAL-is

'Hall's Pink' daylily | streaked pink with orange tinge

A late daylily with orange-tinged pink blossoms that are easy to blend. Flowers are large, abundant, somewhat recurved, and a little flamboyant. Foliage is quite thick and tall.

Sun	Height	Possible bloom time	Zone	Bloom group	Habit Type
☼	Medium (20–30")	2–3 weeks	4–9	Late Summer	

Spring | Early Summer | Midsummer | Late Summer | Fall

Hemerocallis 'Happy Returns' hem-er-o-KAL-is

'Happy Returns' daylily | lemon yellow

A clearer yellow than 'Stella D'Oro', this rebloomer blends easily with other colors. 'Rosy Returns', with melon pink flowers, is similar in bloom length and habit. Good foliage. Blossom edges are slightly ruffled.

Sun	Height	Possible bloom time	Zone	Bloom group	Habit Type
☼	Medium (10–18")	3–6 weeks	3–9	Midsummer	

Spring | Early Summer | Midsummer | Late Summer | Fall

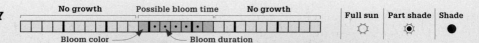
KEY — No growth | Possible bloom time | No growth — Bloom color — Bloom duration Full sun ☼ | Part shade ◉ | Shade ●

Hemerocallis 'Hyperion' hem-er-o-KAL-is

'Hyperion' daylily | light canary yellow

The classic yellow daylily with many good qualities. Fragrant, abundant blossoms open midseason on tall stems held high above the foliage.

Sun	Height	Possible bloom time	Zone	Bloom group	Habit Type
☼◉	**Medium** (24–36")	**3–5 weeks**	**3–9**	**Midsummer**	

Spring | Early Summer | Midsummer | Late Summer | Fall

Hemerocallis 'Ice Carnival' hem-er-o-KAL-is

'Ice Carnival' daylily | near white

Fragrant and easy to blend. Slightly greenish or yellowish cast to flowers. Blossoms can be rather sparse. Especially valuable for its easily blended color and late bloom time. Petals are larger and form a looser, flatter blossom than 'White Temptation'.

Sun	Height	Possible bloom time	Zone	Bloom group	Habit Type
☼◉	**Medium** (16–28")	**3–4 weeks**	**3–9**	**Late Summer**	

Spring | Early Summer | Midsummer | Late Summer | Fall

Hemerocallis lilioasphodelus hem-er-o-KAL-is

Lemon lily | lemon yellow

The earliest blooming daylily, these fragrant flowers look fantastic with Siberian irises. Color is bright and easy to blend. Foliage is more upright than most daylilies and can be crowded out by pushy neighbors. One of the only species daylilies still commonly found at nurseries; usually sold as *Hemerocallis flava*.

Sun	Height	Possible bloom time	Zone	Bloom group	Habit Type
☼◉	**Medium** (24–36")	**2–3 weeks**	**3–9**	**Early Summer**	

Spring | Early Summer | Midsummer | Late Summer | Fall

HABIT TYPES low mound | low mound, blossoms above | tall stems | fan-shaped foliage | low mound, dense mass above | mingled vertical mass | stems form vertical mass | blossoms top vertical mass | matlike foliage | intertwining stems | vase-shaped stemmed blossoms | basal foliage huge blossom

Hemerocallis 'Little Grapette' hem-er-o-KAL-is
'Little Grapette' daylily | dark raspberry/grape

A terrifically useful, easy to blend, and floriferous rebloomer with an irresistably cute name. Slightly ruffled flowers are dark raspberry with an inner band of grape bordering the lime green throat. Compact foliage stays nice all season. 'Siloam Irving Hepner' is a very similar cultivar.

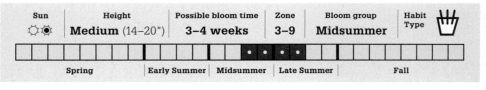

Sun	Height	Possible bloom time	Zone	Bloom group	Habit Type
☼ ◉	Medium (14–20")	3–4 weeks	3–9	Midsummer	

Hemerocallis 'Red Magic' hem-er-o-KAL-is
'Red Magic' daylily | red with yellow throat

Although red and yellow can be harder to blend, this floriferous daylily is worth finding a place for. Great in any garden with a tutti-frutti (anything and everything) color scheme or a garden made up of hot colors.

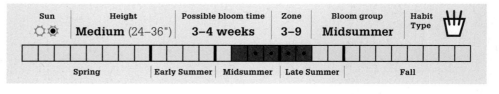

Sun	Height	Possible bloom time	Zone	Bloom group	Habit Type
☼ ◉	Medium (24–36")	3–4 weeks	3–9	Midsummer	

Hemerocallis 'White Temptation' hem-er-o-KAL-is
'White Temptation' daylily | near white

Late blooming and an easy color to blend. Greenish throat. Blossoms can be rather sparse. Petals are slightly ruffled and form a smaller, tighter blossom than 'Ice Carnival'.

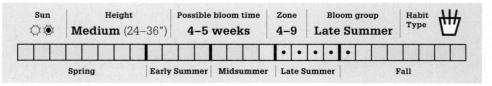

Sun	Height	Possible bloom time	Zone	Bloom group	Habit Type
☼ ◉	Medium (24–36")	4–5 weeks	4–9	Late Summer	

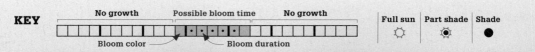

KEY — No growth | Possible bloom time | No growth | Bloom color | Bloom duration | Full sun ☼ | Part shade ◉ | Shade ●

Heuchera 'Amethyst Myst'   HEW-ker-a

'Amethyst Myst' coral bells | purple foliage

Easy and adaptable, this *Heuchera* can hold its own in a mixed bed. Purple leaves with silver overlay; whitish blossoms are rather unremarkable, but flowers are not the main attraction of any purple-leaved coral bells. There are many other good purple-leaved varieties of *Heuchera*. Blooms June-July.

Sun	Height	Possible bloom time	Zone	Bloom group	Habit Type
☼◉	**Short** (8–18")	n/a	4–8	**Foliage**	

| Spring | Early Summer | Midsummer | Late Summer | Fall |

Heuchera 'Mount St. Helens'   HEW-ker-a

'Mount St. Helens' coral bells | vivid coral red

One of my very favorite plants. Plant it at the front of the bed with other short things and enjoy the display of delicate, bell-shaped blossoms on tall stems for months on end. Other green-foliaged, red-flowered varieties, such as *H. sanguinea* 'Splendens', are also good. Extremely long blooming and good for blending. Keeps blooming without any deadheading.

Sun	Height	Possible bloom time	Zone	Bloom group	Habit Type
☼◉	**Short** (8–15")	**8–10 weeks**	3–8	**Midsummer**	

| Spring | Early Summer | Midsummer | Late Summer | Fall |

Heuchera 'Stormy Seas'   HEW-ker-a

'Stormy Seas' coral bells | greenish purple foliage

Similar to 'Amethyst Myst', this *Heuchera* has purple foliage with shades of silver, lavender, and pewter. Many other purple-leaved varieties are also good. Rather unremarkable white blossoms come in June and July. Purple coral bells are grown for their foliage, not for their blossoms.

Sun	Height	Possible bloom time	Zone	Bloom group	Habit Type
☼◉	**Short** (8–18")	n/a	4–8	**Foliage**	

| Spring | Early Summer | Midsummer | Late Summer | Fall |

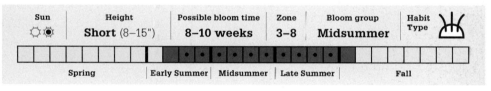

HABIT TYPES   low mound | low mound, blossoms above | tall stems | fan-shaped foliage | low mound, dense mass above | mingled vertical mass | stems form vertical mass | blossoms top vertical mass | matlike foliage | intertwining stems | vase-shaped stemmed blossoms | basal foliage huge blossom

Heuchera villosa 'Autumn Bride' HEW-ker-a

'Autumn Bride' hairy alumroot | white

Large, light green leaves and panicles of long-lasting white flowers make this a great groundcover when massed in a shady spot. Do not crowd in a mixed perennial bed; give it a 16" space and don't let other plants droop or lean onto it. Takes dry shade. Other cultivars are also good. A wonderful and extremely underappreciated plant.

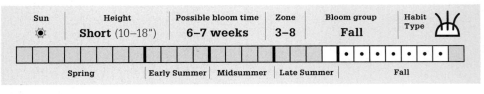

Sun	Height	Possible bloom time	Zone	Bloom group	Habit Type
☀	Short (10–18")	6–7 weeks	3–8	Fall	

Spring | Early Summer | Midsummer | Late Summer | Fall

Hosta 'Kabitan' HOS-ta

'Kabitan' hosta | dark lavender

This small hosta is listed with the flowering plants because of its late summer bloom time when there are fewer plants to choose from. Bright gold leaves with dark edges light up in the shade. Nice groundcover. Slug prone; watch for slugs and snails.

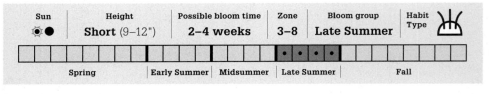

Sun	Height	Possible bloom time	Zone	Bloom group	Habit Type
☀●	Short (9–12")	2–4 weeks	3–8	Late Summer	

Spring | Early Summer | Midsummer | Late Summer | Fall

Hosta 'Patriot' HOS-ta

'Patriot' hosta | white/green foliage

Variegated foliage; quite sun tolerant; do not crowd. Lavender blooms appear in midsummer, but the primary contribution of most hostas is the foliage. Many, many other hosta varieties are also good. Those that are as sun tolerant as 'Patriot' are more adaptable in the mixed perennial bed. Another sun-tolerant hosta is *H. lancifolia*, which has long, pointed, green leaves and dark lilac flowers.

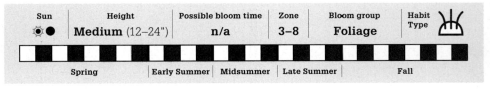

Sun	Height	Possible bloom time	Zone	Bloom group	Habit Type
☀●	Medium (12–24")	n/a	3–8	Foliage	

Spring | Early Summer | Midsummer | Late Summer | Fall

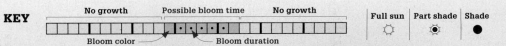

KEY

No growth — Possible bloom time — No growth

Bloom color — Bloom duration

Full sun | Part shade | Shade

Hydrangea macrophylla 'Nikko Blue' hy-DRAN-jee-a

'Nikko Blue' bigleaf hydrangea | French blue

Stays pretty small in Maine, thus fits into a mixed perennial bed. This shrub might get too big to use in a perennial bed in warmer climates. Allow at least 30" for spread. Provide adequate moisture and some shade; prune immediately after bloom (before next year's flower buds begin to form). Apply aluminum sulfate to acidify soil if blossoms are pink instead of blue. 'Endless Summer' is also good.

Sun	Height	Possible bloom time	Zone	Bloom group	Habit Type
☀●	**Medium** (24–36")	**4–6 weeks**	5/6–8	**Late Summer**	⌒

Spring · Early Summer · Midsummer · Late Summer · Fall

Iberis sempervirens 'Alexander's White' eye-BEER-is

'Alexander's White' candytuft | white

Candytuft is an old-fashioned favorite that looks good draping over a wall. The dark green, evergreen foliage looks crisp all season. Actually a woody sub-shrub; other varieties are also good. Requires good drainage. Its one drawback is that it fails the low-maintenance test because it must be cut back hard every couple of years or it becomes an unwieldy mess.

Sun	Height	Possible bloom time	Zone	Bloom group	Habit Type
☼◉	**Short** (6–10")	**3–4 weeks**	3–8	**Spring**	⌒

Spring · Early Summer · Midsummer · Late Summer · Fall

Iris 'Crimson King' EYE-ris

'Crimson King' bearded iris | deep purple

I consider this a "must have" for nearly every garden. Early and very floriferous. The name is misleading, as it is purple, not crimson, and the color is very easy to blend. Looks great with *Aurinia*, which blooms at the same time. Likes lime and good drainage. Abundant, early bloom and possible rebloom. Foliage attractive all season. Check appendix for Web sites that list bloom times of various bearded irises.

Sun	Height	Possible bloom time	Zone	Bloom group	Habit Type
☼	**Medium** (12–22")	**2+ weeks**	4–9	Spring	Ⱳ

Spring · Early Summer · Midsummer · Late Summer · Fall

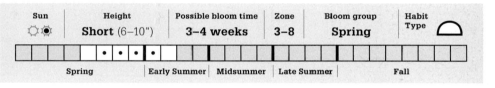

HABIT TYPES low mound | low mound, blossoms above | tall stems | fan-shaped foliage | low mound, dense mass above | mingled vertical mass | stems form vertical mass | blossoms top vertical mass | matlike foliage | intertwining stems | vase-shaped stemmed blossoms | basal foliage huge blossom

Iris cristata EYE-ris

Crested iris | lavender

The extremely short bloom time of this plant is a disadvantage, but the beauty of the flowers and the attractive, spreading habit earned it a place in this list. The white variety, *Iris cristata* 'Alba', is lovely but not quite as vigorous as the lavender or bluish types. Sits well on the edge of a mixed perennial bed where it is somewhat shaded by taller plants. Takes a great deal of shade. Native. Excellent groundcover; great interplanted in a woodland setting.

Sun	Height	Possible bloom time	Zone	Bloom group	Habit Type
☼☀	**Short** (4–8")	**1 week**	**4–8**	**Spring**	

Spring | Early Summer | Midsummer | Late Summer | Fall

Iris ensata 'Mount Fuji' EYE-ris

'Mount Fuji' Japanese iris | white

Prefers good moisture and absolutely requires acidic soil. Large, velvety flowers. There are hundreds of excellent varieties and colors of *Iris ensata*.

Sun	Height	Possible bloom time	Zone	Bloom group	Habit Type
☼	**Medium** (24–36")	**1–2 weeks**	**4–9**	**Midsummer**	

Spring | Early Summer | Midsummer | Late Summer | Fall

Iris ensata 'Royal Robe' EYE-ris

'Royal Robe' Japanese iris | deep wine-purple

Prefers good moisture and absolutely requires acidic soil. Large, velvety flowers. There are hundreds of excellent varieties and colors of *Iris ensata*.

Sun	Height	Possible bloom time	Zone	Bloom group	Habit Type
☼	**Medium** (27–36")	**2–3 weeks**	**4–9**	**Midsummer**	

Spring | Early Summer | Midsummer | Late Summer | Fall

KEY

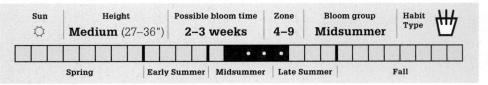

No growth | Possible bloom time | No growth

Bloom color — | — Bloom duration

Full sun | Part shade | Shade
☼ | ☀ | ●

Iris × germanica 'Mexicana' EYE-ris

'Mexicana' bearded iris | yellow/lavender-wine

There are hundreds of good bearded irises, all of which like alkaline soil, good drainage, and full sun. 'Mexicana' has soft lemon yellow standards and veined lavender-wine falls; colors that are easy to blend with others. Its bloom time is in the midrange for bearded irises. Check appendix for Web sites that list bloom times of various bearded irises. 'Mexicana' is an historic iris, bred prior to 1859.

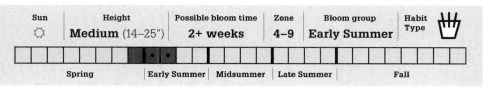

Sun	Height	Possible bloom time	Zone	Bloom group	Habit Type
☼	**Medium** (14–25")	**2+ weeks**	4–9	**Early Summer**	

Spring   Early Summer | Midsummer | Late Summer   Fall

Iris 'Little Episode' EYE-ris

'Little Episode' dwarf bearded iris | wine-purple/purple

Quickly multiplies to form a clump. Looks fantastic with *Aurinia*. Falls are wine-purple with a purple edge; standards are purple. Like regular bearded irises, it likes alkaline soil, good drainage, and full sun. Other dwarf bearded iris (*I. pumila*) cultivars are also good, and valuable for their short height and early bloom. Check appendix for Web sites that list bloom times of various bearded irises.

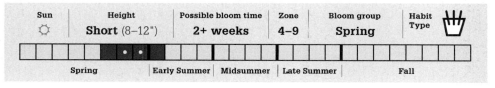

Sun	Height	Possible bloom time	Zone	Bloom group	Habit Type
☼	**Short** (8–12")	**2+ weeks**	4–9	**Spring**	

Spring   Early Summer | Midsummer | Late Summer   Fall

Iris 'Pride of Ireland' EYE-ris

'Pride of Ireland' bearded iris | light greenish yellow

Tall award-winner which blooms at the late end of the genus. Easy color to blend. Needs alkaline soil and good drainage. Check appendix for Web sites that list bloom times of various bearded irises.

Sun	Height	Possible bloom time	Zone	Bloom group	Habit Type
☼ ◉	**Tall** (24–38")	**2+ weeks**	3–8	**Early Summer**	

Spring   Early Summer | Midsummer | Late Summer   Fall

HABIT TYPES | low mound | low mound, blossoms above | tall stems | fan-shaped foliage | low mound, dense mass above | mingled vertical mass | stems form vertical mass | blossoms top vertical mass | matlike foliage | intertwining stems | vase-shaped stemmed blossoms | basal foliage huge blossom

Iris reticulata 'Harmony' EYE-ris

'Harmony' dwarf iris | medium blue

A wonderful, inexpensive bulb for early spring blooms. Often starts blooming in March. There are many fine cultivars, but the light colors show up best against damp, dark spring soil. Plant in swaths to heighten impact.

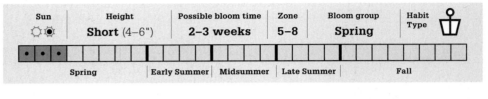

Sun	Height	Possible bloom time	Zone	Bloom group	Habit Type
☼◉	**Short** (4–6")	**2–3 weeks**	**5–8**	**Spring**	

Spring | Early Summer | Midsummer | Late Summer | Fall

Iris sibirica 'Butter and Sugar' EYE-ris

'Butter and Sugar' Siberian iris | white/yellow

'Butter and Sugar' is just one of the hundreds of good varieties of Siberian iris. Foliage is vertical and dramatic, and it usually looks good all season. This cultivar has white standards and bright butter yellow falls. Planting densely with other plants, in keeping with the method described in this book, greatly reduces the need to divide plants that normally require frequent division.

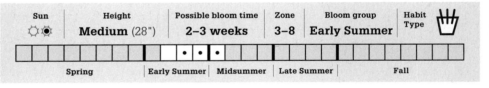

Sun	Height	Possible bloom time	Zone	Bloom group	Habit Type
☼◉	**Medium** (28")	**2–3 weeks**	**3–8**	**Early Summer**	

Spring | Early Summer | Midsummer | Late Summer | Fall

Iris sibirica 'Caesar's Brother' EYE-ris

'Caesar's Brother' Siberian iris | dark purple-violet

'Caesar's Brother' is a widely available tall Siberian iris. Foliage is vertical and dramatic, and it usually looks good all season. Planting densely with other plants, in keeping with the method described in this book, greatly reduces the need to divide plants that normally require frequent division.

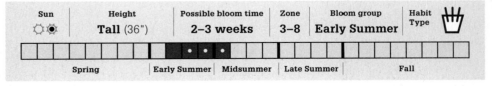

Sun	Height	Possible bloom time	Zone	Bloom group	Habit Type
☼◉	**Tall** (36")	**2–3 weeks**	**3–8**	**Early Summer**	

Spring | Early Summer | Midsummer | Late Summer | Fall

KEY

No growth | Possible bloom time | No growth

Bloom color — Bloom duration

Full sun ☼ | Part shade ◉ | Shade ●

Iris sibirica 'Silver Edge' EYE-ris

'Silver Edge' Siberian iris | sky blue with silver edge

The lovely, sky blue color of 'Silver Edge' blends beautifully with almost any other color. The flowers are more horizontal than many Siberian irises. Foliage is vertical and dramatic, and it usually looks good all season. Planting densely with other plants, in keeping with the method described in this book, greatly reduces the need to divide plants that normally require frequent division.

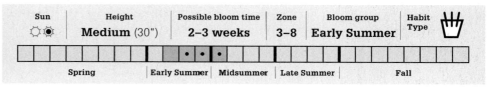

Sun	Height	Possible bloom time	Zone	Bloom group	Habit Type
☼◉	**Medium** (30")	**2–3 weeks**	3–8	**Early Summer**	

Spring | Early Summer | Midsummer | Late Summer | Fall

Kirengeshoma palmata ki-ren-ge-SHOW-ma

Yellow waxbells | creamy yellow

Wonderful, maple-leaf foliage looks fantastic all season. Needs extra space and time to get established. Withstands more sun than expected. Buttery yellow flower buds sometimes open into distorted, pointy shapes.

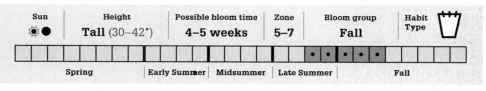

Sun	Height	Possible bloom time	Zone	Bloom group	Habit Type
◉●	**Tall** (30–42")	**4–5 weeks**	5–7	**Fall**	

Spring | Early Summer | Midsummer | Late Summer | Fall

Knautia macedonica NAW-tee-a

Knautia | deep crimson

Knautia has a rather gangly habit, but its color is surprisingly easy to blend. Self-seeding can be a problem, but dense planting and the use of bark mulch usually helps prevent this. Somewhat variable, but generally very long-blooming, especially if deadheaded. Bloom time shown is without deadheading. Also known as *Scabiosa rumelica*.

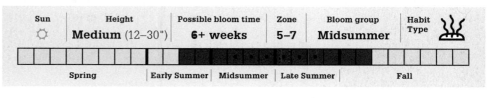

Sun	Height	Possible bloom time	Zone	Bloom group	Habit Type
☼	**Medium** (12–30")	**6+ weeks**	5–7	**Midsummer**	

Spring | Early Summer | Midsummer | Late Summer | Fall

Lamium maculatum 'Shell Pink' LAY-mee-um

'Shell Pink' dead nettle | soft pink

Green leaves with a central white stripe; spreading groundcover. Will spread to fill whatever space is available; spills over walls. Other cultivars are also good. I value this lamium primarily for its flowers, but the foliage also contributes favorably to the planting scheme.

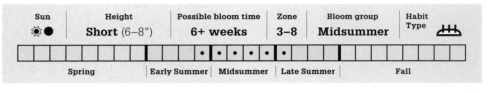

Sun	Height	Possible bloom time	Zone	Bloom group	Habit Type
☀ ●	Short (6–8")	6+ weeks	3–8	Midsummer	

Spring · Early Summer · Midsummer · Late Summer · Fall

Lamium maculatum 'White Nancy' LAY-mee-um

'White Nancy' dead nettle | silver-white/green foliage

Spreading groundcover valuable as a foliage plant. Silvery leaves with green edges and white flowers light up dark corners. Will spread to fill whatever space is available; spills over walls. Blooms Early Summer through Midsummer for four or more weeks. I value this cultivar primarily for its foliage because it contributes a white touch before, during, and after bloom. Other *Lamium* cultivars are also good.

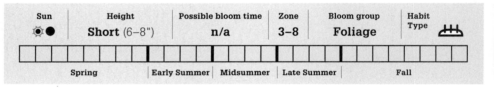

Sun	Height	Possible bloom time	Zone	Bloom group	Habit Type
☀ ●	Short (6–8")	n/a	3–8	Foliage	

Spring · Early Summer · Midsummer · Late Summer · Fall

Lavandula angustifolia 'Munstead' la-VAN-dew-la

'Munstead' lavender | light purple

Needs poor, well-drained soil; don't crowd or shade. *L.* 'Hidcote' has darker blossoms but seems less dependable here on the coast of Maine. 'Munstead' sometimes has major rebloom in the fall.

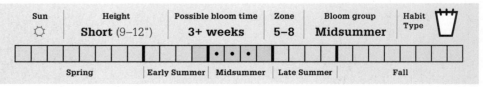

Sun	Height	Possible bloom time	Zone	Bloom group	Habit Type
☼	Short (9–12")	3+ weeks	5–8	Midsummer	

Spring · Early Summer · Midsummer · Late Summer · Fall

KEY

No growth | Possible bloom time | No growth

Bloom color — Bloom duration

Full sun ☼ | Part shade ☀ | Shade ●

Leucanthemum vulgare 'Becky' lew-KAN-the-mum

'Becky' Shasta daisy | white

I think 'Becky' is the best cultivar of Shasta. Good height (not too tall), excellent foliage all season, floriferous, and long-blooming on stout stems. Large blossoms. Seems to need dividing less often than other varieties. Short varieties such as 'Snow Lady' have all disappointed me by being less robust and less floriferous.

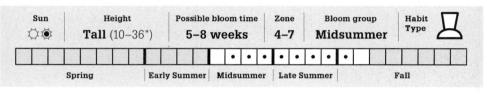

Sun	Height	Possible bloom time	Zone	Bloom group	Habit Type
☼	Tall (10–36")	5–8 weeks	4–7	Midsummer	

Spring | Early Summer | Midsummer | Late Summer | Fall

Liatris spicata 'Kobold' ly-A-tris

'Kobold' gayfeather | lavender

Do not crowd or shade with taller plants, or the bloom will be compromised. Fountain-shaped foliage and blossoms like fat drumsticks. I find *Liatris* slightly difficult to blend, both in color and in habit.

Sun	Height	Possible bloom time	Zone	Bloom group	Habit Type
☼	Medium (24–30")	2–3 weeks	4–9	Midsummer	

Spring | Early Summer | Midsummer | Late Summer | Fall

Ligularia stenocephala 'The Rocket' lig-yew-LAIR-ee-ya

'The Rocket' ligularia | lemon yellow

Ligularia is worth the extra effort to accommodate its need for afternoon shade and moisture. Bold, heart-shaped leaves form a mound from which a cluster of dramatic yellow flower spikes sprout. Leaves droop (but are not damaged) in too much sun, especially in the afternoon.

Sun	Height	Possible bloom time	Zone	Bloom group	Habit Type
◐ ●	Medium (18–36")	3 weeks	5–8	Late Summer	

Spring | Early Summer | Midsummer | Late Summer | Fall

HABIT TYPES   low mound   low mound, blossoms above   tall stems   fan-shaped foliage   low mound, dense mass above   mingled vertical mass   stems form vertical mass   blossoms top vertical mass   matlike foliage   intertwining stems   vase-shaped stemmed blossoms   basal foliage huge blossom

Lilium 'Black Beauty' LIL-ee-um

'Black Beauty' Oriental hybrid lily | dark raspberry/white

A tall, colorful, fragrant lily with recurved petals. Its late bloom time is useful in continuously blooming schemes. Lily leaf beetle is a problem in some areas. Plant as a bulb in fall or spring. Taller than most Oriental hybrid lilies, it requires staking or support from neighboring tall plants.

Sun	Height	Possible bloom time	Zone	Bloom group	Habit Type
☼ ☀	**Tall** (48–84")	**2–3 weeks**	**3–8**	**Late Summer**	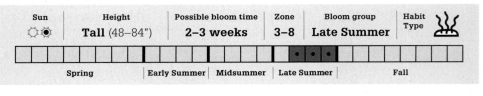

Spring · Early Summer · Midsummer · Late Summer · Fall

Lilium 'Casa Blanca' LIL-ee-um

'Casa Blanca' Oriental hybrid lily | pure white

Valued for its late bloom and dramatic stature, 'Casa Blanca' is one of many good Oriental hybrid lilies. Fragrant. Prone to defoliation by lily leaf beetle in recent years in some parts of the country.

Sun	Height	Possible bloom time	Zone	Bloom group	Habit Type
☼ ☀	**Tall** (36–54")	**3–4 weeks**	**5–8**	**Late Summer**	

Spring · Early Summer · Midsummer · Late Summer · Fall

Lilium 'Lollypop' LIL-ee-um

'Lollypop' Asiatic hybrid lily | pink/white

One of many good varieties of Asiatic hybrid lily. White petals with bright pink tips. Prone to defoliation by lily leaf beetle in recent years in some parts of the country. Plant as a bulb in fall or spring.

Sun	Height	Possible bloom time	Zone	Bloom group	Habit Type
☼ ☀	**Medium** (18–24")	**2–3 weeks**	**4–8**	**Midsummer**	

Spring · Early Summer · Midsummer · Late Summer · Fall

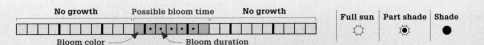

Lilium 'Spirit' LIL-ee-um

'Spirit' Longiflorum-Asiatic (L.A.) hybrid lily | creamy silver-pink

There are many good varieties of L.A. hybrid lily, and 'Spirit' is one of the best for its easy blending color. Prone to defoliation by lily leaf beetle in recent years in some parts of the country. Plant as a bulb in fall or spring.

Sun	Height	Possible bloom time	Zone	Bloom group	Habit Type
☼◉	**Medium** (18–24")	**2–3 weeks**	**4–8**	**Midsummer**	

Spring | Early Summer | Midsummer | Late Summer | Fall

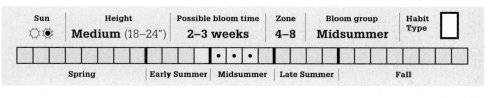

Lilium 'Star Gazer' LIL-ee-um

'Star Gazer' Oriental hybrid lily | raspberry/white

'Star Gazer' is one of the most popular of the many excellent varieties of Oriental hybrid lily. Easy to blend with its pink speckled petals trimmed with white. Extremely fragrant and dependable. Prone to defoliation by lily leaf beetle in recent years in some parts of the country.

Sun	Height	Possible bloom time	Zone	Bloom group	Habit Type
☼◉	**Medium** (24–36")	**3–4 weeks**	**5–8**	**Late Summer**	

Spring | Early Summer | Midsummer | Late Summer | Fall

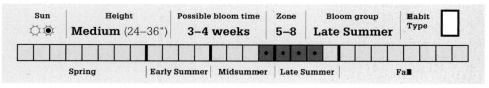

Limonium latifolium li-MOE-nee-um

Sea lavender | lavender-blue

An amazingly adaptable plant, suitable for the rock garden or mixed perennial bed. In nature, it lives at the ocean's edge where it is frequently drenched by sea water — this is a tough plant! Leathery, evergreen foliage topped with a broad, airy spray of tiny lavender flowers; sometimes reblooms. Do not crowd. Needs good drainage.

Sun	Height	Possible bloom time	Zone	Bloom group	Habit Type
☼	**Short** (8–18")	**4–6 weeks**	**3–8**	**Late Summer**	

Spring | Early Summer | Midsummer | Late Summer | Fall

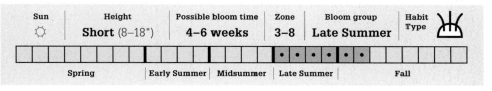

HABIT TYPES — low mound | low mound, blossoms above | tall stems | fan-shaped foliage | low mound, dense mass above | mingled vertical mass | stems form vertical mass | blossoms top vertical mass | matlike foliage | intertwining stems | vase-shaped stemmed blossoms | basal foliage huge blossom

Lychnis chalcedonica LICK-nis

Maltese cross | scarlet

This old-fashioned flower has unfairly (I think) lost popularity, maybe because the color can be hard to blend. Floriferous and self-seeds somewhat. Plants "reach" and grow taller when surrounded by other plants of the same height.

Sun	Height	Possible bloom time	Zone	Bloom group	Habit Type
☼	**Medium** (24–36")	**4–5 weeks**	**3–7**	**Midsummer**	

Spring | Early Summer | Midsummer | Late Summer | Fall

Lychnis coronaria LICK-nis

Rose campion | magenta

Wonderful, feltlike, gray foliage and branching structure. Color blends easily with blues and pinks. Self-seeds; thin excess seedlings in spring. Short-lived perennial; sometimes grows as a biennial. Individual plants may exhibit staggered bloom beyond primary bloom time. Available in seed form; simply sprinkle seeds liberally on bare soil and wait for them to start popping up here and there.

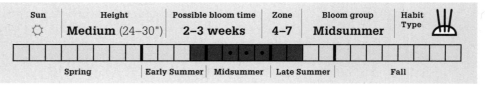

Sun	Height	Possible bloom time	Zone	Bloom group	Habit Type
☼	**Medium** (24–30")	**2–3 weeks**	**4–7**	**Midsummer**	

Spring | Early Summer | Midsummer | Late Summer | Fall

Monarda 'Jacob Cline' mo-NAR-da

'Jacob Cline' bee balm | bright medium red

This Mint Family plant must be used with care, as it can spread too much and is mildew-prone (although 'Jacob Cline' is a mildew-resistant cultivar). Flowers are spectacular and attract hummingbirds. Reblooms. 'Raspberry Wine' is another excellent cultivar with wine red blossoms and good mildew resistance. Plant *Monarda* where it gets good air circulation to minimize mildew. Self supporting.

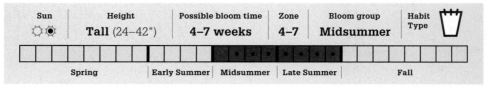

Sun	Height	Possible bloom time	Zone	Bloom group	Habit Type
☼ ◉	**Tall** (24–42")	**4–7 weeks**	**4–7**	**Midsummer**	

Spring | Early Summer | Midsummer | Late Summer | Fall

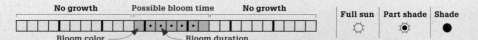

KEY | No growth | Possible bloom time | No growth | Full sun ☼ | Part shade ◉ | Shade ●

Bloom color ←→ Bloom duration

Muscari armeniacum mus-KAR-ee

Grape hyacinth | bluish purple

If I had to choose just one spring bulb, this would be it. Naturalizes (multiplies); long-blooming and fragrant. Plant in clusters for the best effect. Other species of *Muscari* are also good.

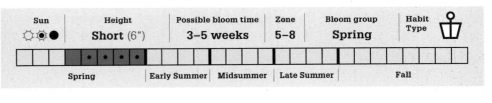

Sun	Height	Possible bloom time	Zone	Bloom group	Habit Type
☼ ◑ ●	Short (6")	3–5 weeks	5–8	Spring	

| | | | Spring | | | Early Summer | Midsummer | Late Summer | | Fall | |

Myosotis sylvatica 'Victoria Blue' my-o-SO-tis

'Victoria Blue' forget-me-not | light blue, turning pink

Once you get a few of these going in your garden, they'll take care of themselves forever by self-seeding. Charming light blue flowers turn pink with time. Other species are also good. Prone to powdery mildew after bloom. Pull out gone-by or mildewy plants by the roots; plenty will materialize next year from seeds invisibly sown. Short-lived perennial or biennial.

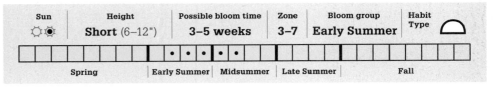

Sun	Height	Possible bloom time	Zone	Bloom group	Habit Type
☼ ◑	Short (6–12")	3–5 weeks	3–7	Early Summer	

| | | | Spring | | Early Summer | Midsummer | Late Summer | | Fall | |

Narcissus 'Hawera' nar-SIS-us

'Hawera' dwarf daffodil | pale canary yellow

Delicate-looking sprays of miniature daffodil blossoms belie the toughness of this plant. Very long bloom; naturalizes. Color is cheerful and bright, but not too harsh. Needs good drainage.

Sun	Height	Possible bloom time	Zone	Bloom group	Habit Type
☼ ◑	Short (8–10")	2–3 weeks	4–9	Spring	

| | | | Spring | | Early Summer | Midsummer | Late Summer | | Fall | |

 HABIT TYPES | low mound | low mound, blossoms above | tall stems | fan-shaped foliage | low mound, dense mass above | mingled vertical mass | stems form vertical mass | blossoms top vertical mass | matlike foliage | intertwining stems | vase-shaped stemmed blossoms | basal foliage huge blossom

Narcissus 'Ice Follies' nar-SIS-us

'Ice Follies' daffodil | white/yellow

White petals and yellow cup that gradually turns white. More subtle and easier to blend than a lot of *Narcissus*. Long bloom. Ensure good drainage and adequate sun.

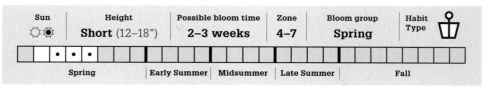

Sun	Height	Possible bloom time	Zone	Bloom group	Habit Type
☼◉	Short (12–18")	2–3 weeks	4–7	Spring	

Spring · Early Summer | Midsummer | Late Summer · Fall

Narcissus 'King Alfred' nar-SIS-us

Trumpet daffodil | bright yellow

'King Alfred' has reigned since 1899 as the standard bearer of classic, large, yellow daffodils. The King needs excellent drainage and prefers full sun. There are many other excellent varieties of *Narcissus* in various colors, sizes, and shapes.

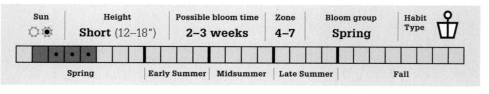

Sun	Height	Possible bloom time	Zone	Bloom group	Habit Type
☼◉	Short (12–18")	2–3 weeks	4–7	Spring	

Spring · Early Summer | Midsummer | Late Summer · Fall

Nepeta sibirica 'Souvenir d'André Chaudron' NEP-e-ta

'Souvenir d'André Chaudron' catmint | lavender-blue

This *Nepeta* has good color, foliage, and height, but it should be used with care, because it can spread aggressively once established. I like to use it in back corners where it is accessible and can only spread in two directions. Thin back to a reasonable clump each spring. Reblooms.

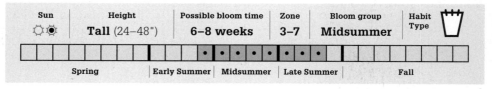

Sun	Height	Possible bloom time	Zone	Bloom group	Habit Type
☼◉	Tall (24–48")	6–8 weeks	3–7	Midsummer	

Spring · Early Summer | Midsummer | Late Summer · Fall

KEY

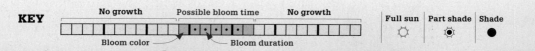

No growth · Possible bloom time · No growth

Bloom color → ← Bloom duration

Full sun ☼ | Part shade ◉ | Shade ●

Nepeta 'Walker's Low'   NEP-e-ta

'Walker's Low' catmint | lavender-blue

Catmint's gray-green foliage and lavender-blue blossoms go with almost any color scheme. It can be a smothering flopper, however — be sure to protect neighboring plants from its sprawling reach. Long-blooming and attractive, if pushy. Reblooms. Cut back completely in midsummer for total flop control. Attractive to cats, but not like catnip. 'Blue Wonder' is also good.

Sun	Height	Possible bloom time	Zone	Bloom group	Habit Type
☼	**Medium (15–24")**	**4–5 weeks**	**4–7**	**Midsummer**	

Spring | Early Summer | Midsummer | Late Summer | Fall

Nipponanthemum nipponicum   nee-po-NAN-the-mum

Montauk daisy | white

An underappreciated season extender, this woody perennial puts out a profusion of daisylike flowers in late September and October, and its succulent foliage looks great all season. Cut back by half (or don't cut back at all; be sure not to cut it to ground level!) for winter and prune any dead tops back to good buds in late spring.

Sun	Height	Possible bloom time	Zone	Bloom group	Habit Type
☼◑	**Medium (24–36")**	**4+ weeks**	**5–8**	**Fall**	

Spring | Early Summer | Midsummer | Late Summer | Fall

Oenothera fruticosa   ee-no-THE-ra

Sundrops | sunny yellow

Oenothera spreads rapidly, forming mats with shallow roots, but it's easy to thin back to manageable clumps in spring. Foliage suffers in dry conditions but rewards you by turning red in the fall.

Sun	Height	Possible bloom time	Zone	Bloom group	Habit Type
☼◑	**Medium (12–20")**	**3–4 weeks**	**4–8**	**Midsummer**	

Spring | Early Summer | Midsummer | Late Summer | Fall

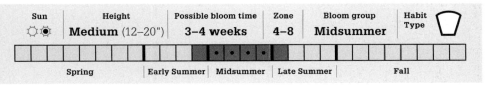

HABIT TYPES   low mound   low mound, blossoms above   tall stems   fan-shaped foliage   low mound, dense mass above   mingled vertical mass   stems form vertical mass   blossoms top vertical mass   matlike foliage   intertwining stems   vase-shaped stemmed blossoms   basal foliage huge blossom

Paeonia 'Karl Rosenfield' pee-ON-ee-a

'Karl Rosenfield' peony | deep reddish pink

This sturdy peony is slightly fragrant and easily supported with a standard peony ring. Foliage looks good all season. There are many other excellent peony cultivars; look for self-supporting ones with strong stems. Peonies make good cut flowers.

Sun ☼☀	Height Tall (30–36")	Possible bloom time 2 weeks	Zone 3–8	Bloom group Early Summer	Habit Type

Spring | Early Summer | Midsummer | Late Summer   Fall

Paeonia 'Miss America' pee-ON-ee-a

'Miss America' peony | white

'Miss America' is at home in any color scheme. It's semidouble, with strong stems. There are many other excellent peony cultivars; look for self-supporting ones with strong stems. Peony foliage is good for hiding maturing tulip or narcissus foliage.

Sun ☼☀	Height Tall (30–36")	Possible bloom time 2 weeks	Zone 3–8	Bloom group Early Summer	Habit Type

Spring | Early Summer | Midsummer | Late Summer   Fall

Paeonia 'Reine Hortense' pee-ON-ee-a

'Reine Hortense' peony | rose-pink

This strong-stemmed pink peony is on the taller side. There are many other excellent peony cultivars; look for self-supporting ones with strong stems (like 'Reine Hortense') or be prepared to support the heavy blossoms with stakes and string or a peony ring.

Sun ☼☀	Height Tall (36–38")	Possible bloom time 2 weeks	Zone 3–8	Bloom group Early Summer	Habit Type

Spring | Early Summer | Midsummer | Late Summer   Fall

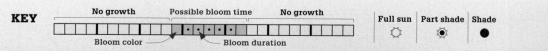

KEY   No growth | Possible bloom time | No growth   Full sun ☼ | Part shade ☀ | Shade ●

Bloom color   Bloom duration

Paeonia suffruticosa pee-ON-ee-a

Tree peony | pink, yellow, white, red, or lavender

Huge blossoms on a small shrub. Blooms before herbaceous peonies. Available in the colors listed, plus some fancy combinations. Burying the trunk with soil or bark mulch causes it to rot (as with any shrub or tree). Do not crowd. Do not cut back for winter.

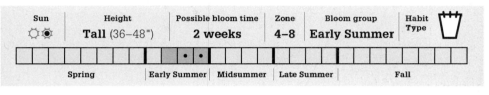

Sun	Height	Possible bloom time	Zone	Bloom group	Habit Type
☼	**Tall** (36–48")	**2 weeks**	**4–8**	**Early Summer**	

Spring · Early Summer · Midsummer · Late Summer · Fall

Papaver orientale 'Türkenlouis' pa-PAH-ver

'Türkenlouis' Oriental poppy | deep, vivid red

Oriental poppies must be used with care, as the plant gets big and has a huge taproot. Place in the middle of the bed to hide the foliage, which goes dormant (looks dead) after bloom. There are many other excellent cultivars in shades of red, orange, pink, and white.

Sun	Height	Possible bloom time	Zone	Bloom group	Habit Type
☼	**Medium** (24–36")	**2–3 weeks**	**4–7**	**Early Summer**	

Spring · Early Summer · Midsummer · Late Summer · Fall

Patrinia gibbosa pah-TRIN-ee-a

Patrinia | soft yellow

Easily overlooked, this modest plant is an excellent blender and team player, with extremely long bloom time and good foliage. Do not bury among much taller plants or it will die out. Looks good with everything.

Sun	Height	Possible bloom time	Zone	Bloom group	Habit Type
☼	**Short** (12–18")	**6–8 weeks**	**5–8**	**Midsummer**	

Spring · Early Summer · Midsummer · Late Summer · Fall

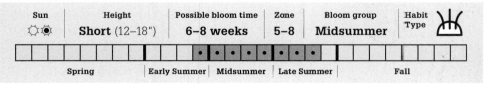

HABIT TYPES — low mound · low mound, blossoms above · tall stems · fan-shaped foliage · low mound, dense mass above · mingled vertical mass · stems form vertical mass · blossoms top vertical mass · matlike foliage · intertwining stems · vase-shaped stemmed blossoms · basal foliage huge blossom

Penstemon digitalis 'Husker Red' pen-STAY-mon
'Husker Red' beardtongue | white

A nice addition if you're planning a garden with repeated purple foliage. The reddish bronze foliage is topped by small blossoms. Looks pretty good all season.

Sun	Height	Possible bloom time	Zone	Bloom group	Habit Type
☼ ◉	**Medium** (24–36")	**2 weeks**	**4–8**	**Early Summer**	

Spring | Early Summer | Midsummer | Late Summer | Fall

Perovskia atriplicifolia 'Filigran' pe-ROF-skee-a
'Filigran' Russian sage | light hyacinth blue

Perovskia has surged in popularity in recent years, but it can look awkward if not supported properly. Has irregular shape. Needs staking or a large, sturdy neighbor to drape itself around. 'Longin' is another good cultivar. Cut woody stems back to 12" for winter.

Sun	Height	Possible bloom time	Zone	Bloom group	Habit Type
☼	**Tall** (36–42")	**6–10 weeks**	**5–9**	**Late Summer**	

Spring | Early Summer | Midsummer | Late Summer | Fall

Perovskia atriplicifolia 'Little Spire' pe-ROF-skee-a
'Little Spire' Russian sage | medium violet

Although self-supporting, this smaller *Perovskia* is still irregularly shaped and needs careful placement to look good. It helps to use cleanly shaped, good foliage plants like *Baptisia* or peonies behind and beside it. Cut woody stems back to 12" for winter.

Sun	Height	Possible bloom time	Zone	Bloom group	Habit Type
☼	**Medium** (18–24")	**6–10 weeks**	**4–9**	**Late Summer**	

Spring | Early Summer | Midsummer | Late Summer | Fall

KEY

No growth | Possible bloom time | No growth

Bloom color — Bloom duration

Full sun ☼ | Part shade ◉ | Shade ●

Phlox carolina 'Miss Lingard' floks

'Miss Lingard' Carolina phlox | white

Beautiful, clear white blossoms above crisp, dark green foliage. Can be difficult to establish; needs some elbow room. Blooms earlier and is shorter than garden phlox (below).

Sun	Height	Possible bloom time	Zone	Bloom group	Habit Type
☼	**Medium** (24–36")	**2–4 weeks**	**5–8**	**Midsummer**	

Spring | Early Summer | Midsummer | Late Summer | Fall

Phlox 'David' floks

'David' garden phlox | white

'David' is an especially mildew-resistant cultivar of *Phlox paniculata*. Forms a large clump; needs a 24" space. Cut woody stems off bluntly in fall to avoid painful pointy stubs during spring cleanup.

Sun	Height	Possible bloom time	Zone	Bloom group	Habit Type
☼	**Tall** (30–36")	**5–7 weeks**	**4–8**	**Late Summer**	

Spring | Early Summer | Midsummer | Late Summer | Fall

Phlox 'Starfire' floks

'Starfire' garden phlox | magenta-red

Garden phlox (*Phlox paniculata*) comes in colors that tend to be hard to blend, but I think 'Starfire' is an exception. Requires good air circulation to avoid powdery mildew. Cut woody stems off bluntly in fall to avoid painful pointy stubs during spring cleanup.

Sun	Height	Possible bloom time	Zone	Bloom group	Habit Type
☼	**Tall** (30–36")	**3–5 weeks**	**4–8**	**Late Summer**	

Spring | Early Summer | Midsummer | Late Summer | Fall

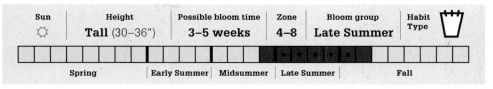

HABIT TYPES   low mound | low mound, blossoms above | tall stems | fan-shaped foliage | low mound, dense mass above | mingled vertical mass | stems form vertical mass | blossoms top vertical mass | matlike foliage | intertwining stems | vase-shaped stemmed blossoms | basal foliage huge blossom

Physocarpus opulifolius 'Diabolo' fy-so-KAR-pus

'Diabolo' ninebark | dark red foliage

A purple-leaved shrub, more irregularly shaped than *Cotinus*. Useful when planning a garden with repeated purple foliage. Adds structure to the back of a bed. Cut back hard in spring to encourage flush of new foliage. Heights given are for this method; plant will grow taller if not cut back in spring. Can become too huge for a mixed border if not cut back regularly.

Sun	Height	Possible bloom time	Zone	Bloom group	Habit Type
☼	**Tall** (48–72")	n/a	3–7	Foliage	〰

Spring	Early Summer	Midsummer	Late Summer	Fall

Platycodon grandiflorus 'Fuji Blue' pla-tee-KO-don

'Fuji Blue' balloonflower | purplish blue

One of the very best plants. Other varieties are also good (for example, 'Hybrid Blue' and 'Florist Blue'). Blue *Platycodon* is sturdier and more floriferous than white or pink. Very late to emerge in spring; plant crocus around the base to remind yourself not to trample it. Quite variable in bloom time, even among adjacent specimens of the same type. Deadhead individual blossoms for longer bloom, then cut off whole stem tops to encourage new bud formation at stem tips. Bloom time is for deadheaded plants.

Sun	Height	Possible bloom time	Zone	Bloom group	Habit Type
☼◑	**Medium** (24–36")	4–6 weeks	4–7	Late Summer	〰

Spring	Early Summer	Midsummer	Late Summer	Fall

Platycodon grandiflorus 'Florist White' pla-tee-KO-don

'Florist White' balloonflower | white

See comments for blue balloonflower above. Other varieties are also good. Less floriferous and less robust than the blue varieties.

Sun	Height	Possible bloom time	Zone	Bloom group	Habit Type
☼◑	**Medium** (24–30")	4+ weeks	4–7	Late Summer	〰

Spring	Early Summer	Midsummer	Late Summer	Fall

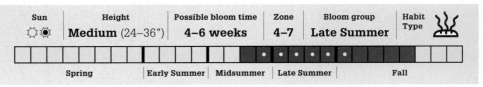

Platycodon grandiflorus 'Hybrid Pink'   pla-tee-KO-don
'Hybrid Pink' balloonflower | pastel pink

See comments for blue balloonflower above. Other varieties are also good. Less floriferous and less robust than the blue varieties.

Sun	Height	Possible bloom time	Zone	Bloom group	Habit Type
☼◉	**Medium** (24–30")	**4+ weeks**	**4–7**	**Late Summer**	

Spring | Early Summer | Midsummer | Late Summer | Fall

Prunella grandiflora 'Pink Loveliness'   prue-NEL-a
'Pink Loveliness' selfheal | purplish pink

Twines nicely among its neighbors. Grows taller among medium-height plants. Bloom time includes rebloom (which is significant). Other varieties are also good.

Sun	Height	Possible bloom time	Zone	Bloom group	Habit Type
☼◉	**Short** (8–16")	**6+ weeks**	**5–7**	**Late Summer**	

Spring | Early Summer | Midsummer | Late Summer | Fall

Pulmonaria rubra 'Bowles Red'   pul-mo-NAIR-ee-a
'Bowles Red' lungwort | rich pink

Unlike most *Pulmonarias*, this one has plain (not spotted) leaves. Much more sun-tolerant than *P. saccharata* cultivars like 'Mrs. Moon'. In Maine it can be planted in full sun, although some drooping will occur on hot, sunny days. Very long-blooming. Self-seeding can be unwelcome. *P. rubra* 'Redstart' is similar.

Sun	Height	Possible bloom time	Zone	Bloom group	Habit Type
◉●	**Short** (10–12")	**6–8 weeks**	**4–7**	**Spring**	

Spring | Early Summer | Midsummer | Late Summer | Fall

HABIT TYPES   low mound | low mound, blossoms above | tall stems | fan-shaped foliage | low mound, dense mass above | mingled vertical mass | stems form vertical mass | blossoms top vertical mass | matlike foliage | intertwining stems | vase-shaped stemmed blossoms | basal foliage huge blossom

Pulmonaria 'Victorian Brooch'   pul-mo-NAIR-ee-a
'Victorian Brooch' lungwort | magenta-coral

This beautiful *Pulmonaria* has large, silver-spotted leaves and a long bloom time. There are many other good varieties of shade-loving *Pulmonaria*, such as *P. saccharata* 'Mrs. Moon', which has pink flower buds turning to light blue flowers.

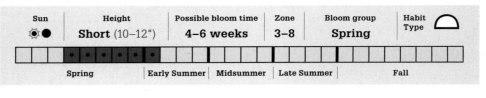

Sun	Height	Possible bloom time	Zone	Bloom group	Habit Type
☀●	**Short** (10–12")	**4–6 weeks**	**3–8**	**Spring**	

Spring   Early Summer   Midsummer   Late Summer   Fall

Rudbeckia fulgida 'Goldsturm'   rud-BEK-ee-a
'Goldsturm' black-eyed Susan | orange-gold

'Goldsturm' is one of the longest blooming and most floriferous perennials. No dead-heading is required, and seed heads are somewhat attractive. Color can be difficult to blend.

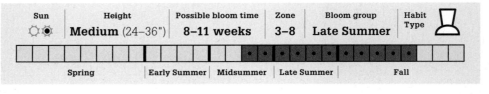

Sun	Height	Possible bloom time	Zone	Bloom group	Habit Type
☼☀	**Medium** (24–36")	**8–11 weeks**	**3–8**	**Late Summer**	

Spring   Early Summer   Midsummer   Late Summer   Fall

Rudbeckia laciniata 'Goldquelle'   rud-BEK-ee-a
'Goldquelle' cutleaf coneflower | yellow-gold

An old-fashioned plant that deserves more attention. 'Goldquelle' is shorter than some other types of *Rudbeckia laciniata*. Double blossoms, late bloom time, and attractive, divided leaves. Some people confuse this with the older cultivar 'Golden Glow' which is taller, more invasive, floppier, and more attractive to aphids. Self supporting.

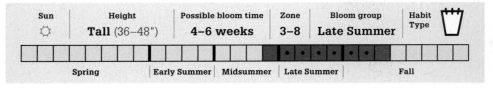

Sun	Height	Possible bloom time	Zone	Bloom group	Habit Type
☼	**Tall** (36–48")	**4–6 weeks**	**3–8**	**Late Summer**	

Spring   Early Summer   Midsummer   Late Summer   Fall

KEY

No growth   Possible bloom time   No growth

Bloom color   Bloom duration

Full sun ☼   Part shade ☀   Shade ●

Salvia nemerosa 'May Night' SAL-vee-a

'May Night' sage | rich, dark violet

Salvia has a lot to offer, if you don't object to the smell it gives off when brushed. Requires full sun. Other varieties are also good, but I think 'May Night' is the best for attractive flowers and easy-to-blend color.

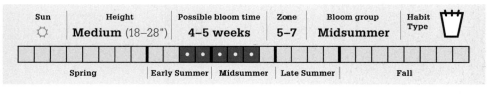

Sun	Height	Possible bloom time	Zone	Bloom group	Habit Type
☼	**Medium** (18–28")	**4–5 weeks**	**5–7**	**Midsummer**	

Spring   Early Summer   Midsummer   Late Summer   Fall

Salvia verticillata 'Purple Rain' SAL-vee-a

'Purple Rain' sage | deep violet-purple

One of the very best plants. Very long-blooming and reblooming. Works in the perennial border or in the rock garden. Faded flowers sometimes hold their purple color long after actual bloom period ends. 'Purple Rain' has larger leaves than *S. nemerosa* and fluffier, slightly curled flower panicles.

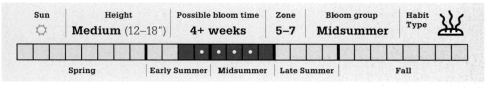

Sun	Height	Possible bloom time	Zone	Bloom group	Habit Type
☼	**Medium** (12–18")	**4+ weeks**	**5–7**	**Midsummer**	

Spring   Early Summer   Midsummer   Late Summer   Fall

Saponaria ocymoides sa-po-NAH-ree-a

Soapwort | medium pink

I prefer *Saponaria* to moss phlox (*Phlox subulata*) for the edge of a bed, because its color is easier to blend and its foliage stands up better through the summer. Shear back after bloom. Requires excellent drainage; best on the edge of a stone wall or raised bed.

Sun	Height	Possible bloom time	Zone	Bloom group	Habit Type
☼◑	**Short** (4–8")	**3–4 weeks**	**2–7**	**Early Summer**	

Spring   Early Summer   Midsummer   Late Summer   Fall

HABIT TYPES   low mound | low mound, blossoms above | tall stems | fan-shaped foliage | low mound, dense mass above | mingled vertical mass | stems form vertical mass | blossoms top vertical mass | matlike foliage | intertwining stems | vase-shaped stemmed blossoms | basal foliage huge blossom

Scabiosa columbaria 'Butterfly Blue' ska-bee-OH-sa
'Butterfly Blue' pincushion flower | lavender-blue

Tolerates no crowding; classed as "short" because basal foliage must receive sun. Likes poor, dry soil. Deadhead for long bloom and to encourage rebloom.

Sun	Height	Possible bloom time	Zone	Bloom group	Habit Type
☼	**Short** (12–18")	**4+ weeks**	**5–7**	**Midsummer**	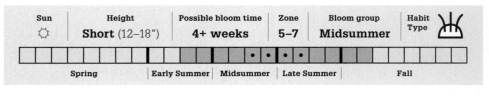

Spring | Early Summer | Midsummer | Late Summer | Fall

Scabiosa columbaria 'Pink Mist' ska-bee-OH-sa
'Pink Mist' pincushion flower | soft pink

Tolerates no crowding; classed as short because basal foliage must receive sun. Likes poor, dry soil. Deadhead for long bloom and to encourage rebloom.

Sun	Height	Possible bloom time	Zone	Bloom group	Habit Type
☼	**Short** (12–18")	**4+ weeks**	**5–7**	**Midsummer**	

Spring | Early Summer | Midsummer | Late Summer | Fall

Scilla siberica SILL-la
Siberian squill | sky blue

One of the earliest spring bulbs, *Scilla* is best planted in masses. Naturalizes (increases). Looks great mixed up with little species tulips such as *Tulipa humilis*. Several good types exist.

Sun	Height	Possible bloom time	Zone	Bloom group	Habit Type
☼ ◉	**Short** (4–6")	**2–4 weeks**	**3–7**	**Spring**	

Spring | Early Summer | Midsummer | Late Summer | Fall

KEY

No growth   Possible bloom time   No growth

Bloom color —   — Bloom duration

Full sun | Part shade | Shade
☼ | ◉ | ●

Sedum 'Autumn Joy' SEE-dum

'Autumn Joy' stonecrop | deep, dusty pink

Foliage looks good all season. Buds and seed heads are attractive before, during, and after bloom, unless you don't like the look of broccoli. Leave the plants intact for winter interest. Some gardeners around here say they have luck with this in a fair amount of shade.

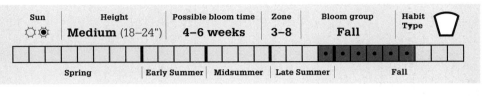

Sun	Height	Possible bloom time	Zone	Bloom group	Habit Type
☼ ◉	**Medium** (18–24")	**4–6 weeks**	**3–8**	**Fall**	

Spring | Early Summer | Midsummer | Late Summer | Fall

Sedum 'Bertram Anderson' SEE-dum

'Bertram Anderson' stonecrop | dusty pink

Attractive, deep purple foliage, which sometimes gets chewed by insects. Habit tends to be prostrate. Growing in a raised bed seems to help minimize insect damage.

Sun	Height	Possible bloom time	Zone	Bloom group	Habit Type
☼	**Short** (6–12")	**4–5 weeks**	**5–8**	**Fall**	

Spring | Early Summer | Midsummer | Late Summer | Fall

Sedum 'Matrona' SEE-dum

'Matrona' stonecrop | pale pink

This sedum always catches my eye with its excellent shape and lovely coloring. Reddish stems, deep grayish foliage with red overtones. A very classy, well-dressed plant that always looks great.

Sun	Height	Possible bloom time	Zone	Bloom group	Habit Type
☼	**Medium** (18–30")	**4–5 weeks**	**3–8**	**Fall**	

Spring | Early Summer | Midsummer | Late Summer | Fall

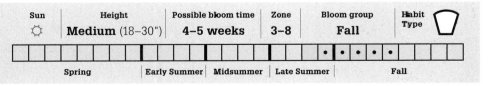

HABIT TYPES | low mound | low mound, blossoms above | tall stems | fan-shaped foliage | low mound, dense mass above | mingled vertical mass | stems form vertical mass | blossoms top vertical mass | matlike foliage | intertwining stems | vase-shaped stemmed blossoms | basal foliage huge blossom

Sedum 'Purple Emperor' SEE-dum

'Purple Emperor' stonecrop | deep wine-purple foliage

One of the very best plants. Blooms throughout most of the late summer and early fall, but its primary contribution is its beautiful, dark purple foliage, which makes a great foil all season long. Plants in partial shade are floppy and exhibit mottled greenish purple foliage.

Sun	Height	Possible bloom time	Zone	Bloom group	Habit Type
☼	**Medium** (12–18")	**5–7 weeks**	**3–7**	**Foliage**	

Spring · Early Summer | Midsummer | Late Summer · Fall

Sedum 'Rosy Glow' SEE-dum

'Rosy Glow' stonecrop | deep pink

One of my favorite plants, this sedum has nice foliage, nice form, and beautiful flowers. Good buds and seed heads. Also known as 'Ruby Glow'. Can be grown in more shade than most sedums without becoming bedraggled.

Sun	Height	Possible bloom time	Zone	Bloom group	Habit Type
☼◉	**Short** (6–12")	**5–7 weeks**	**3–8**	**Late Summer**	

Spring · Early Summer | Midsummer | Late Summer · Fall

Sedum sieboldii SEE-dum

October daphne | crisp light pink

Extraordinarily beautiful, scalloped, pink-edged gray-green foliage. Buds, which are what you'll be looking at most of the season, are very nice. Valuable for its extremely late bloom, although frost usually kills it back in Maine before the blossoming is done. Best in a raised bed in full sun; prone to insect damage in ground-level bed.

Sun	Height	Possible bloom time	Zone	Bloom group	Habit Type
☼	**Short** (4–8")	**2–4 weeks**	**3–8**	**Fall**	

Spring · Early Summer | Midsummer | Late Summer · Fall

Sedum spectabile 'Brilliant'   SEE-dum
'Brilliant' stonecrop | bright pink

Lime-green foliage and true pink blossoms make this easier to blend than 'Autumn Joy', which it otherwise resembles. But unlike 'Autumn Joy', the foliage deteriorates soon after bloom. Nice buds before bloom.

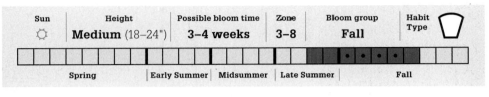

Sun	Height	Possible bloom time	Zone	Bloom group	Habit Type
☼	**Medium** (18–24")	**3–4 weeks**	**3–8**	**Fall**	

Spring | Early Summer | Midsummer | Late Summer | Fall

Sedum spurium 'Fuldaglut'   SEE-dum
'Fuldaglut' stonecrop | dark red

Foliage varies from deep red to mottled green; generally redder in full sun. Excellent groundcover, nice contrast with short, gray-foliaged plants like *Sedum sieboldii* or woolly thyme. Valuable in a color scheme featuring repeated purple foliage, and the lovely flowers are an added bonus.

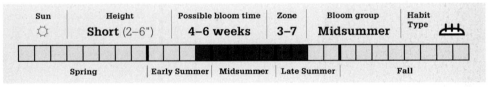

Sun	Height	Possible bloom time	Zone	Bloom group	Habit Type
☼	**Short** (2–6")	**4–6 weeks**	**3–7**	**Midsummer**	

Spring | Early Summer | Midsummer | Late Summer | Fall

Sedum spurium 'Tricolor'   SEE-dum
'Tricolor' stonecrop | light pink

This is a topnotch plant that contributes a lot, whether or not it's in bloom. Beautiful variegated foliage mixes with plain green sometimes as it spreads; pinch out green leaves if you want only the variegated foliage. Nice groundcover. Spills over edges of a stone wall. Tolerates more shade than some sedums.

Sun	Height	Possible bloom time	Zone	Bloom group	Habit Type
☼ ☼	**Short** (2–6")	**4–6 weeks**	**3–7**	**Midsummer**	

Spring | Early Summer | Midsummer | Late Summer | Fall

HABIT TYPES   low mound | low mound, blossoms above | tall stems | fan-shaped foliage | low mound, dense mass above | mingled vertical mass | stems form vertical mass | blossoms top vertical mass | matlike foliage | intertwining stems | vase-shaped stemmed blossoms | basal foliage huge blossom

Solidago rugosa 'Fireworks' so-li-DAH-go

'Fireworks' goldenrod | bright golden yellow

The diagonal blossoming stems, which resemble shooting fireworks, make this really dynamic at the back of a perennial border. Don't let the common name scare you away; this goldenrod is not like the weedy wildflower. Needs a little extra room to strut its stuff. Easy to grow, and foliage is good all season. Self supporting.

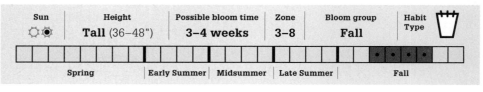

Sun	Height	Possible bloom time	Zone	Bloom group	Habit Type
☼◉	**Tall** (36–48")	**3–4 weeks**	**3–8**	**Fall**	

Spring | Early Summer | Midsummer | Late Summer | Fall

Stylophorum diphyllum sty-LAH-for-rum

Celandine poppy | canary yellow

This is recommended with reservations, as it self-seeds rampantly. Excess seedlings must be removed in spring (which is easily done as they pop right out), or this will soon be the only plant in your garden. That said, it has lovely lobed foliage and a long bloom time. Cut back in late summer if foliage becomes unsightly. Native.

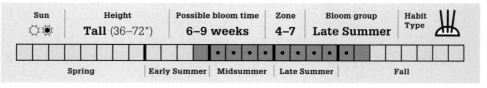

Sun	Height	Possible bloom time	Zone	Bloom group	Habit Type
◉	**Medium** (12–18")	**6–8 weeks**	**4–8**	**Spring**	

Spring | Early Summer | Midsummer | Late Summer | Fall

Thalictrum rochebrunianum tha-LICK-trum

Meadow-rue | lavender

Tall and airy with layers of columbine-like foliage topped by a single spray of pale purple flowers. Self-supporting and excellent in masses. Watch for powdery mildew, which can be a problem.

Sun	Height	Possible bloom time	Zone	Bloom group	Habit Type
☼◉	**Tall** (36–72")	**6–9 weeks**	**4–7**	**Late Summer**	

Spring | Early Summer | Midsummer | Late Summer | Fall

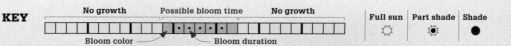

Tiarella cordifolia tee-a-REL-a
Foamflower | white

This native plant is well-suited to general garden use. Spreads quickly by runners; may need to be pulled back from less robust neighbors. There are many excellent cultivars which spread less than the species and might therefore be even better choices for a mixed planting. Other species and cultivars, such as the clumping, pink-blossomed *T. wherryi* 'Oakleaf' with burgundy-splashed leaves, are also good.

Sun	Height	Possible bloom time	Zone	Bloom group	Habit Type
☼ ●	**Short** (6–12")	**3–4 weeks**	**3–8**	**Spring**	

Spring | Early Summer | Midsummer | Late Summer | Fall

Trollius chinensis 'Golden Queen' TRO-lee-us
'Golden Queen' globeflower | vivid yellow-orange

The long root makes this difficult to transplant and it dislikes sitting in a pot. Tolerates heavy clay soil, but needs good moisture to thrive. Color is luminous and mixes well. Prefers a somewhat shady, moist site. Flowers are a bit small for a rather large plant with long stems, but the color is a knockout. 'Lemon Queen' is light yellow and easy to blend.

Sun	Height	Possible bloom time	Zone	Bloom group	Habit Type
○ ☼	**Medium** (24–36")	**3–4 weeks**	**5–7**	**Midsummer**	

Spring | Early Summer | Midsummer | Late Summer | Fall

Tulipa 'Apeldoorn' TEW-li-pa
'Apeldoorn' Darwin hybrid tulip | bright red

Darwin hybrid tulips are the best large tulips that come back year after year (not to be confused with Darwin tulips, which are grown as annuals). There are hundreds of good varieties, with reds probably being the most robust. Plant in middle of bed, as browning foliage must be left intact for six weeks after bloom. Plant in clusters of five or more.

Sun	Height	Possible bloom time	Zone	Bloom group	Habit Type
○ ☼	**Medium** (20–24")	**2–3 weeks**	**3–7**	**Spring**	

Spring | Early Summer | Midsummer | Late Summer | Fall

HABIT TYPES — low mound | low mound, blossoms above | tall stems | fan-shaped foliage | low mound, dense mass above | mingled vertical mass | stems form vertical mass | blossoms top vertical mass | matlike foliage | intertwining stems | vase-shaped stemmed blossoms | basal foliage huge blossom

Tulipa batalinii 'Apricot Jewel' TEW-li-pa
'Apricot Jewel' tulip | luminous apricot

Although they are rather short in bloom time and in stature, the *T. batalinii* cultivars seem to emit a soft glow from their lovely urn-shaped blossoms. Foliage is a beautiful, smooth gray that complements the blooms. There are several good cultivars of *T. batalinii*, and many other good species tulips. Plant in clusters of five or more.

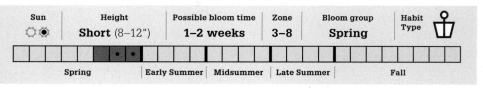

Sun	Height	Possible bloom time	Zone	Bloom group	Habit Type
☼◉	**Short** (8–12")	**1–2 weeks**	**3–8**	**Spring**	

Spring | Early Summer | Midsummer | Late Summer | Fall

Tulipa 'Flaming Purissima' TEW-li-pa
'Flaming Purissima' Emperor or Fosteriana tulip | ivory/pink/yellow

The Emperor or Fosteriana tulips are shorter than Darwin hybrids (which bloom at about the same time), but they have more elongated blossoms. 'Madame Lefeber' (sometimes sold as 'Red Emperor') is another great tulip in this family and blooms somewhat earlier than 'Flaming Purissima'. In my experience some of the other colors (white 'Purissima', 'Golden Emperor', and 'Solva', also sold as 'Pink Emperor') are less robust. Plant in clusters of five or more.

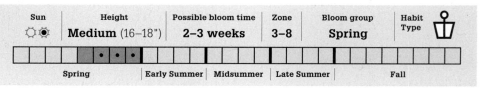

Sun	Height	Possible bloom time	Zone	Bloom group	Habit Type
☼◉	**Medium** (16–18")	**2–3 weeks**	**3–8**	**Spring**	

Spring | Early Summer | Midsummer | Late Summer | Fall

Tulipa humilis 'Persian Pearl' TEW-li-pa
'Persian Pearl' tulip | deep magenta/yellow

Species tulips like *T. humilis* have deservedly gained popularity in recent years. 'Persian Pearl' is one of my favorites with its magenta petals opening to expose a bright yellow eye in full sun, then closing up as the day wanes. They mix wonderfully with *Scilla siberica*. There are several other good cultivars of *T. humilis*, and many other good species tulips. Plant in masses.

Sun	Height	Possible bloom time	Zone	Bloom group	Habit Type
☼◉	**Short** (4–6")	**2 weeks**	**4–8**	**Spring**	

Spring | Early Summer | Midsummer | Late Summer | Fall

KEY

No growth | Possible bloom time | No growth

Bloom color ← → Bloom duration

Full sun ☼ | Part shade ◉ | Shade ●

Tulipa Kaufmanniana Type TEW-li-pa

Waterlily tulip | cream/red/yellow

Usually the earliest-blooming, Kaufmanniana hybrid tulips are short in height and long-blooming. 'Kaufmanniana Type', which dates from 1877, is one of many multicolored varieties, most of which display combinations of cream, red, and yellow. Foliage is often striped or slightly mottled. Plant in clusters of five or more.

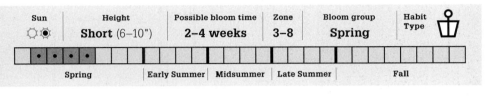

Sun	Height	Possible bloom time	Zone	Bloom group	Habit Type
☼◉	**Short** (6–10")	**2–4 weeks**	3–8	**Spring**	

Spring | Early Summer | Midsummer | Late Summer | Fall

Tulipa 'Red Riding Hood' TEW-li-pa

'Red Riding Hood' Greigii tulip | dark red

Shorter and earlier than Darwin hybrids, the Greigii tulips have wonderful striped or splotched foliage. There are many good varieties, mostly in combinations of red, yellow, and near-white. Plant behind perennials that will hide the tulips' maturing foliage for six weeks. Plant in clusters of five or more.

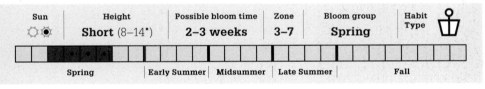

Sun	Height	Possible bloom time	Zone	Bloom group	Habit Type
☼◉	**Short** (8–14")	**2–3 weeks**	3–7	**Spring**	

Spring | Early Summer | Midsummer | Late Summer | Fall

Tulipa saxatilis TEW-li-pa

Species tulip | rose/lilac/yellow

Another lovely species tulip; the lighter color of *T. saxatilis* shows up well against dark, moist spring soil. This sweet little tulip sports petals of alternating rose and lilac with a yellow eye. Plant in masses. There are many other good species tulips.

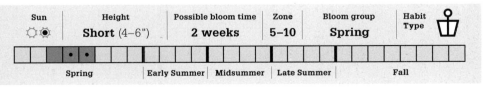

Sun	Height	Possible bloom time	Zone	Bloom group	Habit Type
☼◉	**Short** (4–6")	**2 weeks**	5–10	**Spring**	

Spring | Early Summer | Midsummer | Late Summer | Fall

HABIT TYPES low mound | low mound, blossoms above | tall stems | fan-shaped foliage | low mound, dense mass above | mingled vertical mass | stems form vertical mass | blossoms top vertical mass | matlike foliage | intertwining stems | vase-shaped stemmed blossoms | basal foliage huge blossom

Vernonia noveboracensis ver-NO-nee-a
New York ironweed | purple-pink

Extremely tall, but a wonderful late-blooming plant for the back of a big border. Foliage is a dark bluish green. Give it at least 30" and be prepared for it to overshadow its neighbors. The very long and late bloom time of this plant leads me to include it here in spite of its extreme height and girth. Native. Self supporting.

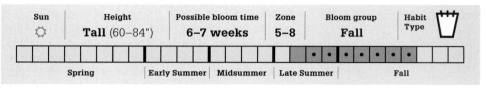

Sun	Height	Possible bloom time	Zone	Bloom group	Habit Type
☼	**Tall** (60–84")	**6–7 weeks**	**5–8**	**Fall**	

Spring · Early Summer | Midsummer | Late Summer | Fall

Veronica austriaca 'Crater Lake Blue' ve-RON-i-ka
'Crater Lake Blue' speedwell | bright medium blue

'Crater Lake Blue' is easy to grow in Maine, unlike the fussier *V. longifolia* cultivars. It can flop if not supported by neighboring plants, but then it makes a good draping edge plant. Cut back after bloom. When unsupported, it should be classed as "short."

Sun	Height	Possible bloom time	Zone	Bloom group	Habit Type
☼	**Medium** (12–18")	**2–3 weeks**	**4–7**	**Early Summer**	

Spring | Early Summer | Midsummer | Late Summer | Fall

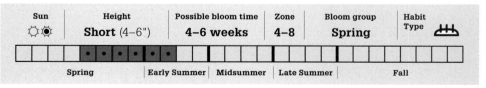

Veronica umbrosa 'Georgia Blue' ve-RON-i-ka
'Georgia Blue' speedwell | intense blue

'Georgia Blue' sometimes disappears over the winter, but new plants quickly produce a neat mat of foliage and a long-lasting flush of charming blue flowers. Needs good drainage. Reblooms. Foliage looks terrific all season and often reddens in the fall.

Sun	Height	Possible bloom time	Zone	Bloom group	Habit Type
☼ ☀	**Short** (4–6")	**4–6 weeks**	**4–8**	**Spring**	

Spring | Early Summer | Midsummer | Late Summer | Fall

KEY

No growth — Possible bloom time — No growth

Bloom color ← → Bloom duration

 Full sun ☼ | Part shade ☀ | Shade ●

Veronicastrum virginicum ve-ron-i-KAS-trum
Culver's root | white

One of the best structural plants. Dramatic, spiky blossoms and good foliage all season. Best planted in a mass of three or more. This genus has a number of good varieties in pale blues and pinks, including the one below. Wonderful foliage looks like stars skewered on long stems and often turns golden in fall. Can take a bit of shade. Native. Self supporting.

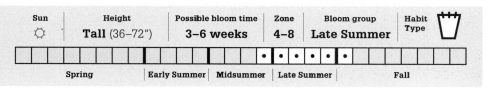

Sun	Height	Possible bloom time	Zone	Bloom group	Habit Type
☼	**Tall** (36–72")	**3–6 weeks**	**4–8**	**Late Summer**	

Spring | Early Summer | Midsummer | Late Summer | Fall

Veronicastrum virginicum 'Fascination' ve-ron-i-KAS-trum
'Fascination' Culver's root | pale violet-blue

'Fascination' blooms slightly earlier than the species but is otherwise the same. Can take a bit of shade. *V. sibiricum* (another blue type) is also good. Self supporting.

Sun	Height	Possible bloom time	Zone	Bloom group	Habit Type
☼	**Tall** (36–72")	**3–5 weeks**	**4–8**	**Late Summer**	

Spring | Early Summer | Midsummer | Late Summer | Fall

Viola tricolor VYE-o-la
Johnny jump up | purple/yellow

Self-seeding perennial grown as a hardy annual. Extremely long bloom time and easy-to-blend colors make this a terrific addition to almost any garden. Unwanted seedlings are easily weeded out. Be sure you're not buying annual pansies, which do not reseed the way johnny jump ups do. Usually sold in six-packs with the annuals.

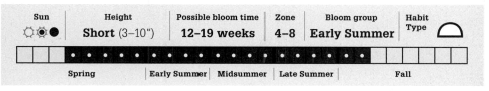

Sun	Height	Possible bloom time	Zone	Bloom group	Habit Type
☼ ◐ ●	**Short** (3–10")	**12–19 weeks**	**4–8**	**Early Summer**	

Spring | Early Summer | Midsummer | Late Summer | Fall

HABIT TYPES   low mound | low mound, blossoms above | tall stems | fan-shaped foliage | low mound, dense mass above | mingled vertical mass | stems form vertical mass | blossoms top vertical mass | matlike foliage | intertwining stems | vase-shaped stemmed blossoms | basal foliage huge blossom

APPENDIXES

The gorgeous green pinwheels of Maidenhair fern (*Adiantum pedatum*) are the perfect companions for a mossy rock.

PLANTS FOR SPECIAL CONDITIONS

This section includes some favorite perennials that don't quite fit in the standard densely planted continuously blooming garden but which are worthy of use under certain circumstances. You probably won't want a densely planted continuously blooming bed in every corner of your yard, and I hope the plants in this section will give you some ideas for dealing with typical trouble spots such as shady corners; hot, dry areas; or tall, bare fences. You can still use the Blueprint to organize and evaluate your bloom times for all the plantings (including flowering trees and shrubs) in your yard.

The plants in this section are especially suitable for shady spots (where the sun rarely, if ever, reaches) or dry, sunny places. Most of these selections are groundcovers, meaning they will spread to cover the ground and they tend to provide good foliage throughout the growing season. Shady spots and hot, sunny places are generally not much good for growing grass, so I hope you'll try some of these plants here and there instead. Special thanks to Leslie van Berkum of Van Berkum Nursery in New Hampshire for reviewing and adding to this list.

PLANTS FOR SHADE

Anemonella thalictroides (rue anemone). Luminous white or pinkish blooms in spring. Withstands competition with tree roots. Prefers moist, well-drained soil. Grows 8 to 10 inches tall. Native.

Anemonella thalictroides

Asarum canadense (wild ginger) and A. europaeum (European ginger). Elegant foliage, if somewhat difficult to establish. *A. canadense* is native and grows 4 to 8 inches tall. *A. europaeum* is 6 to 8 inches tall. Both have inconspicuous brown flowers.

Aster macrophyllus (large-leaved aster). This native groundcover can be found growing in woods, where it can take dry conditions. Abundant, coarse, dark green, heart-shaped foliage topped by a spray of small, bluish white blossoms in late summer and fall. Grows about 12 inches tall.

Convallaria majalis (lily of the valley). Lovely old-fashioned fragrant favorite. It spreads aggressively once established, so avoid using it in a mixed planting. Grows 8 to 12 inches tall and prefers moist conditions.

Epimedium × rubrum (barrenwort). Cool, irregularly heart-shaped multicolored foliage. Best massed; do not crowd. Grows 8 to 12 inches tall, flowering in spring.

Epimedium × versicolor 'Sulphureum' ('Sulphureum' barrenwort). Same as for *E. × rubrum*.

Ferns. Many ferns are easy to grow and look terrific in the shade garden. Some of my favorites are maidenhair fern (*Adiantum pedatum*), the diminutive oak fern (*Gymnocarpium dryopteris*), and the evergreen Christmas fern (*Polystichum acrostichoides*).

Galium odoratum (sweet woodruff). Spreading, fragrant woodland plant fills any partly shady space, even in dry areas under trees. 6 to 8 inches tall, blooming in spring.

Helleborus foetidus (bears foot hellebore). My favorite *Helleborus*, with large, distinctive foliage and chartreuse and rose purple blossoms. I think these are best planted on a wall or steep bank where you can better appreciate the downward-facing blossoms. Grows 15 to 18 inches; spring bloom.

Helleborus orientalis (Lenten rose). These are enjoying a surge of popularity, and like the entry above, they benefit from planting where you'll be able to appreciate the downward-facing blossoms, which come in pinks, white, and rosy purple in spring. Leathery evergreen leaves grow 15 to 18 inches tall.

Hostas. Some hostas are more sun-tolerant and a couple of them are listed in the Plant Palette. This listing is for the vast majority of hostas, which are best grown in shade or partial shade. The small number of hostas common to the nursery trade do not begin to represent the wonderful variety available — blue foliage, miniature, giant, ribbed, variegated, ruffled, and so on. A good hosta nursery (such as Fernwood in Swanville,

Maine) will quickly renew your enthusiasm for these great plants. Good in dry shade; spreading and indestructible. A few of my favorites are: 'Striptease', *H. sieboldiana* 'Elegans', and the large and lovely *H. montana* 'Aureomarginata'. Vary in height from several to 48 inches; bloom times are usually in the summer.

Lamiastrum galeobdolon 'Florentinum' (yellow archangel). A little too aggressive for the regular list, this attractive groundcover with silver variegated leaves and yellow blossoms is good in partial shade and under trees. Grows 12 inches tall; blooms in spring.

Lysimachia nummularia 'Aurea' (golden creeping Jenny). If you have a shady spot, even on a rather steep slope, this plant will spread aggressively to cover the earth. Often sold in small pots as an annual for container plantings. The light golden yellow of the foliage lights up dark corners. The species is plain green and is on several invasive species lists, and people in Zone 6 often complain that even 'Aurea' is too aggressive. Check your local invasive species list before buying this. Use with care, or just try something else. Grows 1 to 2 inches tall; small white blossoms in the fall.

Lysimachia nummularia 'Aurea' in a rocky, mossy nook.

Marshallia grandiflora (Barbara's buttons). An unusual, compact perennial for part shade with pink, cushion-shaped flowers. Grows 12 inches tall; blooms in summer.

Meehania cordata (Meehan's mint). A lovely, noninvasive groundcover with bright lavender blue flowers for shade or part shade. Can be hard to find. Grows 3 to 8 inches tall; blooms in spring or early summer.

Primula denticulata (drumstick primrose) and P. japonica (Japanese primrose). In a moist, well-drained spot in part shade these tall, jewel-toned primroses crank out wonderful, crinkled foliage, as they spread by self-seeding. Excellent on a shady slope below a stone wall where moisture tends to be constant but drainage is good. *P. denticulata* is 12 inches tall and blooms in spring; *P. japonica* is 20 inches tall and blooms slightly later in late spring or early summer. Like all primroses, *P. japonica* thrives on riverbanks where the soil is moist but also well-drained. The conditions at the sloping base of a stone retaining wall are similar.

Rodgersia (Rodger's flower). The dramatic foliage will draw your eye to this plant, even if it's tucked back under trees at the edge of the garden. Likes a moist spot. Several different species are all good. *R. pinnata* (a nice selection) is 36 to 48 inches tall and puts out pink flowers in early summer.

Saxifraga × arendsii (saxifrage). Tends to be short-lived and requires moist, well-drained soil, but the incredible, vivid flowers make this plant worth growing. Grows 5 to 8 inches tall; blooms in spring.

Viola labradorica (Labrador violet). A strong groundcover in sun or shade, these violets look good all season and reseed to boot. Too aggressive for a mixed planting. Grows 4 inches tall; blooms in spring.

Waldsteinia ternata (Siberian barren strawberry). Adaptable to sun or shade, this groundcover has great foliage all season and bright little yellow flowers in spring. Grows 4 to 6 inches tall; blooms in spring.

SUNNY GROUNDCOVERS

Sometimes the site I'm trying to work with is sunny and dry and just not hospitable to ordinary plant life. Instead of fighting the site with heroic measures, such as trucking in massive amounts of topsoil, I like to use plants that thrive in the dry sun. Matching the plants to the site cuts down drastically on maintenance. Garden Five (see page 102) shows a rock garden I created in just such a space. Some of the plants in the Plant Palette are suitable for sunny dry conditions, and below I'm offering a few more selections (which didn't make the cut for the Plant Palette because they are not suited to general garden conditions for one reason or another). I hope you can use these plants as a starting point if you want to try building a rock garden or if you need to fill a sunny, dry space.

When I put together a rock garden I like to make a special planting mixture of ⅓ topsoil, ⅓ peat moss, and ⅓ stone chips or stone dust (preferably granite, not limestone, because most rock garden plants prefer acid soil). This mixture provides the good drainage and lean fertility that most sunny groundcovers prefer. Most of the plants in this section are very drought-tolerant once established, but they should be watered like any other new plant while getting established.

Achillea tomentosa 'Aurea' ('Aurea' dwarf yarrow). A low-growing, creeping yarrow with bright gold flowers in early summer. Up to 6" tall. Also sold as *A. tomentosa* 'Maynard's Gold'.

Allium senescens 'Glaucum' ('Glaucum' circle chives). Blue-gray foliage topped with pink blossoms in the fall. Growth pattern is a wonderful spiral or whorl shape. Grows 4 to 6 inches tall.

Arabis × sturii (dwarf rockcress). A tight mat of mouse-ear-shaped leaves produces masses of white flowers in spring. Its diminutive stature (3 to 4 inches tall), tendency to clump instead of draping, and relative scarcity in the nursery trade are the only reasons

this fantastic plant is not included in the Plant Palette (where you will find its draping cousin, *Arabis caucasica* 'Snowcap').

Empetrum nigrum (black crowberry). This native, woody groundcover creeps between and onto rocks. Delicate feathery strands of foliage sport black berries. Turns reddish in fall. Grows 6 to 8 inches tall.

Erodium chrysanthum (heron's bill). Soft yellow flowers adorn 6-inch silvery-gray filigree foliage in the summer. Do not crowd; needs excellent drainage. Can be very hard to find, probably because it hates to be in a pot. Prefers alkaline soil.

Erodium chrysanthum with *Sedum spurium* 'Fuldaglut', *Campanula poscharskyana,* and woolly thyme.

Geranium dalmaticum (Dalmatian cranesbill). Lovely smooth foliage, which turns red in autumn; spreads quickly without being invasive. Dwarf habit; 4 to 6 inches tall. Blooms pinkish purple in spring.

Lewisia 'Little Plum' ('Little Plum' bitterroot). An explosion of bright pink blossoms above a rosette of fleshy, pointed foliage. Blooms in spring. Grows 12 inches tall.

***Sagina subulata* (pearlwort).** Tiny (1 to 2 inch tall) mat-forming groundcover with white blooms in summer. Requires excellent drainage. Tends to develop dead patches with time. Also suitable for partial shade.

***Sedum reflexum* 'Angelina' ('Angelina' stonecrop).** A rather delicate sedum, but worth growing for its amazing luminous goldish yellow–needled foliage. Do not crowd. Grows 3 to 6 inches tall; yellow flowers (which hardly show against the bright yellow foliage) in summer.

Sedum reflexum 'Angelina'

***Sedum spurium* 'John Creech' ('John Creech' stonecrop).** An excellent low-growing, fast-spreading blossoming groundcover for sunny spots. Grows 2 inches tall; blooms pink in early summer.

***Sempervivum* (hens and chicks).** While the commonly sold forms are familiar to many, there are many more interesting species and cultivars. Look for odd ducks like the cobwebby *Sempervivum arachnoideum* or the purple-leaved *S.* 'Purple Beauty'. Needs full sun and good drainage, but that's about it; I had a clump that got left sitting on a piece of cardboard where it lived happily for many years. Grows 2 to 8 inches tall; puts up weird blooming pedistals in summer.

***Thalictrum kiusianum* (Kyushu meadow rue).** If you can find it, this choice groundcover has deep blue-green foliage topped by fuzzy lilac purple blossoms. Needs good drainage. Best draping over the edge of a stone wall. Grows 4 to 6 inches tall and blooms in summer.

***Thymus* 'Elfin' ('Elfin' creeping thyme).** Tidier and shinier than woolly thyme, elfin thyme is extremely low-growing and dense. It has beautifully shaped pinkish blossoms. Won't take foot traffic as well as woolly thyme, though. Grows 1 to 2 inches tall; blooms in summer or later.

Thymus praecox 'Pseudolanuginosus' (woolly thyme)

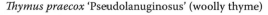

***Thymus praecox* 'Pseudolanuginosus' (woolly thyme).** The best thyme to plant between stepping stones, it will fill in quickly if fertilized every two weeks with a standard liquid fertilizer. Also wonderful in mixed rock garden plantings. Goes especially well with red sedums and campanulas. Grows 2 inches tall; blooms in late spring or summer. In the photo above, woolly thyme mingles with *Sedum* 'Fuldaglut'.

***Veronica pectinata* (comb speedwell).** Forms a tidy mat of gray-green foliage that looks great all season. Beautiful blue blossoms in spring. Grows 3 to 6 inches tall.

CALCULATING THE NUMBERS: SKIP THE GRAPH PAPER

If you prefer not to use graph paper, you can follow this method instead.

1. Multiply the bed's length and depth to get the square footage.

2. Choose a ratio of short/medium/tall. For example, 30% short, 50% medium, and 20% tall works in many situations, or you can choose your own ratio.

3. Multiply the square footage by each of the height percentages.

4. Enter these figures into the column marked "Number of Squares" in the table in Step 3 (page 11), then continue following the directions from there. Or simply refer to the chart, which has all the math worked out for you.

Garden Size (sq.ft.)	Ratio (Short-Medium-Tall)				
	20-50-30%	25-35-40%	20-55-25%	30-50-20%	20-40-40%
	Number of Plants (Short-Medium-Tall)				
20	3-7-3	3-5-4	3-7-3	6-10-4	3-5-4
30	4-10-5	5-7-6	4-11-4	9-15-6	4-8-6
40	5-13-6	7-9-8	5-15-5	12-20-8	5-11-8
50	7-17-8	8-12-10	7-18-6	15-25-10	7-13-10
60	8-20-9	10-14-12	8-22-8	18-30-12	8-16-12
70	9-23-11	12-16-14	9-26-9	21-35-14	9-19-14
80	11-27-12	13-19-16	11-29-10	24-40-16	11-21-16
90	12-30-14	15-21-18	12-33-11	27-45-18	12-24-18
100	13-33-15	17-23-20	13-37-13	30-50-20	13-27-20
110	15-37-17	18-26-22	15-40-14	33-55-22	15-29-22
120	16-40-18	20-28-24	16-44-15	36-60-24	16-32-24
130	17-43-20	22-30-26	17-48-16	39-65-26	17-35-26
140	19-47-21	23-33-28	19-51-18	42-70-28	19-37-28
150	20-50-23	25-35-30	20-55-19	45-75-30	20-40-30
160	21-53-24	27-37-32	21-59-20	48-80-32	21-43-32

Match square footage and ratio to find your plant numbers.

PLANT USAGE LISTS

These lists help identify the best plants for certain conditions. Only plants from the Plant Palette are included. Thanks primarily to Van Berkum Nursery (www.vanberkumnursery.com), and also to *Armitage's Garden* *Perennials: A Color Encyclopedia* by Allan M. Armitage, *Taylor's Guide to Perennials* by Norman Taylor, and *Perennial Reference Guide* by Karleen Shafer and Nicole Lloyd for most of the information in these lists.

GOOD CUT FLOWERS

Achillea
Aconitum
Alcea
Alchemilla
Allium
Amsonia
Anemone
Anthemis
Aquilegia
Artemisia ludoviciana
   'Valerie Finnis'
Aster
Astilbe
Astrantia
Baptisia
Bergenia
Boltonia
Campanula (some)
Centaurea
Chrysanthemum
Coreopsis
Corydalis
Delphinium
Dianthus
Dicentra
Digitalis
Echinacea
Eryngium
Eupatorium
Gaillardia
Gypsophila
Helenium
Heliopsis

Heuchera
Hosta
Iris (most)
Knautia
Lavandula
Leucanthemum
Liatris
Lilium
Limonium
Lychnis
Monarda
Muscari
Narcissus (some)
Nepeta
Nipponanthemum
Paeonia
Penstemon
Perovskia
Phlox carolina
Phlox paniculata
Platycodon
Rudbeckia
Salvia
Scabiosa
Sedum (some)
Solidago
Thalictrum
Trollius
Tulipa (some)
Veronica
Veronicastrum
Viola

ATTRACT BUTTERFLIES AND BUTTERFLY LARVAE

Achillea
Alcea
Anthemis tinctoria
Artemisia ludoviciana
Aster novae-angliae
Baptisia australis
Echinacea purpurea
Eupatorium purpureum
Filipendula rubra
Gaillardia
Heliopsis
Heuchera (green-leaved, pink-flowered types)
Lavandula
Liatris
Monarda
Nepeta
Penstemon
Perovskia
Rudbeckia fulgida
Scabiosa
Sedum spectabile
Solidago rugosa
Veronica austriaca

ATTRACT HUMMINGBIRDS

Ajuga
Alcea rosea
Aquilegia
Campanula
Delphinium
Dianthus
Dicentra
Digitalis
Hemerocallis
Heuchera (green-leaved, pink-flowered types)
Hosta
Iris (bearded)
Iris cristata
Iris ensata
Iris sibirica
Lavandula
Liatris
Lilium (some)
Lychnis
Monarda
Penstemon digitalis
Phlox paniculata
Platycodon

ATTRACT HONEYBEES

Achillea
Allium sphaerocephalon
Aruncus dioicus
Aster
Campanula glomerata
Coreopsis lanceolata
Digitalis
Echinacea
Eupatorium
Filipendula
Gaillardia
Lamium
Lavandula
Leucanthemum
Nepeta
Nipponanthemum
Perovskia
Rudbeckia fulgida
Scabiosa
Veronica

WILL GROW IN MOIST SOIL AND FULL SUN

Note: Some of these plants may require some shade in more southerly climates.

Achillea
Aconitum
Ajuga
Alcea
Alchemilla
Allium
Amsonia
Aquilegia
Aster
Aurinia
Baptisia
Boltonia
Centaurea
Coreopsis verticillata
Delphinium
Digitalis
Echinacea
Eupatorium
Euphorbia
Filipendula
Gentiana
Geranium
Gypsophila
Helenium
Hemerocallis
Heuchera
Hosta 'Patriot'
Iberis
Iris

Monarda
Myosotis
Nepeta
Nipponanthemum
Oenothera
Paeonia
Papaver
Patrinia
Penstemon
Phlox
Prunella
Rudbeckia
Salvia
Scabiosa
Sedum
Solidago
Thalictrum
Veronica

WILL GROW IN DRY SOIL AND FULL SUN

Note: Most of these plants prefer well-drained soil and some moisture. They must be established before they can withstand the conditions of dry sun.

Achillea
Anthemis
Arabis
Artemisia
Aurinia
Baptisia
Campanula glomerata
Campanula poscharskyana
Centaurea
Coreopsis
Dianthus
Echinacea
Eryngium
Euphorbia
Gaillardia
Geranium
Gypsophila
Heliopsis
Hemerocallis
Iberis
Iris (bearded)
Knautia
Lavandula
Limonium
Nepeta
Oenothera
Perovskia
Platycodon
Rudbeckia
Salvia
Saponaria
Scabiosa
Sedum
Solidago
Trollius
Vernonia

WILL GROW IN PARTIAL SHADE

Aconitum
Actaea
Ajuga
Alcea
Alchemilla
Allium 'Globemaster'
Amsonia
Anemone
Aquilegia
Arabis
Aruncus
Aster 'Schneegitter'
Aster novi-belgii
Astilbe
Astrantia
Baptisia
Bergenia
Brunnera
Campanula (most, except
    C. glomerata and C.
    'Elizabeth')
Chionodoxa
Chrysanthemum weyrichii
    'White Bomb'
Coreopsis verticillata
Corydalis
Crocus
Dicentra
Digitalis
Echinacea
Eupatorium
Euphorbia dulcis
    'Chameleon'
Filipendula
Gentiana
Geranium
Helenium
Heliopsis
Hemerocallis

Heuchera
Hosta
Hydrangea
Iberis
Iris cristata
Iris reticulata
Iris sibirica
Kirengeshoma
Lamium
Leucanthemum
Liatris
Ligularia
Lilium
Monarda
Muscari
Myosotis
Narcissus
Nepeta sibirica
Nipponanthemum
Oenothera
Paeonia
Patrinia
Penstemon
Phlox carolina
Platycodon
Prunella
Pulmonaria
Rudbeckia fulgida
Saponaria
Scilla
Solidago
Stylophorum
Thalictrum
Tiarella
Trollius
Tulipa
Veronica peduncularis
Viola

WILL GROW IN DEEP SHADE

Actaea
Ajuga
Astilbe
Bergenia
Brunnera
Campanula persicifolia
Campanula
    poscharskyana
Corydalis
Dicentra
Heuchera
Hosta
Iris cristata
Kirengeshoma
Lamium
Pulmonaria
Tiarella
Viola

WILL GROW IN DRY SOIL AND PARTIAL SHADE

Alchemilla
Brunnera
Campanula persicifolia
Campanula
    poscharskyana
Coreopsis verticillata
Dicentra
Euphorbia polychroma
Hemerocallis
Heuchera villosa
Hosta
Iberis
Lamium
Muscari
Pulmonaria
Rudbeckia
Sedum spurium
Tiarella
Viola

WILL GROW IN BOGGY SOIL

Actaea
Ajuga
Aruncus
Astilbe
Astrantia
Bergenia
Brunnera
Campanula glomerata
Echinacea
Eupatorium
Filipendula
Helenium
Hemerocallis
Iris ensata
Ligularia
Monarda
Prunella
Vernonia

WILL GROW IN HEAVY CLAY SOIL

Ajuga
Alchemilla
Anemone
Aruncus
Aster
Bergenia
Digitalis
Echinacea
Eupatorium
Helenium
Heliopsis
Hemerocallis
Hosta
Lamium
Liatris
Ligularia
Monarda
Rudbeckia
Stylophorum
Thalictrum
Trollius

GOOD PURPLE FOLIAGE

Actaea (purple-leaved cultivars)
Ajuga (purple-leaved cultivars)
Cotinus (purple-leaved cultivars)
Eupatorium rugosum 'Chocolate'
Euphorbia dulcis 'Chameleon'
Heuchera (purple-leaved cultivars)
Penstemon digitalis 'Huskers Red'
Physocarpus (purple-leaved cultivars)
Sedum (purple-leaved cultivars)

GOOD GRAYISH FOLIAGE

Achillea 'Coronation Gold' and 'Moonshine'
Artemisia
Aurinia
Dianthus
Dicentra 'Zestful'
Lavandula
Lychnis coronaria
Nepeta 'Walker's Low'
Perovskia
Sedum (some)

GOOD FALL FOLIAGE COLOR

Note: This can be quite variable, depending on weather and growing conditions.

Aconitum carmichaelii 'Arendsii' (yellow)
Amsonia (yellow)
Arabis (red)
Astrantia (yellow)
Bergenia (red-purple)
Eupatorium (gold)
Euphorbia (red)
Geranium (red)
Oenothera (red)
Patrinia (yellow)
Phlox carolina (yellow)
Platycodon (yellow)
Sedum sieboldii (pink)
Tiarella (red)
Veronica peduncularis (red)
Veronicastrum (golden)

GOOD FOLIAGE MOST OF THE SEASON

Achillea 'Coronation Gold'
Achillea 'Moonshine'
Aconitum carmichaelii 'Arendsii'
Ajuga
Amsonia
Anemone
Arabis
Aster 'Schneegitter'
Aurinia
Baptisia
Bergenia
Brunnera
Campanula carpatica
Campanula portenschlagiana
Chrysanthemum weyrichii 'White Bomb'
Corydalis
Cotinus
Dianthus
Euphorbia
Heuchera
Hosta
Hydrangea
Iberis
Iris
Kirengeshoma
Lamium
Lychnis coronaria
Nipponanthemum
Paeonia
Patrinia
Physocarpus
Saponaria
Sedum
Thalictrum
Tiarella
Vernonia
Veronica peduncularis
Veronicastrum

DRAPE OVER WALLS

Note: This means they can be planted right up against the outer edge of a raised bed.

Arabis
Aster 'Schneegitter'
Aurinia
Campanula carpatica
Campanula poscharskyana
Chrysanthemum weyrichii 'White Bomb'
Coreopsis lanceolata
Corydalis
Dianthus
Geranium
Gypsophila repens
Iberis
Lamium
Saponaria
Sedum (low varieties)
Tiarella

DEER RESISTANT

Note: These plants are probably less attractive to deer than many others, but a very hungry deer will eat anything. If you have a lot of trouble with deer, consider spraying plants with the nontoxic, bitter product called Tree Guard.

Achillea (repels deer)
Aconitum
Actaea
Ajuga
Alcea
Alchemilla
Allium (repels deer)
Amsonia
Anemone
Aquilegia
Artemisia
Aruncus
Aster
Astilbe
Aurinia
Baptisia
Bergenia
Boltonia
Brunnera
Campanula
Centaurea
Chionodoxa
Clematis
Coreopsis
Corydalis
Delphinium
Dianthus
Dicentra
Digitalis
Echinacea
Eryngium
Eupatorium
Euphorbia
Filipendula
Geranium
Gypsophila
Heuchera
Iberis
Iris (bearded)
Iris reticulata
Kirengeshoma
Knautia
Lamium
Lavandula (repels deer)
Leucanthemum
Liatris
Limonium
Monarda
Muscari
Myosotis
Narcissus
Nepeta (repels deer)
Oenothera
Paeonia
Papaver
Perovskia
Platycodon
Rudbeckia
Salvia (repels deer)
Scabiosa
Scilla
Sedum (low varieties)
Solidago
Stylophorum
Tiarella
Veronica
Veronicastrum

POISONOUS PLANTS

Achillea
Aconitum (very poisonous)
Actaea
Alcea (skin irritant only)
Allium (may cause dermatitis or allergies)
Anemone
Aquilegia
Artemisia
Chrysanthemum
Clematis
Corydalis
Cotinus (skin irritant only)
Delphinium (very poisonous)
Dianthus
Dicentra (skin irritant only)
Digitalis purpurea (very poisonous)
Eupatorium 'Chocolate'
Euphorbia
Gaillardia (skin irritant only)
Gypsophila paniculata (skin irritant only)
Helenium
Hydrangea (very poisonous)
Iberis (skin irritant only)
Iris
Lilium
Narcissus (bulb)
Paeonia
Papaver
Scilla (very poisonous)
Sedum
Thalictrum
Tulipa (bulb)
Veronica (some)

Delphinium Belladonna Group

Scilla siberica

PLANTS TO BE WARY OF

Thanks to many wonderful clients, I've been fortunate to have the opportunity to plant over 8,000 perennials (plus thousands of bulbs) in hundreds of gardens over the course of a dozen or so years. I wish I could say they all lived long and happy plant lives, but losses are inevitable due to disease, siting errors, weather and, well, bad plant genes. If killing beautiful plants counts against karma, I'm definitely coming back in my next lifetime as a toadstool.

Learning something from the dead plants can help give meaning to an otherwise unfortunate situation, and I'd like to pass along my experience with a few plants I've had trouble with. These are divided into two groups: "Proven Losers" (a.k.a. "Thugs"), which I don't recommend under any circumstances, and "Disappointments", which are plants that didn't work for me in Maine using this dense planting system. The second group could work for you if your growing conditions are different or if you don't plant them densely, so please don't feel I'm condemning them outright. I offer this second group simply as a list of things I've tried and failed with. Some of the plants that appear in the "Disappointments" list are simply too shy and polite — they might be appreciated in a special place but are unsuited to the competitive, free-for-all conditions of the densely planted continuously blooming bed.

PROVEN LOSERS (A.K.A. THUGS)

These plants, especially the first one, should be avoided.

***Aegopodium podagraria* (goutweed or bishop's weed).** This most evil of all plants usually arrives in a division from a well-meaning friend or neighbor. You can even get it in a delivery of topsoil. Rampantly invasive, it spreads by tiny nodes the more you try to weed it out. In one client's garden, it killed a patch of (the usually indestructible) *Rosa rugosa*. The variegated type is slightly less invasive, but this plant is virtually impossible to eradicate. Run the other way.

***Artemisia ludoviciana* 'Silver King' ('Silver King' wormwood).** The King will lay siege to your garden and rule its hapless subjects by sending runners all over. What starts out as pleasant, silvery gray foliage soon turns to scraggly 3-foot tatters. Other wormwoods like silver mound (*Artemisia schmidtiana*) and 'Valerie Finnis' (*Artemisia* 'Valerie Finnis') behave much better.

***Centaurea montana* (perennial bachelor's buttons).** *Taylor's Guide to Perennials* calls this "Invasive and a floppy grower with a weak floral display . . ." If that's not enough, it's also prone to powdery mildew.

***Lysimachia clethroides* (gooseneck loosestrife).** The arched and tapered white blossoms look so elegant and innocent one would never guess this plant invades its neighbors like a flock of angry geese. Frequently shows up next door or on the wrong side of a stone wall.

***Tradescantia virginiana* (spiderwort).** The vivid, photogenic triangular blossoms of this plant have enticed many an unwary catalog-shopping victim. The blooms are dwarfed by masses of untidy foliage that all lies down like a wet collie in a mud puddle after the blossoms fade. To add insult to injury, it spreads invasively.

DISAPPOINTMENTS

These are plants I had trouble with in my densely planted beds in Maine, but you might want to try them if your climate is different or in beds that are not densely planted.

***Aconitum cammarum* 'Bicolor' ('Bicolor' monkshood).** Not as vigorous as common monkshood (*A. napellus*) or azure monkshood (*A. carmichaelii* 'Arendsii'). Tends to shrivel up, doesn't thrive, doesn't compete well. Beautiful photos of the two-tone blossoms made me try and try again with this one.

***Aconitum septentrionale* (monkshood).** Not as vigorous as common monkshood (*A. napellus*) or azure monkshood (*A. carmichaelii* 'Arendsii'); disappeared over first winter.

***Anemone blanda* (Grecian windflower).** Beautiful, but short-lived — tends to disappear in second or third year. Some sources list it as Zone 6; that could explain my problem here in Zone 5.

Anemone × hybrida 'Honorine Jobert' (Japanese anemone). These gorgeous plants always die out tragically in their second or third year, even when given plenty of room. Might be a hardiness problem (although it's listed as Zone 5) or just a climate problem.

Aquilegia flabellata 'Ministar' (dwarf columbine). Failed to thrive; always died out during the first winter.

Armeria maritima (thrift). Forms a thick grassy clump of slightly tousled foliage that blooms less and less.

Artemisia stellariana 'Boughton Silver'' ('Boughton Silver' wormwood). Easily overshadowed by neighboring plants against which it can't compete. Excellent drainage too important; becomes bedraggled.

Asclepias tuberosa (butterfly weed). Because it is so beautiful and so attractive to butterflies, I tried and tried to grow this in the ordinary perennial border. But it's really at home in a sharply drained field in poor soil, plus it has a taproot and hates to be transplanted and kept in a pot. Too bad!

Aster laevis 'Blue Bird' ('Blue Bird' smooth aster). Just couldn't get it to thrive.

Aster linariifolius (stiff-leaved aster). Couldn't keep this alive in a dense perennial border.

Aster novi-belgii 'Winston Churchill' ('Winston Churchill' New York aster). I was attracted by the color but could never get this plant to establish itself. Other cultivars, such as 'Professor Kippenberg' aster (*Aster novi-belgii* 'Professor Kippenberg') are shorter but much more likely to survive and thrive.

Astilbe chinensis 'Pumila' ('Pumila' astilbe). I always found this purpley pink shade unattractive and difficult to blend, like PJM Rhododendrons. It's not purple, and it's not pink. Otherwise, this is a great groundcover plant with a useful spreading habit.

Cerastium tomentosum (snow in summer). Lovely gray, felty foliage with a profusion of snowy blossoms tends to become straggly and unsightly after bloom and as the years progress. On the plus side, it will grow in pure sand if you're searching for a plant that does that.

Ceratostigma plumbaginoides (leadwort). Many sources list this as Zone 5, but it usually dies in Maine's cold winters. Beautiful blue flowers late in the season; probably a fantastic plant in Zone 6.

Corydalis flexuosa 'China Blue' (blue corydalis). Though lovely and charming with sky blue flowers, this corydalis is frail, sparse, and difficult to establish. Looks great in pictures and maybe with a lot of TLC in a special place. Not designed for shouldering its way in a crowded continuously blooming perennial border.

Dianthus deltoides 'Zing Rose' ('Zing Rose' maiden pinks). Deep pink blossoms and darker foliage drew me to this plant, but I could never get it to come back the next year. Perfectly fine grown as an annual.

Doronicum orientale 'Magnificum' ('Magnificum' Caucasian leopard's bane). Very touchy about being touched by neighbors; never seemed to thrive. Too bad, because it's very attractive and early blooming for a daisy-type flower.

Echinacea Meadowbrite cultivars (Meadowbrite coneflowers). These cultivars don't seem to thrive, at least not in my area.

Echinops ritro (globe thistle). Although this thistle has cool-looking blossoms, it reseeds rampantly and really needs drier, poorer soil than the average perennial bed provides. Sea holly (*Eryngium planum*), which is one of the plants I do recommend, could be on this list for the same reasons as *Echinops ritro*, but I think it's better adapted to average garden soil.

Geranium 'Johnson's Blue' ('Johnson's Blue' cranesbill). This plant looks great in photos, but it quickly becomes a large, smothering thug that looks scruffy when gone by. Smaller geraniums like Lancaster geranium (*G. sanguineum* var. *striatum*) are more useful, since they leave a smaller hole if they need to be cut back hard.

Helianthus 'Lemon Queen' ('Lemon Queen' perennial sunflower). Although the flowers are pretty and the bloom time is convenient, I think this Jerusalem artichoke cousin just spreads too much to be useful in a mixed perennial bed.

Leucanthemum 'Snow Lady' ('Snow Lady' dwarf shasta daisy). Has not thrived in my gardens. Too bad, because a dwarf habit is just what you need sometimes.

Lilium martagon (Turk's cap lily). Withered away in densely planted beds.

Lupinus (lupine, all cultivars). Although you can't beat lupines for showy flowers, the plant cannot withstand crowding. Another problem is the spent foliage attracts aphids and tends to dissolve into a blackened mass. Best left to the wildflower planting.

Ornamental grasses. Require too much space to be at their best in the tightly planted continuously blooming perennial bed. Very small ornamental grasses like blue fescue are a possible exception. This is not a condemnation of ornamental grasses in general, just a note that they need more room to spread their glorious foliage. Large ornamental grasses do make a terrific backdrop for a densely planted continuously blooming bed.

Phlox subulata (moss phlox). Foliage is prickly and usually looks unkempt after bloom; grass creeps in easily and is very hard to remove without killing the phlox; colors are a bit harsh for my taste. For bed edgings I prefer to use *Arabis* 'Snow Cap', *Aster* 'Schneegitter', *Aurinia*, *Campanula* 'Blue Clips' or 'White Clips', *Iberis*, and *Saponaria*.

Physostegia virginiana (obedient plant). It's not obedient.

Platycodon grandiflorus 'Mariesii' ('Mariesii' balloonflower). This dwarf balloonflower is not as vigorous as larger varieties. Not a bad plant if you can wait several years for it to get established. Does not bloom as much as tall blue balloonflower.

Rudbeckia nitida 'Herbstsonne' ('Herbstsonne' coneflower). Seems too gangly and sparse to me; takes quite a while to create a thickish clump. Can be effective in just the right setting, but not generally useful for a continuously blooming bed.

Sedum 'Vera Jameson' ('Vera Jameson' stonecrop). Seems to die out within a year or two, not as vigorous as other tallish sedums. I just couldn't get it to look good.

Stachys byzantina (lamb's ears). Soft, felty gray leaves look and feel fabulous to begin with, then they collapse into a ratty pile of gray mush. Prone to foliar diseases. Improves after cutting back, but that leaves a temporary gap at the crucial front of the border. Flowers are awkward-looking and are best removed completely. I consider it a high-maintenance plant, which is fine if you're into maintenance.

Veronica 'Sunny Border Blue' ('Sunny Border Blue' speedwell). I killed about a dozen of these before giving up; I could never get them to live more than a year. You will be rewarded with terrific blue spikes if you can grow these in your zone or with your weather.

INDEX OF COMMON PLANT NAMES

COMMON NAME	SCIENTIFIC NAME
Allium, azure	*Allium caeruleum* (a.k.a. *A. azureum*)
Allium, drumstick	*Allium sphaerocephalon* (a.k.a. *A. sphaerocephalum*)
Alumroot, hairy	*Heuchera villosa*
Anemone, grapeleaf	*Anemone tomentosa*
Aster, New England	*Aster novae-angliae*
Aster, New York	*Aster novi-belgii*
Baby's breath	*Gypsophila paniculata*
Baby's breath, creeping	*Gypsophila repens*
Balloonflower	*Platycodon grandiflorus*
Basket of gold	*Aurinia*
Beard tongue	*Penstemon*
Bee balm	*Monarda*
Bellflower	*Campanula*
Bellflower, clustered	*Campanula glomerata*
Bellflower, Dalmatian	*Campanula portenschlagiana*
Bellflower, 'Kent Belle'	*Campanula* 'Kent Belle'
Bellflower, peachleaf	*Campanula persicifolia*
Bellflower, Serbian	*Campanula poscharskyana*
Black-eyed Susan	*Rudbeckia fulgida*
Blanketflower	*Gaillardia × grandiflora*
Bleeding heart, fringed	*Dicentra eximia*
Blue star flower	*Amsonia*
Bolton's aster	*Boltonia*

COMMON NAME	SCIENTIFIC NAME
Bugbane	*Actaea* (formerly *Cimicifuga*)
Bugleweed	*Ajuga*
Bugloss, Siberian	*Brunnera macrophylla*
Campion, rose	*Lychnis coronaria*
Candytuft	*Iberis sempervirens*
Catmint	*Nepeta*
Celandine poppy	*Stylophorum*
Clematis, solitary	*Clematis integrifolia*
Columbine	*Aquilegia*
Columbine, golden	*Aquilegia chrysantha*
Coneflower, cutleaf	*Rudbeckia laciniata*
Coneflower, purple	*Echinacea purpurea*
Coral bells	*Heuchera*
Coreopsis, lanceleaf	*Coreopsis lanceolata*
Coreopsis, threadleaf	*Coreopsis verticillata*
Cranesbill	*Geranium*
Creeping Jenny	*Lysimachia nummularia*
Culver's root	*Veronicastrum virginicum*
Daisy, Montauk	*Nipponanthemum nipponicum* (formerly *Chrysanthemum nipponicum*)
Daisy, Shasta	*Leucanthemum vulgare* (formerly *Dendranthema vulgare*)
Daphne, October	*Sedum sieboldii*
False spirea	*Astilbe*
Foamflower	*Tiarella*
Forget-me-not	*Myosotis*
Foxglove, yellow	*Digitalis grandiflora*
Gayfeather	*Liatris spicata*
Gentian	*Gentiana*
Globeflower	*Trollius*
Glory of the snow	*Chionodoxa*
Goat's beard	*Aruncus*
Goldenrod	*Solidago*

COMMON NAME	SCIENTIFIC NAME	COMMON NAME	SCIENTIFIC NAME
Harebell, Carpathian	*Campanula carpatica*	Peony, tree	*Paeonia suffruticosa*
Helen's flower	*Helenium*	Phlox, garden	*Phlox paniculata*
Hollyhock	*Alcea*	Phlox, moss	*Phlox subulata*
Hyacinth, grape	*Muscari*	Pigsqueak	*Bergenia*
Hydrangea, bigleaf	*Hydrangea macrophylla*	Pincushion flower	*Scabiosa*
Indigo, false	*Baptisia australis*	Pinks	*Dianthus*
Iris, bearded	*Iris germanica*	Poppy, oriental	*Papaver orientale*
Iris, crested	*Iris cristata*	Queen of the prairie	*Filipendula rubra*
Iris, dwarf	*Iris reticulata*	Rock cress, wall	*Arabis caucasica*
Iris, dwarf bearded	*Iris pumila*	Sage	*Salvia*
Iris, Japanese	*Iris ensata*	Sage, Russian	*Perovskia*
Iris, Siberian	*Iris sibirica*	Sea holly	*Eryngium planum*
Ironweed, New York	*Vernonia noveboracensis*	Sea lavender	*Limonium*
Joe-Pye weed	*Eupatorium maculatum*	Self heal	*Prunella*
Johnny jump up	*Viola tricolor*	Silver Mound	*Artemisia schmidtiana*
Knapweed	*Centaurea hypoleuca*	Smokebush	*Cotinus coggygria*
Lady's mantle	*Alchemilla mollis*	Snakeroot	*Actaea* (formerly *Cimicifuga*)
Lady's mantle, dwarf	*Alchemilla alpina*		
Lavender	*Lavandula*	Sneezeweed	*Helenium autumnale*
Lily	*Lilium*	Soapwort	*Saponaria*
Lily, lemon	*Hemerocallis lilioasphodelus*	Speedwell	*Veronica*
		Spurge	*Euphorbia*
Lungwort	*Pulmonaria*	Spurge, cushion	*Euphorbia polychroma*
Maltese cross	*Lychnis chalcedonica*	Squill, Siberian	*Scilla siberica*
Marguerite, golden	*Anthemis tinctoria*	Star of Persia	*Allium christophii*
Masterwort	*Astrantia*	Stonecrop	*Sedum*
Meadow-rue	*Thalictrum*	Sundrops	*Oenothera fruticosa*
Meadowsweet	*Filipendula*	Tulip	*Tulipa*
Monkshood, common	*Aconitum*	Tulip, Darwin hybrid	*Tulipa* (Darwin Hybrids)
Monkshood, azure	*Aconitum carmichaelii* 'Arendsii'	Tulip, Greigii	*Tulipa greigii*
		Tulip, waterlily	*Tulipa* (Kaufmanniana Hybrids)
Mums (hardy)	*Chrysanthemum*		
Nettle, dead	*Lamium*	Waxbells, yellow	*Kirengeshoma palmata*
Ninebark	*Physocarpus opulifolius*	Wormwood	*Artemisia ludoviciana*
Onion, ornamental	*Allium*	Yarrow	*Achillea*
Peony	*Paeonia*		

FURTHER READING AND OTHER RESOURCES

BOOKS

Applied Plant Research. *List of Names of Perennials (Naamlijst van Vaste Planten)*. Boskoop, The Netherlands: Applied Plant Research, 2005. (authority on currently accepted botanical names)

Armitage, Allan M. *Armitage's Garden Perennials: A Color Encyclopedia*. Portland, Oregon: Timber Press, 2000.

Armitage, Allan M. *Herbaceous Perennial Plants: A Treatise on their Identification, Culture, and Garden Attributes*. Champaign, Illinois: Stipes Publishing, 1997 (Second Edition).

Dirr, Michael A. *Dirr's Hardy Trees and Shrubs: An Illustrated Encyclopedia*. Portland, Oregon: Timber Press, 1997.

Disabato-Aust, Tracy. *The Well-Tended Perennial Garden: Planting & Pruning Techniques*. Portland, Oregon: Timber Press, 1998.

Mineo, Baldassare. *Rock Garden Plants: A Color Encyclopedia*. Portland, Oregon: Timber Press, 1999.

Rice, Graham, editor. *Encyclopedia of Perennials* (American Horticultural Society). New York: DK Publishing, 2006.

Shafer, Karleen and Nicole Lloyd. *Perennial Reference Guide*. Champaign, Illinois: Stipes Publishing, 2007.

Taylor, Norman. *Taylor's Guide to Bulbs*. Boston: Houghton Mifflin Company, 1961.

Taylor, Norman. *Taylor's Guide to Perennials*. Boston: Houghton Mifflin Company, 1961.

OTHER SOURCES, INCLUDING INTERNET

American Hemerocallis Society. *Daylilydatabase.org*. 2007. http://daylilydatabase.org (13 December 2007).

Argyle Acres. *Argyleacres.com*. 2007. http://argyleacres.com (13 December 2007). (for bearded iris information)

Filmer, Ann King. "Toxic Plants." 1997. *Ann Filmer's Web Page*. www.plantsciences.ucdavis.edu/ce/king/PoisPlant/Tox-SCI.htm (9 December 2007).

Michigan State University Extension and Michigan Nursery and Landscape Association. *Msue.msu.edu*. 1999. http://web1.msue.msu.edu/imp/modzz/masterzz.html (13 December 2007). (Ornamental Plants plus Version 3.0 database)

Missouri Botanical Garden Kemper Center for Home Gardening. *Mobot.org*. 2007. www.mobot.org/gardeninghelp/plantinfo.shtml (13 December 2007). (Plant database and bloom data)

O'Donal's Nursery. *Odonalsnurseries.com*. 2007. www.odonalsnurseries.com (13 December 2007). (Plant information)

Royal Horticulture Society (United Kingdom) Plant Finder. 2008. Online version of the annual publication (authority on currently accepted botanical names) www.rhs.org.uk/rhsplantfinder/plantfinder.asp

Schreiners Iris Gardens. *Schreinersgardens.com*. 2007. www.schreinersgardens.com (13 December 2007). (Iris information)

The Lily Gallery. *Lilyregister.com*. 2007. http://lilyregister.com/register (13 December 2007). (Searchable lily database based on data from the Royal Horticultural Society Register)

University of Hull. *Clematis.hull.ac.uk*. 2007. www.clematis.hull.ac.uk (13 December 2007). (Searchable clematis database from the University of Hull)

Van Berkum Nursery. *Vanberkumnursery.com*. 2007. www.vanberkumnursery.com (13 December 2007). (Plant information)

ACKNOWLEDGMENTS

I am grateful to many people for helping with this book.

For offering comments on my first feeble drafts, thanks to Debby Smith, Liz Stanley, Nick von Hoffman (the Flower Piggy), Susan Dooley and Debby Atwell. Thanks to Dinnie Thorndike and Phil Roberts for telling me to resubmit the book to more publishers when I was ready to give up after my first rejection. Thanks to Jennifer Benner, the editor who saw potential in the huge, disorganized binder I sent her and distilled it into a one-page summary of my technique for *Fine Gardening* magazine.

A huge thank you to Judy Galipeau, owner of Sisters Two Hair Design, and to Barbara Noyes, intrepid leader of the volunteers at the Farnsworth Victorian Garden, who gave me my first opportunities as an unproven garden designer. Thanks also to the many clients who let me design gardens for them, especially Pam and Jim Watson and Susan Schor, whose gardens appear in the examples section. Apologies to clients who ended up with some of my earlier efforts when I was still figuring out what to do.

For meticulously reviewing the plant data and offering many helpful comments and suggestions, thanks to Leslie van Berkum of Van Berkum Nursery and to my dear friend Debby Smith, landscape designer, who kindly provided my author photo. Thanks to Schreiners Gardens for the photo of *Iris* 'Pride of Ireland' on page 161.

Thanks to Merryspring Nature Park for hosting my design workshops year after year, and to the many participants who offered feedback and encouragement, especially Stevie Kumble and Naomi Howe who generously offered their comments for the book cover. Thanks to the Farnsworth Art Museum and Jackson Memorial Library, which also hosted workshops.

Many friends (gardeners and not) too numerous to name helped in many ways, especially the Friday morning Camden group, who offered support and urged me on when the going was tough. I'm very grateful to the members of my gardening crew, past and present, who made gardening fun and made all these gardens possible. Among them, I owe special thanks to Noah Gottlieb, Liz Stanley, Cindy Waite, Wang Chen Dorje, Steve Moore, Phil Roberts, Julie Rogers, Denise Hylton, and Scott Graham. I am also very grateful to Liz Stanley for photographing the preparation and planting sequences that appear in the book.

Many thanks to Cole Burrell and Lucy Hardiman for encouragement and feedback at their excellent four-day intensive garden writing seminar at New England Wildflower Society.

Last but not least, I owe a great debt of gratitude to editors Gwen Steege and Liz Stell at Storey Publishing for their thoughtful and sensitive reorganization of my material and painstaking review of its contents, which I believe improved the book immeasurably.

INDEX

NUMBER OF SQUARES	PLANT SPACING ADJUSTER	TARGET QUANTITIES
TALL ▶	÷ 1.5 =	
MED ▶	÷ 1.5 =	
SHORT ▶	÷ 2 =	

ENTER THESE NUMBERS IN BLUEPRINT

ENTER # OF PLANTS	◀ SHORT actual: _____	◀ MEDIUM actual: _____	◀ TALL actual: _____
FOLIAGE			
SPRING			
EARLY SUMMER			
MIDSUMMER			
LATE SUMMER			
FALL			

	NUMBER OF SQUARES	PLANT SPACING ADJUSTER		TARGET QUANTITIES
TALL ▶		÷ 1.5	=	
MED ▶		÷ 1.5	=	
SHORT ▶		÷ 2	=	

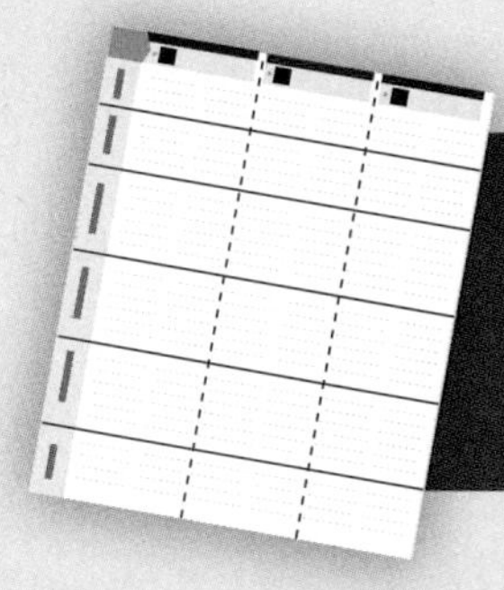

ENTER THESE NUMBERS IN BLUEPRINT

ENTER # OF PLANTS	☐ ◀ SHORT actual: _____	☐ ◀ MEDIUM actual: _____	☐ ◀ TALL actual: _____
FOLIAGE			
SPRING			
EARLY SUMMER			
MIDSUMMER			
LATE SUMMER			
FALL			